Cognitive Digital Twins for Smart Lifecycle Management of Built Environment and Infrastructure
Challenges, Opportunities and Practices

Editor

Ibrahim Yitmen
Department of Construction Engineering & Lighting Science
Jönköping University, Jönköping, Sweden

CRC Press
Taylor & Francis Group
Boca Raton London New York

CRC Press is an imprint of the
Taylor & Francis Group, an **informa** business

A SCIENCE PUBLISHERS BOOK

First edition published 2023
by CRC Press
6000 Broken Sound Parkway NW, Suite 300, Boca Raton, FL 33487-2742

and by CRC Press
4 Park Square, Milton Park, Abingdon, Oxon, OX14 4RN

© 2023 Ibrahim Yitmen

CRC Press is an imprint of Taylor & Francis Group, LLC

Library of Congress Cataloging-in-Publication Data (applied for)

ISBN: 978-1-032-13626-4 (hbk)
ISBN: 978-1-032-13628-8 (pbk)
ISBN: 978-1-003-23019-9 (ebk)

DOI: 10.1201/9781003230199

Typeset in Palatino
by Radiant Productions

Preface

This book aims to provide knowledge into Cognitive Digital Twins for smart lifecycle management of built environments and infrastructure focusing on challenges and opportunities. It focuses on the challenges and opportunities of data-driven cognitive systems by integrating heterogeneous data from multiple resources that can easily be used in a machine learning model and adjusting the algorithms. This book comprises Digital Twins incorporating cognitive features that will enable sensing complex and unpredicted behavior and reason about dynamic strategies for process optimization to support decision-making in the lifecycle management of the built environment and infrastructure.

This book introduces the Knowledge Graph (KG)-centric framework for Cognitive Digital Twins involving process modeling and simulation, ontology-based Knowledge Graph, analytics for process optimizations, and interfaces for data operability. This book presents the integration of Digital Twins, Blockchain, and Artificial Intelligence in the Metaverse focusing on enabling technologies, ecosystems, and challenges. This book offers the contributions of Cognitive Digital Twins for the integration of IoT, Big data, Artificial Intelligence, smart sensors, machine learning, and communication technologies, all connected to a novel paradigm of self-learning hybrid models with proactive cognitive capabilities. This book introduces the integration of Digital Twins, Blockchain, and Artificial Intelligence in the Metaverse focusing on enabling technologies, ecosystems, and challenges. This book presents the topologies of models described for autonomous real time interpretation and decision-making support of complex system development based on Cognitive Digital Twins with applications in critical domains such as maintenance of complex engineering assets in built environment and infrastructure.

This book offers the essential material to enlighten pertinent research communities of the state-of-the-art research and the latest development in the area of Cognitive Digital Twins, as well as a valuable reference for planners, designers, developers, and ICT experts who are working towards the development and implementation of autonomous Cognitive IoT based on big data analytics and context–aware computing.

Ibrahim Yitmen

Acknowledgements

I am grateful to all those with whom I have had the pleasure to work during the co-production of this book.

The completion of this book could not have been accomplished without the participation and assistance of the many contributors.

I cannot express enough thanks to all the contributors and individual chapter authors for their excitement in participation and assistance in the accomplishment of this book.

Nobody has been more important to me in the pursuit of this book than the members of my family. Most importantly, I wish to thank my loving and supportive wife and my wonderful son who provide unending inspiration.

Ibrahim Yitmen

Contents

Preface		iii
Acknowledgements		iv
List of Figures		vii
List of Tables		x
About the Contributors		xi
Acronyms		xvii
Introduction		xxi

1. **Enabling Technologies for Cognitive Digital Twins Towards Construction 4.0**
   Ibrahim Yitmen and *Sepehr Alizadehsalehi* — 1

2. **Synopsis of Construction 4.0-based Digital Twins to Cognitive Digital Twins**
   Ibrahim Yitmen and *Sepehr Alizadehsalehi* — 20

3. **Integration of Digital Twins, Blockchain and AI in Metaverse: Enabling Technologies and Challenges**
   Ibrahim Yitmen, Sepehr Alizadehsalehi, Muhammed Ernur Akiner and *Ilknur Akiner* — 39

4. **AI-Driven Digital Twins for Predictive Operation and Maintenance in Building Facilities**
   Ibrahim Yitmen, Habib Sadri and *Afshin Taheri* — 65

5. **Knowledge Graph-based Approach for Adopting Cognitive Digital Twins in Shop-floor of Modular Production**
   Ibrahim Yitmen, Sepehr Alizadehsalehi, Ilknur Akiner and *Muhammed Ernur Akiner* — 79

6. **Improving Sustainability in the Built Environment through**   101
   a BIM-based Integration of Digital Twin and Blockchain: An
   Analysis of Prefabricated Modular Construction
   Karoline Figueiredo, Ahmed WA Hammad and *Assed Haddad*

7. **Digital ID Framework for Human-Centric Smart Management** 123
   of the Indoor Environment
   Min Deng, Carol C Menassa and *Vineet R Kamat*

8. **Semi-Autonomous Digital Twins to Support Sustainable**   158
   Outcomes in Construction 4.0
   Marzia Bolpagni, Angelo Luigi Camillo Ciribini, Davide Simeone,
   Sara Comai, Silvia Mastrolembo and *Maud Santamaria*

9. **Cognitive Digital Twin Framework for Life Cycle Assessment** 177
   Supporting Building Sustainability
   Lavinia Chiara Tagliabue, Tassiane Feijó Brazzalle, Stefano Rinaldi
   and *Giovanni Dotelli*

Index   207

About the Editor   215

List of Figures

1.1: Different aspects of Construction 4.0. 4
1.2: Summary of main research topics and their corresponding 7
AI approaches
1.3: Overview of CDT ecosystems from a broad perspective. 16
2.1: Comparison between DTs and CDTs. 28
2.2: Relation between DT and CDT. 29
2.3: Cognitive engineering journey. 30
2.4: Framework of CDTC reference architecture. 31
2.5: Reference architecture of CDT based on RAMI4.0. 32
2.6: Outline of the process flow of CDTsBLM. 34
3.1: Enabling technologies and ecosystems for Metaverse. 41
3.2: The metaverse's primary areas divided into technology and 42
ecosystem.
3.3: Illustration of artificial intelligence technologies. 43
3.4: Different scenarios of wireless blockchain for virtual 45
and physical services in the Metaverse.
3.5: The Metaverse's three-layer architecture. 48
3.6: The three-layer design of the link between physical world 52
and the metaverse with the approach of applying DT
in Metaverse.
3.7: The AEC industry achieving real-time physical/virtual 54
synchronization of the Metaverse and intelligent edge
networks.
3.8: A plan for three-stage metaverse growth toward surreality. 55
4.1: General structure of a ML-based predictive model. 71
4.2: Technical architecture of the AI-driven DT framework. 73
4.3: Modular ML architecture of the AI-driven DT framework. 74
5.1: Knowledge graph-based IIoT data fusion framework towards 83
cognitive modular production.
5.2: Knowledge graph-based cognitive reasoning. 85
5.3: Constructing shop-floor CDT through the MBSE: the 89
implementation process.
5.4: Human synchronization technology scheme. 91

5.5:   IoT-based data communication scheme.   91
5.6:   Real-time data used to create a continuous transient   92
       simulation framework.
5.7:   Constructing a shop-floor CDT: Implementation process   93
       using MBSE.
6.1:   Components of a building digital twin.   104
6.2:   Stages of the building life cycle.   110
6.3:   First steps to integrate Digital Twin and Blockchain.   111
6.4:   Advantages of integrating concepts during the fabrication   113
       and assembly stages.
6.5:   Framework to integrate BIM, digital twin and blockchain   114
       across various stages of the building life cycle.
6.6:   Proposed semantic architecture for the integrated framework.   115
6.7:   An example of a role mapping with permissions defined   116
       for each entity.
7.1:   Components and information flow of the DID-based system.   125
7.2:   Components of Digital ID.   126
7.3:   The schematic diagram for the establishment, access, and   128
       update of the database.
7.4:   The proposed method for model training.   130
7.5:   Computation of the scores for building rooms.   131
7.6:   The schematic diagram for the original optimization problem.   134
7.7:   Computation of function loss.   136
7.8:   The trade-off between thermal comfort and energy   138
       consumption.
7.9:   Comparison between the initial and optimized thermal   139
       comfort distribution.
7.10: Match of occupants and rooms before (left) and after   140
       optimization (right).
7.11: Framework for measurement and prediction of work   142
       engagement under different lighting levels.
7.12: Experimental setup.   143
7.13: Experimental procedures for each session.   143
7.14: Locations of F3 and F4 electrodes.   144
7.15: Indication system of work engagement for 5-scale.   145
7.16: Classification of EV using ML.   145
7.17: Example rooms (1006, 1140, and 1105).   147
7.18: The layout of the GGB basement.   147
7.19: Estimation of thermal sensation and work engagement using   148
       physiological responses.
7.20: The developed real-time visualization platform based   151
       on unity.
8.1:   Electronic attendance records and feedback stations.   163

8.2: Data sample from sensors. 164
8.3: Extraction of bathroom usage per floor per gender. 165
8.4: Data flow process of case study 1. 166
8.5: Diagram of future application. 167
8.6: Data flow process of case study 2. 169
8.7: The atrium organization in zones 170
8.8: Profile settings used in flow simulations. The speed of a 171
     child was considered in m/s while the personal space was
     imposed by the CTS.
8.9: Simulation in the collective scenario. 172
8.10: Proximity map. Low density identified by the blue color, 172
     high density indicated by the red color.
8.11: The simulation components within the game engine Unity3D. 173
9.1: Workflow for retrieving information from BIM and the 182
     calculation model.
9.2: New parameters for energy assessment in the enriched 183
     digital model.
9.3: Data transfer from the ISO standard to the calculation 184
     model and to the BIM model.
9.4: Dynamo script for the automatic generation of Schedule 185
     in the BIM model.
9.5: BIM model of the test house and tested insulation materials. 186
9.6: Phases considered in the LCA procedure. 186
9.7: Workflow for machine readable EPD to BIM. 187
9.8: The new type created with Dynamo included in Revit 2021. 187
9.9: Creation of the analytical model for BEM starting from 189
     the BIM.
9.10: LCA, EN-15978 - All impact categories. 195
9.11: The cognitive layer used to enhance the LCA. 196

List of Tables

1.1: Summary of the AI type, clusters and descriptions.   8

2.1: Diverse CDT applications in various fields of industry.   25

2.2: Diverse CDT definitions in various fields of industry.   27

7.1: Details of the example database.   136

7.2: Room environments before and after optimization.   140

7.3: Overall classification accuracies.   146

7.4: Details of the personal prediction model for thermal sensation and work engagement.   149

7.5: Example of the feedback regarding the thermal environment of different rooms.   150

7.6: Example of the feedback regarding the lighting levels of different rooms.   150

9.1: Thermal transmittance limits for II-level major and minor renovation (EPBD 2021, Climate zone E).   181

9.2: Percentage of recycled material for the insulation materials as reported in the EPD.   188

9.3: Wall Thermal properties values for Phase 01 and Phase 02.   188

9.4: Consumption and cost – Phase and Materials.   190

9.5: Exported energy calculation results.   191

9.6: Environmental impacts quantified in the EPDs.   192

9.7: Data input for LCA Saas with specification on Input Model and results.   193

9.8: Material cost and LCA results by material and LCA calculation.   194

About the Contributors

Ilknur Akiner graduated from the Architecture Department of Istanbul Technical University in 1997. She completed her MS study in Architecture at the same university in 2000. Dr. Akiner received her Ph.D. in Project and Construction Management in Architecture from Istanbul Technical University in 2004. She published several scientific publications on architecture, mainly in the field of project and construction management and environmental issues in architecture. Her research interests include cognitive digital twins, innovation, culture in construction, organizational culture, international construction, strategic alliancing, and the performance improvement in construction, sustainability, and LEED (Leadership-in energy-and-Environmental-Design).

Muhammed Ernur Akiner graduated from the Civil Engineering Department of Eastern Mediterranean University in 2002. He completed his MS study in Structural Mechanics at the same university in 2004. He held another MS degree in Environmental Engineering from SUNY at Buffalo in 2007. Dr. Akiner obtained his Ph.D. from the Civil Engineering Department of Boğaziçi University in 2012. He published several scientific publications on engineering, mainly in the field of environmental engineering. His research interests include cognitive digital twins, environmental engineering, water resources, ecology, civil engineering, construction, and building technology.

Sepehr Alizadehsalehi received his B.Sc. in Civil Engineering, M.Sc. in Civil Engineering-Construction Management, M.Sc. in Project Management, and Ph.D. in Civil Engineering-Construction Management. He is a research associate at Northwestern University's Department of Civil and Environmental Engineering's Master of Project Management (MPM) program. He is also an experienced construction manager who has worked on projects in the Middle East, Europe, and North America for many years. Dr. Alizadehsalehi's research aims to explore and research the most relevant and applicable construction management technologies such as BIM, Extended Reality (XR), Metaverse, Smart Infrastructure, Cognitive Digital Twins, Reality Capture Technologies, and Lean and

Collaborative Working in Construction. Dr. Alizadehsalehi has authored more than 25 peer-reviewed journal and conference publications. He is also on the editorial board of a few journals and is an active reviewer for more than ten journals in the field published by the ASCE, Elsevier, Springer, and Tayler & Francis.

Marzia Bolpagni is Head of BIM International at Mace where she develops and implements Digital Construction Strategies for international clients. In addition, she is task group leader of CEN/TC442 on Level of Information Need, Honorary Lecturer at UCL, member of BIM Excellence Initiative, Associate Editor of the BIMdictionary, Ambassador of the UK BIM Alliance, Chair of the EC3 Modelling and Standards Committee, Founder of Italians in Digital Transformations UK and Visiting Professor at Northumbria University.

Tassiane Feijó Brazzalle collaborates in the private sector as a BIM specialist creating and managing data within construction projects following the AEC sector's digitalization process. The architecture and urban planner bachelor's degree and Master Business Environmental degree, both acquired at Universidade Federal do Rio de Janeiro lead the way to BIM A+ European Master in Building Information Modelling program, toughed in Portugal and Italy. The knowledge acquired from these experiences enhanced digital modelling skills and virtual energy calculation oriented to the calculation of LCA focused on renovation works.

Angelo Luigi Camillo Ciribini acts as a Full Professor in Construction Management at the University of Brescia. He is the convenor of the CEN TC 442 WG8 (Competence). He has been a member of the Steering Committee of the EU BIM Task Group and has been involved in numerous national and international research programmes. He is involved in the UNI and ISO standardization activities, too. He is the author of a large number of papers and books.

Sara Comai is a research fellow at the Department of Civil, Environmental, Architectural Engineering and Mathematics of the University of Brescia. Her research focuses on digital innovation applied to the design, management, and coordination of construction processes. She holds a Master of Science (2020) in Architectural Engineering from the University of Brescia.

Min Deng is a Ph.D. candidate in Civil and Environmental Engineering at the University of Michigan, where he is also expected to obtain an M.S. degree in robotics. His current research interest is human-infrastructure interaction including human state prediction using physiological sensing in buildings and autonomous vehicles. He has several published peer-reviewed journal and conference papers. He received both his bachelor's degree (1st class honors) from the University of Nottingham, M.Sc. and M.Phil. degrees from Hong Kong University of Science and Technology.

Giovanni Dotelli graduated with laude in Chemical Engineering (1989) and received his Ph.D. in Materials Engineering (1993). He is a full Professor of Materials Science and Engineering at the Department of Chemistry, Materials, and Chemical Engineering "G. Natta", Politecnico di Milano). He is the team leader of Materials for Energy and Environment (Mat4En2), and a laboratory member of the Ph.D. board in Materials Engineering of the Politecnico di Milano. He is a Member of the Technical Secretariat of Product Environmental Footprint (PEF) for batteries nominated by the European Automobile Manufacturers Association (ACEA). His research interests are the design and selection of sustainable materials for different engineering sectors, and the Life Cycle Assessment of products and industrial processes.

Karoline Figueiredo is a Civil Engineer with a Master's degree in Environmental Engineering, and she is currently a doctoral candidate at Universidade Federal do Rio de Janeiro (UFRJ), Brazil. She was a Visiting Researcher at Universitat Rovira i Virgili, Spain, and Western Sydney University, Australia, and in both situations, she developed research in the life cycle assessment of construction materials. Her research focuses on improving sustainability in construction projects by applying Building Information Modeling (BIM), Life Cycle Sustainability Assessment (LCSA) and Blockchain.

Assed Haddad is a Full Professor and Head of the Construction Engineering Department at the Universidade Federal of Rio de Janeiro, Brazil. B.S. in Civil Engineering, Juris Doctor, M.S. in Civil Engineering, and Ph.D. in Production Engineering. He was a Visiting Professor at the University of Florida, Universitat Politècnica de Catalunya, Universitat Rovira i Virgili, and Western Sydney University. Guest Editor of the International Journal of Construction Management, Frontiers in Built Environment Journal, Energies Journal, Infrastructures Journal, and Sustainability Journal. Prof Haddad has more than 250 papers in journals and peer-reviewed conferences, many book chapters, and edited books.

Ahmed WA Hammad is a Senior Lecturer at UNSW Built Environment, UNSW Sydney. His research focuses on the use of operational research (OR) techniques, including machine learning and mathematical optimization, linked with digital engineering platforms such as Building Information Modelling (BIM) and City Information Modelling (CIM), for enhancing decision-making and sustainability in the built environment.

His past works included the introduction of a systematic framework that relies on neural networks and BIM for building performance enhancement, along with proposing a mathematical optimization platform for organizing construction sites to improve productivity and enhance safety by minimizing high noise level exposure. Dr. Hammad has an extensive industry background in BIM implementation, virtual reality, prefabrication, optimized design, and scheduling techniques.

Vineet R Kamat is the John L. Tishman Family Professor of Construction Management and Sustainability, and Professor of Civil and Environmental Engineering at the University of Michigan. His research is focused on automation and robotics, virtual and augmented reality visualization, mobile computing, and their applications in the construction and operation of the built environment. He received a BE degree in Civil Engineering from Goa University in India in 1998, and MS and Ph.D. degrees in Civil Engineering from Virginia Polytechnic Institute and State University in 2000 and 2003 respectively.

Carol C Menassa is a Professor and John L. Tishman Faculty Scholar in the Department of Civil and Environmental Engineering at the University of Michigan (U-M). Carol directs the Intelligent and Sustainable Civil Infrastructure Systems Laboratory at U-M. Her research focuses on understanding and modeling the interconnections between the human experience and the built environment. Her research group designs autonomous systems that support wellbeing, safety, and productivity of office and construction workers, and provides them with opportunities for lifelong learning and upskilling. Carol has more than 120 peer reviewed publications. Carol currently serves as a member of the Board of Governors of the ASCE (American Society of Civil Engineers) Construction Institute. She previously served as chair of the ASCE Construction Research Congress Executive Committee. Carol is an Associate Editor for the ASCE Journal of Computing in Civil Engineering and Assistant Specialty Editor for the ASCE Journal of Construction Engineering and Management. Carol is the recipient of the 2021 ASCE Arthur M. Wellington Prize, the 2021 ASCE Collingwood Prize, the 2017 ASCE Daniel Halpin Award, the 2017 ASCE Alfred Noble Prize, the 2017 Outstanding Early Career Researcher from Fiatech, the 2015 CII Distinguished Professor Award and the 2014 NSF Career award. She also received several best paper awards.

Stefano Rinaldi received an M.S. degree (Hons.) in electronic engineering and a Ph.D. degree in electronic instrumentation from the University of Brescia, Brescia, Italy in 2006 and 2010, respectively. He is an Associate Professor with the Department of Information Engineering, University of Brescia. He is the author of more than 180 articles published in international journals. He is a member of several international standardization organizations. His current research interest includes industrial real-time Ethernet network, smart grids, the Internet of Things, the design of FPGA SoC design and Linux embedded systems, and cognitive buildings.

Habib Sadri is a doctoral student at Jönköping University – Sweden, working on a research project, entitled "Integration of Blockchain and Digital Twin for Smart Asset Lifecycle Management". Born in 1986 in Iran, he has a background is in civil engineering, a master's degree in Sustainable Building Information Management from the School of Engineering, Jönköping University, and a second master's degree in Engineering Management from Jönköping International Business School.

Maud Santamaria is redefining workplace services to deliver an exceptional experience for businesses and their employees. In addition to leading workplace strategies for our clients, Maud is also responsible for creating Mace's own workplace experience. Maud's passion and experience for what makes a workplace engaging and effective have led to her transforming corporate offices. From a career that started in office furniture to leading Mace's workplace experience strategy, creating inspiring workplaces has always been Maud's ambition.

Davide Simeone is an engineer and digital construction expert with 10+ years of experience, holds a Ph.D. and M.Sc. in Architectural Engineering from the Sapienza University of Rome. Former post-doc at Sapienza, and has been visiting scholar at Technion Israel Institute of Technology and Berkeley University of California. He is a member of the BIM Management Department of the international general contractor Webuild, and the author of more than 60 international publications on BIM and digital construction.

Lavinia Chiara Tagliabue is an Associate Professor of Construction Management, at the Computer Science Department, University of Turin, a member of the BIMGroup, Department of Architecture, Built environment and Construction Engineering, Politecnico di Milano. She is interested in sustainability at the building and district level, environmental and energy protocols, energy saving, renewable energies, energy retrofit, NZEB, interoperability BIM to BEM (building information modelling to building energy modelling), cognitive buildings, behavioral design, probabilistic models, building management systems (BMS). She is an international expert in the project Integration of Blockchain and Digital Twin for Smart Asset Lifecycle Management and invited lecturer at the course Intensive knowledge in BIM and International expert University of Jönköping, Sweden; Conference Chair European Conference in Computing in Construction E3 2023.

Afshin Taheri is a BIM consultant at Pythagoras AB, a company specializing in integrated workspace management systems (IWMS), based in Sweden. Part of his role is to contribute to a project, entitled "Integration of Blockchain and Digital Twin for Smart Asset Lifecycle Management". Afshin was born in 1991 in Iran, he obtained a bachelor's degree in civil engineering followed by a master's degree in Sustainable Building Information Management from Jönköping University in Sweden.

Silvia Mastrolembo Ventura is an Assistant Professor at the Department of Civil, Environmental, Architectural Engineering and Mathematics of the University of Brescia. Her research falls at the intersection of design and construction management with a focus on project coordination and management procedures enabled by digital innovation. She holds a Doctor of Philosophy (2019) in Architecture, Built Environment and Construction Engineering from Politecnico di Milano and a Master of Science (2013) in Architectural Engineering from the University of Brescia.

Acronyms

ABW	Activity-based Workplaces
AC-DT	Associative Cognitive Digital Twin
AEC	Architecture Engineering Construction
AECO	Architecture Engineering Construction Operation
AI	Artificial Intelligence
AI-PPP	Artificial Intelligence Public Private Partnership
ANN	Artificial Neural Networks
AR	Augmented Reality
AV	Air velocity
BAS	Building Automation Systems
BCI	Brain-computer Interface
BDVA	Big Data Value Association
BEM	Building Energy Modelling
BFO	Basic Formal Ontology
BIM	Building Information Modelling
BiPV	Building Integrated Photovoltaic
BioS	bio-CO_2 Storage
BLM	Building Lifecycle Management
CBLE	Cognitive Building Lifecycle Environment
CDT	Cognitive Digital Twins
CDTC	Cognitive Digital Twin Core
CMMS	Computerized Maintenance Management Systems
CNN	Convolutional neural networks
COC	Computation-oriented Communication
CPS	Cyber Physical Systems
CPPS	Cyber-physical Production System
CV	Computer Vision
CVE	Calculation Virtual Environments
CYB	Cybex
DCA	Deep Cognition Agent
DEDS	Discrete Event Dynamic Systems

DeFi	Decentralized Finance
DEX	Decentralized Exchange
DID	Digital ID
DLT	Distributed Ledger Technology
DOLCE	Descriptive Ontology for Linguistic and Cognitive Engineering
DRL	Deep learning-based Reinforcement Learning
DT	Digital Twin
DT-II	DT-enhanced Industrial Internet
EEG	Electroencephalogram
EPBD	Energy Performance in Building Directive
EPD	Environmental Product Declaration
ERP	Enterprise Resource Planning
ES	Energy-saving
EV	Engagement Vote
FACTLOG	Energy-aware Factory Analytics for Process Industries
FAI	Frontal Asymmetry Index
FEL	Future Event List
FM	Facility Management
GA	Genetic Algorithm
GBS	Green Building Studio
GHGs	Greenhouse Gases
GSR	Galvanic Skin Response
gNB	gNodeB
GTC	Gas Treatment Center
HR	Heart rate
HVAC	Heating Ventilation Air Conditioning
ICT	Information Communication Technology
IEA	International Energy Agency
IFC	Industry Foundation Class
IIoT	Industrial Internet of Things
iMMS	Indoor Mobile Mapping Survey
IOF	International Ontology Framework
IoT	Internet of Things
KG	Knowledge Graph
KPI	Key Performance Indicas
LN	Local Area Network
LCA	Life Cycle Assessment
LLCLCC	Life Cycle Cost
LC-ZEB	Life Cycle – Zero Energy Building

LNS	Large Neighborhood Search
LOD	Level of Development
LP-WAN	Low Power Wide Area Network
MBSE	Model-based Systems Engineering
MoEs	Measurement of Effectiveness
MEP	Mechanical Electrical Plumbing
MES	Manufacturing Execution System
MEV	Miner Extractable Value
ML	Machine Learning
MR	Mixed Reality
NFT	Non-fungible Tokens
NLP	Natural Language Processing
NPS	Net Promoter Score
nZEB	Nearly Zero Energy Building
OM	Operation and Maintenance
OWL	Web Ontology Language
P2P	Peer-to-Peer
PLM	Product Lifecycle Management
PSO	Particle Swarm Optimization
PVGIS	Photovoltaic Geographical Information System
QoE	Quality of experience
QU4LITY	Digital Reality in Zero Defect Manufacturing
RBF	Radial Basis Function
RDBMS	Relational Database Management Systems
RFID	Radio Frequency Identification
RH	Relative humidity
RL	Reinforcement Learning
RMPFQ	Resource, Material, Process, Feature/Function, Quality
RT	Room Temperature
SA	Simulated Annealing
SaaS	Software as a Service
SAS	Symbiotic Autonomous Systems
SCA	Shallow Content Agents
SCADA	Supervisory Control and Data Acquisition
SDT	Shop-floor Digital Twins
SE	Systems Engineering
SEDIT	Semantic Digital Twin
SLA	Service Levels Agreements
ST	Skin Temperature
SVM	Support Vector Machines

TMC	Total Material Cost
TPE	Total Use of Primary Energy
UAV	Unmanned Aerial Vehicles
UGC	User-generated Content
UI	User Interfaces
UWB	Ultra-wide Band
VPL	Visual Programming Language
VR	Virtual Reality
XML	Extensible Markup Language
XR	Extended Reality

Introduction

Digital transformation in the construction industry has gained momentum worldwide in the last decade. Construction projects across the world are increasingly adopting digital technologies for various functions and operations. The key drivers of Construction 4.0 are the various digital technologies and their interaction with each other. These technologies were augmented using Artificial Intelligence (AI), Machine Learning (ML), Semantic technologies, Big Data Analytics, Blockchain, the Internet of Things (IoT), Cloud Computing, and Cognitive computing. The research studies have demonstrated the usefulness and relevance of different technological advancements. The fundamental design principles of construction 4.0 are information transparency, decentralized decision making, seamless information flow, technical assistance through robotics and automation, and interconnectivity and interoperability among these applied technologies.

The Metaverse as a computer-generated universe has been defined through vastly diversified concepts, such as lifelogging, collective space in virtuality, embodied internet/spatial Internet, a mirror world, and an omniverse: a venue of simulation and collaboration. The Metaverse is one of the most concerned and promising smart applications (Extended Reality, User Interactivity (Human-Computer Interaction), Artificial Intelligence, Blockchain, Computer Vision, IoT and Robotics, Edge and Cloud computing) in the next generation of wireless network intelligent applications. At the core of the metaverse stands the vision of an immersive Internet as a gigantic, unified, persistent, and shared realm. This signifies that the Metaverse places higher demands on the current edge AI architecture.

The digital twin (DT) is an emerging concept whereby a digital replica can be built of any physical object. DTs are becoming mainstream to monitor, analyze, and simulate physical assets and processes in built environments and infrastructure. The current studies have attempted to enhance the cognition capabilities of DTs with semantic technologies. Cognitive digital twins (CDT) are an extension of existing DTs with additional capabilities of communication, analytics, and intelligence in three levels: (i) access, (ii) analytics, and (iii) cognition. CDT uses real time data from IoT sensors and other sources to enable learning, reasoning, and automatic adjusting for improved decision making. CDTs as the next generation of Digital Twins enhanced with cognitive capabilities through a knowledge graph and artificial intelligence models provide insights and decision-making options to the users. The knowledge graph describes the domain-specific knowledge regarding entities and interrelationships related to a design/construction/operation setting. The knowledge graph provides semantic descriptions and contextualization of the design/ construction/operation and processes, including data identification and simulation or artificial intelligence algorithms and forecasts used to support them.

CDTs can be leveraged to draw intelligent conclusions from data by identifying the faults and recommending precautionary measures ahead of critical events. Empowering CDTs with blockchain in industrial use-cases targets key challenges of disparate data repositories, untrustworthy data dissemination, and the need for predictive maintenance. Researchers recently addressed the requirements of trustworthy data management, data security, and predictive maintenance through a provenance-enabled blockchain-based DT framework by introducing data integration and interoperability components (such as data fusion, data wrangler, and composability) and data synchronization. Although CDTs offer a variety of advantages, they may pose limitations. For instance, how to analyze the huge volume of data for creating actionable insights in real-time. AI can address these limitations through the predictive capability of Machine Learning (ML) algorithms. For instance, blockchain and AI can provide intelligent and trusted CDTs.

Chapter 1 introduces an overview of enabling technologies for CDTs towards Construction 4.0 focusing on AI, semantic technologies, ontology engineering, knowledge graph, industrial data management systems, cloud/fog/edge computing, distributed ledger technology, cognitive computing, and ecosystem of CDTs.

Chapter 2 presents the synopsis of Construction 4.0-based DTs to CDTs focusing on the emergence of CTDs, the vision of CDT, DT vs. CDT, CDT reference architecture, applications in different industries, CDT framework for building lifecycle management, and challenges in the implementation of CDTs.

Chapter 3 presents the integration of DT, Blockchain and AI in Metaverse focusing on enabling technologies, ecosystems, and challenges.

Chapter 4 presents an AI-Driven Digital Twins for predictive operation and maintenance in building facilities focusing on maintenance approaches, deep learning overview, and Hierarchical Diagnosis and Prognosis system.

Chapter 5 introduces a knowledge graph-based approach for adopting CDTs in shop-floor modular production focusing on cognition-driven knowledge graph-based data representation and the implementation process of constructing shop-floor CDT.

Chapter 6 focuses on an analysis of prefabricated modular construction for improving sustainability in the built environment through the integration of Digital Twins and Blockchain.

Chapter 7 depicts the digital ID framework for human-centric smart management of the indoor environment presenting personal prediction models for human comfort and work engagement.

Chapter 8 presents semi-autonomous digital twins to support sustainable outcomes in Construction 4.0 focusing on Case study 1 involving the integration of IoT for office buildings in the UK to improve customer service, and Case Study 2 Agent-based simulations in Italian schools to enable better user experience.

Chapter 9 introduces a framework to outline the structure of a Cognitive Digital Twin to upkeep sustainable operation of the building and evaluated emphasizing the benefits and the procedures that can be activated to increase asset efficiency and reduce the carbon footprint.

Chapter 1

Enabling Technologies for Cognitive Digital Twins Towards Construction 4.0

Ibrahim Yitmen[1,*] and *Sepehr Alizadehsalehi*[2]

1.1 Introduction

Technology automation and data exchange, also known as Industry 4.0, refer to the current trend in technology automation and data exchange that includes cyber-physical systems (CPSs), the Internet of things (IoT), cloud computing, cognitive computing, and developing smart businesses in the Architecture Engineering Construction and Operation (AECO) industry (Irizarry 2020). The construction engineering and management professions are continually changing in the direction of digitalization and more intelligent systems to reach considerable levels of automation, productivity, and reliability in the field (Pan and Zhang 2021, Rahimian et al. 2019). The term "cyber-physical systems" (CPS) refers to systems that function by utilizing different sensors to understand physical components, automatically transferring collected data to cyber components, analyzing and processing data, and then converting the data into required information through the use of cyber systems that can be used to make appropriate decisions and take the required action. One

[1] Department of Construction Engineering and Lighting Science, School of Engineering, Jönköping University, Gjuterigatan 5, 551 11, Jönköping, Sweden.
[2] Project Management Program, Department of Civil and Environmental Engineering, Northwestern University, Evanston, IL, USA.
Email: sepehralizadehsalehi2018@u.northwestern.edu
* Corresponding author: ibrahim.yitmen@ju.se

example of a CPS is intelligent building systems. Building components and elements, as well as air conditioning, are used as physical resources in such a system, and data is gathered via sensors attached to these resources, which make up the cyber component of the system. The transmission of data used to monitor and manage physical resources occurs regularly over a communication channel. On the cyber side, optimization calculations are carried out to maximize resource utilization, and an appropriate choice is made depending on which physical resources are to be handled in the future. CPS, which comprises networked and integrated smart technologies, has the potential to transform the AEC sector and contribute to the development of Construction 4.0. CPS applications are projected to have a significant impact on construction projects that are planned, managed, developed, and linked to other autonomous systems (Yitmen and Alizadehsalehi 2021a). Currently, technologies such as value-added monitoring of sensor network data, data management in safe and resilient storage systems based on semantic models, and engineering system modeling and optimization are having a growing impact on the design, construction, and operation processes (Boje et al. 2020).

Sensors, communication, processing, and control are all included in a large-scale cyberinfrastructure via the use of CPS, which defines how various physical systems may work together to integrate. On the other hand, DT construction is a new engineering approach for coordinating construction performance that leverages data streaming and the unique capabilities of numerous site-monitoring systems (Sacks et al. 2020). In the AEC industry, a DT performs artificially intelligent activities like providing accurate status information, proactively analyzing and optimizing ongoing design and planning, and generating new solutions to maximize its value. Researchers in the Architecture Engineering Construction (AEC) industry have made remarkable advances and considerable advancements to stay up with the rapidity with which DL is being implemented (Galanos and Chronis 2021, Hou et al. 2021, Ma et al. 2020, Zhong et al. 2020). The fast development of graphics processing unit (GPU)-accelerated calculation methods, as well as the availability of structured and labeled data, have all contributed to the widespread use of DLs in the AEC industry (Akinosho et al. 2020).

While there are numerous cutting-edge enabling technologies, applications, and implementations of Digital Twins (DT) in the AEC industry, there are still numerous significant knowledge gaps that must be addressed through ongoing research to make DT more capable, reliable, and practical in real-world applications (Alizadehsalehi and Yitmen 2021, Yitmen and Alizadehsalehi 2021b).

Some of these issues include the expense of obtaining technology, software, and hardware, as well as the challenge of hiring and educating professional staff. Some of the other challenges include a lack of fully automated systems and codes; a lack of computing; a lack of storage; a lack of network capacity; and a lack of rules, policies, security, and processes (Alizadehsalehi and Yitmen 2021). Even with advanced IoT technologies in use today, data loss during the transfer process continues to be a problem due to a variety of factors, including software incompatibility and data fading. There is a lack of correlation between existing simulation approaches for the AEC environment and real-time environmental data in most instances (ur Rehman et al. 2019, Wang et al. 2020). Furthermore, the next generation of DT not only allows for real-time visualization and prediction to support in decision-making, but also enables autonomous feedback and control of the built environment (Deng et al. 2021).

1.2 Construction 4.0

Construction 4.0 is the AEC industry's version of Industry 4.0, and it is the process of deploying CPSs to stimulate the digitalization of the construction industry in order to achieve maximum performance. Construction 4.0, which integrates technology that enables smart construction sites, simulation, and virtualization, is designed to ensure that projects function to their greatest potential. Prefabrication, 3D printing, automation, extended reality (XR), unmanned aerial vehicles (UAVs), different kinds of sensors, robotics, and big data are just a few examples of technologies that are being used to enhance real-time decision-making processes (Alizadehsalehi et al. 2020, Alizadehsalehi et al. 2018). A general classification of Construction 4.0 may be broken down into three main scenarios: (I) Digital end-to-end engineering integration and technology for the automation of the physical construction environment are two terms that relate to the physical domain/automation of a construction environment; (II) interchangeably; (III) Digitalization refers to digital end-to-end engineering integration and technology for physical construction automation.

Companies will be able to boost productivity, decrease project delays and costs, manage complexity, and improve safety, quality, and resource efficiency as a result of Construction 4.0 (Craveiroa et al. 2019). As new and creative technology and materials are produced, AEC projects are becoming more attractive, energy-efficient, comfortable, economical, safe, and sustainable. Due to recent developments in materials and cutting-edge technologies such as artificial intelligence, robotics, nanotechnology, 3D printing, and biotechnology, the construction industry has entered a new age (Qi et al. 2018). Massive transformations are being driven by the potential provided by big data and the Internet of Things, as well as technological advancements that are bringing down the cost of sensors, data storage, and computer services.

A complete overview of advancements in materials, emerging trends, cutting-edge technologies, and strategies in smart building design, construction, and operation is provided by advanced technology, tools, and materials for the digital transformation of the construction industry. As shown in Fig. 1.1, all of these variables contribute to the development of Construction 4.0.

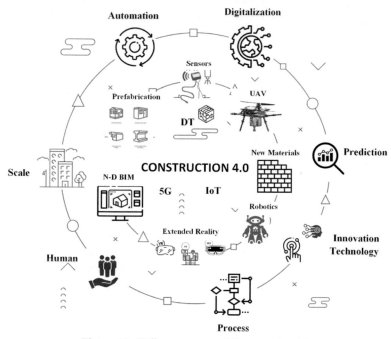

Figure 1.1: Different aspects of Construction 4.0.

1.3 Cognitive Digital Twins (CDT)

When the DT idea is used, the physical equivalent can be mirrored in virtual space, and data can be exchanged between the two spaces (Hartmann and Van der Auweraer 2021, Kor et al. 2022). The CDT concept is a progression from the DT concept. It has been designed to meet the requirements of monitoring complex industrial processes and to make use of the same trade model, shadow, and thread as DTs in order to do so efficiently (Abburu et al. 2020). It is critical from an economic standpoint for all businesses to maintain a balance between rapidity, resolution, and exception management (Alizadehsalehi and Yitmen 2021). As a consequence of virtualization in a dynamic run-time process, the digital counterpart's behavioral model may be continually adjusted to mimic the behaviors of the physical element, resulting in the CDT (Continuous Dynamic Transformation) (Rozanec et al. 2020). Virtualization is a dynamic design-time process that begins with the use of computational approaches to model the physical feature and evolves into a complex run-time process that allows the behavioral model of the digital counterpart to be constantly adjusted to reflect the physical element's actions, resulting in the CDT. The CDT is a DT that has cognitive capacities, such as anomaly detection and behavioral learning, as well as the ability to identify physical twin behaviors in order to enhance the metrics characterizing its condition or function (Eirinakis et al. 2020). As a result, a CDT uses optimization techniques to enhance decision-making and analyzes data from the physical twin using analytics or machine learning (Yitmen et al. 2021).

The CDT is envisioned as a reliable control and monitoring mechanism that is also a significant aspect of the decision-making process that leads to system optimization. The use of optimization methods at the core of the cognitive twin, as well as the effect of these approaches, is the major differentiating factor between it and presently existing DT solutions (Eirinakis et al. 2020). Abburu et al. (2020) developed a three-layer framework to define the sorts of twins that would be required to transition from physical assets in the form of digital replicas to cognitive advancement. Abburu et al. (2020) established a three-layer framework to define the sorts of twins required to shift from physical assets to cognitive advancement: digital, hybrid, and cognitive. The three-layer division is defined by the need to develop separate models of systems for anomaly detection, to interconnect the models for predicting unusual behavior, and to develop problem-solving abilities for dealing with uncertain scenarios. Advanced semantic abilities to detect mechanisms of virtual model evolution, enhance DT-based decision-making, and foster the interpretation of virtual model interrelationships are what distinguish CDT in DT. CDT is characterized by advanced semantic abilities to detect mechanisms of virtual model evolution, enhance DT-based decision-making, and foster the interpretation of virtual model interrelationships (Kalaboukas et al. 2021). It is the CDT's responsibility to ensure that assets are properly managed and challenges involving parties other than technical stakeholders are addressed by adopting Internet of Things (IoT) technologies (Lu et al. 2020).

CDTs may be intelligent enough to replicate human cognitive processes and undertake conscious actions with no or little human interaction (Zhang et al. 2020). The CDT Knowledge Core has semantic-driven recognition, learning, inference, estimation, and decision qualifications, which are comprised of a set of prediction and ML models developed using data from multiple sources, such as physical equivalents and sensors, from all aspects of industrial systems' operational conditions. Furthermore, it combines data and processes from the supply chain, as well as domain knowledge from experts. As a consequence, the CDT can learn and enhance its ability to represent and show the current status and operational circumstances of the physical asset in real time. Furthermore, by bridging the gap between the digital and physical worlds, the CDT can recognize, evaluate, deduce, predict, and make decisions for the dual physical system's current and prospective activities, all while interconnecting machines and humans.

Lu et al. (Qiuchen Lu et al. 2019) proposed a new cognitive twins definition, referred to as the CT definition, as well as a knowledge graph-centric framework for the CT process. Du et al. (2020) investigated how to develop personalized information systems for future smart cities using a human-centered DT simulation method for cognitive processes. In the context of process industries, Eirinakis et al. (Eirinakis et al. 2020) proposed an Enhanced Cognitive Twin, also known as an ECT, which introduces enhanced cognitive abilities to the DT asset that enable aiding decisions to allow DTs to react to internal or external stimulation. The ECT may be utilized at a variety of levels in the supply chain hierarchy, including sensor, device, process, workforce, and manufacturing stages, and it can be combined to allow for lateral and vertical interaction between the various stages.

1.4 Key Enabling Technologies for Cognitive Digital Twins

1.4.1 Artificial Intelligence

Different AI approaches and techniques have been designed to allow machines to mimic human cognitive processes in terms of learning, reasoning, and self-correcting. The AI techniques that have been developed are divided into four broad categories: expert systems, fuzzy logic, machine learning (ML), and optimization algorithms. Further, an expert system is an understandable and straightforward approach to intelligent decision-making that includes expert knowledge and reasoning for complicated problems to be addressed. Fuzzy logic works with input data that is unclear, uncertain, imprecise, or incomplete by converting and transforming it into computer readable forms, and then responds depending on a set of fuzzy rules that are applied to the data. Machine learning is an important step in artificial intelligence because it teaches machines how to discover patterns buried in enormous amounts of data and to make data-driven predictions about future activities. Deep learning and reinforcement learning, which are emerging as new trends in machine learning, have been developed at a greater degree of sophistication as the field progresses. The goal of an optimization algorithm is to find the best possible solution from a collection of available alternatives, either locally or globally. Furthermore, process mining is a relatively new subject that is attempting to bridge the gap between process management and data science. The use of process mining to monitor, diagnose, analyze, and improve the actual process has not garnered enough attention yet, despite the fact that it makes extensive use of event logs (Pan and Zhang 2021).

It is well acknowledged that the application domains of artificial intelligence (AI) are highly numerous, but some of the most promising study topics in building 4.0, as identified by Pan and Zhang (Pan and Zhang 2021) and shown in Fig. 1.2, are as follows:

Different AI systems have been used in various studies for a variety of objectives, including the detection and mitigation of risk, understanding the nature of the project for better planning and adjustment, and more. Furthermore, these concepts are significantly related to the clusters pertaining to AI approaches in Table 1.1, which is shown as a result of the correlation between them. For example, the topic of knowledge representation and reasoning is associated with the clusters of expert system and knowledge representation; the topics of information fusion, computer vision, and neural language processing are associated with the clusters of the hybrid model and neural network, the topic of intelligent optimization is associated with the cluster of artificial bee colony; the topic of process mining is associated with the clusters of expert system and knowledge representation; and the topic of process mining is associated with the clusters of expert system and knowledge representation (Pan and Zhang 2021).

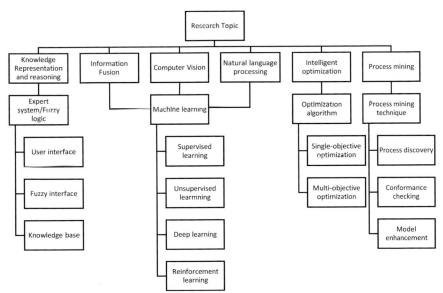

Figure 1.2: Summary of main research topics and their corresponding AI approaches (Adapted from Pan and Zhang 2021).

Table 1.1: Summary of the AI type, clusters and descriptions.

Type	Cluster Topic	Description
Method	Expert System	Multicriteria decision making, profiling, agreement option, decision support systems, computer programming
	Hybrid model	Computational intelligence, machine learning, hybrid method, multivariate regression, fuzzy logic
	Artificial bee colony	Optimization, swarm intelligence optimization, genetic algorithm, structural design, sustainability
	Neural network	Neural networks, artificial neural network, fuzzy neural networks, differential evolution, crack detection
	Knowledge representation	Software prototyping, intelligent agents, product individual characteristics identification, probabilistic methods, fuzzy logic
Application/ Purpose	Digital transformation	BIM, industry foundation classes (IFC), big data, internet of things (IoT), digital twin
	Information technology	Construction cost management, control variable, communications and control systems, safety, data mining
	Fog	Smart contract, smart oracle, blockchain, cloud, storage

AI has been discovered to automate and speed up the process of learning, reasoning, and perceiving from massive data in the context of Construction 4.0, indicating that it has enormous potential in solving various engineering projects based on their unique features. The artificial intelligence-based solutions used in building projects are not all the same. The strategic choices that are appropriate for a particular project will be informed without the need for human interaction in complex and unpredictable contexts. Apart from that, this kind of tactical decision-making may potentially be adjusted in response to changing circumstances, allowing for ongoing optimization of project operations and the delivery of smarter construction management over the project's entire lifecycle. The practical value of these important research subjects, it can be properly concluded, is in tackling the challenges that arise from the features of Construction 4.0, which include uniqueness, labor-intensiveness, dynamics, complexity and unpredictability. In general, artificial intelligence makes sense of large amounts of data to provide deeper insights. This is accomplished via three main steps: data capture and preprocessing, data mining based on suitable models, and knowledge discovery and analysis. In the long run, many AI-related technologies may finally accomplish the three key functions listed below, which are useful to Construction 4.0 in terms of automation, risk reduction, high efficiency, digitalization, and computer vision, as well as other aspects (Pan and Zhang 2021).

1.4.1.1 Modelling and Pattern Detection

Modeling is the process of developing conceptual models in a standardized, consistent, and predictable way, according to a set of rules. While modeling is a necessary precondition for additional knowledge interpretation and reasoning to be used for complex construction issues, the quality and reliability of the model that has been produced will have a substantial influence on the outcomes of analytical procedures. Knowledge representation approaches based on rules, logic, and schemas have been made to help researchers design the study model in a way that computers can comprehend. Additionally, the model should integrate extensive information about the actual project, such as declarative, procedural, structural, meta, and heuristic knowledge. Another effective technique for extracting information from data is pattern recognition, which can easily and automatically find and recover essential patterns and regularities buried in enormous datasets. As a result, pattern detection can simplify complicated problems by breaking them down into smaller pieces and returning outputs based solely on the characteristics of the data itself. This has demonstrated application potential in areas such as process mining, computer vision, natural language processing, and others. Using process discovery algorithms, for example, you may automatically define and map the end-to-end construction process into a clear process model in a digital representation, which can then be used as a basis for fact-based analysis to optimize the construction process. Apart from that, pattern recognition is particularly useful in extracting features from images or videos, which can automatically identify damage-like, crack-like, and unsafety condition-like patterns for infrastructure condition assessment and construction safety assurance, amongst other applications (Pan and Zhang 2021).

1.4.1.2 Prediction

AI-powered analytical tasks based on machine learning are often prediction tasks, in which the AI learns from provided sets of historical data to generate exact predictions about future observations. Specific to classification and regression, supervised learning may give a class label to data or predict future values and trends based on past data values and trends. The goal of unsupervised learning for clustering is to split data points without labels into many meaningful clusters, with data in the same group possessing comparable characteristics to that in the other groups. Instead of relying on empirical techniques in the construction business, prediction is a key strategic goal for project management in that industry.

Artificial intelligence is expected to classify, quantify, and forecast potential risks related to project performance and their relevant impacts to conduct reliable diagnosis and analysis ahead of time concerning broad aspects of project performance, such as planning, constructability, and safety, as well as other aspects of productivity and efficiency. As a consequence, the expected outcomes can serve as the foundation for proactive project management, to ensure the efficacy and dependability of the project's progress toward its objectives. For example, because unavoidable delays will inevitably result in decreased efficiency, cost overruns, and other negative consequences, the prediction of potential delays in the construction process can aid in the identification of key factors related to bottlenecks and the pursuit of high-accuracy project duration estimation. The use of artificial intelligence (AI) can aid in accurately detecting the safety risk of structural systems in advance, even when there is uncertainty and dynamic behavior. This is accomplished via the complete analysis of multiple factors, as well as their interrelationships. Based on this, urgent steps may be made to cope with the potential risk to lessen the possibility of the risk event happening (Pan and Zhang 2021).

1.4.1.3 Optimization

Optimization may be thought of as a decision-making process for identifying and implementing realistic sustainable construction solutions. Optimization can be used to make a process completely adhere to a set of criteria and constraints by maximizing the effects that are predicted. Popular meta-heuristic optimization algorithms, such as GA, SA, and PSO, among others, have traditionally been used extensively in the construction industry for project planning, construction, and maintenance tasks. They can provide recommendations continuously to not only reduce time and expense, but also to increase productivity and safety as well. Using optimized project goals, for example, suitable plans in terms of strategy, operation, and schedule can be developed during the planning stage as a critical precondition for project success, which can then be implemented. The phase of performing construction work on a challenging site is aided by optimization because it allows for better resource allocation, better personnel organization, better facility layout determination, and the ability to make appropriate alterations in a reasonable and timely way. In conclusion, O&M optimization aims to ensure that daily operations are carried out responsibly and that maintenance actions are carried out appropriately and at the lowest possible cost to preserve the infrastructure in a suitable shape. It also helps to reduce waste and energy consumption in buildings, which is important for long-term sustainability (Pan and Zhang 2021).

1.4.2 Semantic Technologies

Semantic technologies are recognized as the foundation of the CDT idea due to their advantages in terms of data interoperability and cognitive capability development. CDT models often involve heterogeneous data, information, and knowledge, making it challenging to coordinate efforts across multiple DTs and stakeholders. Ontologies and knowledge graphs, among other semantic technologies, provide promising solutions to these challenges (Zheng et al. 2021).

1.4.3 Ontology Engineering

Ontology is seen as a potential core for cognitive systems due to its ability to formalize the ontological properties of physical entities in a way that is consistent with human common sense (El Kadiri and Kiritsis 2015). Specifically, ontological engineering refers to a collection of activities that include the ontology creation process and lifecycle, as well as the techniques and processes for developing ontologies, as well as the tool suites and programming languages that support them (Gruber 1993, El Kadiri and Kiritsis 2015).

There are a variety of sophisticated approaches, tools, and programming languages available today to assist in ontology construction. However, a large number of ontologies have been developed using a variety of languages and tools to address a wide range of application cases. It becomes a difficult challenge to combine several ontologies into a unified framework and ensure that they are interoperable with one another. As a result, when creating CDT models for complex systems, this is a typical issue to encounter. Using a hierarchical approach to unify the application ontologies under a single top-level ontology, which has a collection of generic vocabularies that are widely used across all domains, may be a viable option. These vocabularies have been appropriately organized and explicitly developed following a certain methodological framework. Developing top-level ontologies like these serves as a common core component for the development of lower-level ontologies like domain-specific ontologies and more complex application ontologies. It is possible to achieve semantic interoperability between various lower-level ontologies because of the adoption of the top-level ontology. Several high-level ontologies have been established and extensively used by various groups, including the Basic Formal Ontology (BFO) (Arp and Smith 2008) and the Descriptive Ontology for Linguistic and Cognitive Engineering (DOLCE) (Borgo et al. 2022).

Certain top-level ontologies have been the focus of recent initiatives aimed at unifying and standardizing the many domain ontologies that have been built up. Consider the Industrial Ontologies Foundry (IOF), which is an ongoing endeavor with the goal of co-creating a collection of open ontologies to help to manufacture for industrial purposes while also encouraging data interchange. A multi-layer architecture is provided by the International Ontology Framework (IOF) to guide ontology development. The architecture is divided into four layers: a top-level foundation ontology, domain-level reference ontologies (domain independent and domain specific), subdomain ontologies, and application ontologies. It makes use of the BFO as a basis, on which experts from many industry fields collaborate to develop open and principles-based ontologies for usage in various applications (Zheng et al. 2021).

A top-level ontology facilitates the semantic interoperability of lower-level ontologies belonging to the same family of ontologies. On the other hand, several top-level ontologies have been produced, and each one has its own set of adherents. It is vital to produce uniform specifications for these top-level ontologies via cross-domain partnerships with the most relevant stakeholders to ensure that they are used consistently. To incorporate top-level ontologies that are already in use and generally accepted, a set of standards and specifications is required. Aside from that, some ontology alignment approaches should be able to optimize the usage of current domain ontologies that have been developed under various top-level ontologies (Zheng et al. 2021).

1.4.4 Knowledge Graph

In terms of enabling the CDT goal, the knowledge graph is often regarded as the most promising tool. It makes use of a graph model made up of nodes and edges to describe the topology of both structured and unstructured data, allowing for the formal, semantic, and structured representation of knowledge to be achieved (Nguyen et al. 2020). Knowledge graph nodes are used to represent entities or raw data encoded as literals, while linked edges are used to define the semantic relationships between nodes and between nodes and connected edges. The creation of semantic links across diverse data sources and the extraction of underlying knowledge from them is feasible via the use of knowledge graphs. This is particularly critical for the CDT vision, which involves a vast quantity of data and models (Zheng et al. 2021).

Since 2012 (Singhal and Rogers 2012), when Google launched its knowledge graph for its search engine, the knowledge graph and related technologies have garnered substantial interest from academic researchers and industry professionals alike (Ehrlinger and Wöß 2016, Nguyen et al. 2020). Among the information technology domains covered by this research are recommendation systems, question-answering systems, cybersecurity systems, semantic search systems, and other similar systems, among others Nguyen et al. (2020). The application of knowledge graphs in the manufacturing sector is still in its early stages. Recent studies (Banerjee et al. 2017, Boschert et al. 2018, Gómez-Berbís and Amescua-Seco 2019, Lu et al. 2020) have shown that CDT is effective in improving digital twins, which is one of the primary driving forces behind the development of the concept of CDT as discussed previously. When utilized in combination with ontologies, knowledge graphs are often used in the creation of a knowledge base or knowledge management system. Typical approaches include using knowledge graphs to gather information from raw data and integrating that information into an ontology, from which a reasoner may be operated to extract new knowledge (Ehrlinger and Wöß 2016, Nguyen et al. 2020).

The Industrial Internet of Things (IIoT) is a subset of the Internet of Things (IoT) that has applications in the industrial arena. It is characterized by the deployment of a large number of smart things in industrial systems to allow real-time sensing, gathering, and processing. Whenever it comes to ensuring high production performance, IIoT systems typically demand greater levels of security and more reliable connections than traditional systems (Liao et al. 2018, Khan et al. 2020). The fast growth of the Internet of Things and related technologies has been one of the primary driving factors behind Industry 4.0 and smart manufacturing, which is also the cornerstone of CDT's mission. Data created by IIoT devices is sent into the data ingestion and processing layer of the CDT reference architecture, which is then used to build data-driven services as the foundation for the CDT reference architecture (Zheng et al. 2021).

Because of the substantial investment made around the world in IIoT technologies and applications over the last decade, a significant amount of effort has been expended in both academia and industry on it. Since these efforts have been completed, the CDT can proceed to the next stage of its development, which is the correct use and reuse of advanced techniques when they are applied to the CDT vision. The widespread use of IIoT devices in current industrial systems creates a massive amount of industrial data in a variety of various types and structures. CDT's data-driven services are built on the foundation of this massive amount of industrial data. On the other hand, the collecting, storage, sharing, and processing of this data continues to be a difficult operation that necessitates the use of a variety of complex technology (Zheng et al. 2021).

1.4.5 Cloud/Fog/Edge Computing

The usage of cloud computing has been identified as one of the most essential techniques for dealing with big data problems in a variety of industries. When a mature market has been established, it has evolved into a crucial digital infrastructure for numerous industrial businesses in that area. Companies such as Amazon, Google, IBM, and Microsoft, among others, are delivering flexible computing services and solutions via the use of their cloud computing platforms, or platforms provided by third parties (Qi and Tao 2019). Furthermore, transmission between the cloud server and local data sources demands a large bandwidth, which is incompatible with many application scenarios, particularly those using CDT vision, where real-time processing is crucial. To address this issue, the concepts of fog computing and edge computing have been suggested, which would bring cloud computing closer to data generators and consumers, respectively (Mohan and Kangasharju 2016). Cloud computing is believed to be a subset of fog and edge computing (Roman et al. 2018). Edge computing, in contrast to fog computing, uses edge devices such as tablets, smartphones, nano data centers, and single board computers, as a cloud to perform basic computing tasks (Chandra et al. 2013, Ordieres-Meré et al. 2019). Fog and edge computing are techniques of transferring a portion of the computing, storage, and networking capabilities of the cloud to the local network, allowing for low latency, real-time response, and traffic reduction, among other benefits (Wang et al. 2020) and Qi and Tao (2019). As a result of these features, they are crucial components of intelligent industrial systems. They are critical enablers for the physical entity layer and the data ingestion and processing layer of the proposed CDT reference architecture when it comes to establishing the fundamental connections between the physical and digital worlds.

1.4.6 Distributed Ledger Technology

For a CDT system to function properly, data from various stakeholders must be integrated. The primary issues about data sharing are data security and privacy, as well as the protection of intellectual property (IP). Reliable cybersecurity infrastructure and data encryption mechanisms are required to overcome this challenge. Boschert et al. (2018) outlined two strategies for managing the degree of transparency of CDTs: encapsulated models to guarantee IP and open models to enable integrated development processes. Recent advancements in Distributed Ledger Technologies (DLT), particularly blockchain, present a decentralized approach to ensuring data security and privacy while exchanging data. In contrast to conventional data sharing systems, DLT eliminates the dominating administrator and central database, enabling safe data exchange in a trustless environment. It has recently garnered an increased amount of attention from researchers and practitioners. DLT systems and platforms have been created for a variety of applications, including private ledgers, permissioned ledgers, and public ledgers, among others (Zheng et al. 2021). As an example, Sun et al. (Sun et al. 2020) developed an IIoT data handling architecture that makes use of a public ledger and IOTA Tangle (Chen et al. 2020) to assure data privacy and data ownership on a distributed platform, as well as to protect data ownership. Given the benefits of DLT, it is a potential technology for accelerating the CDT vision and should be considered in future CDT development.

1.4.7 Cognitive Computing

This is a broad term that refers to a collection of technologies that include big data, machine learning, cognitive algorithms, and artificial intelligence. It attempts to recreate human thought processes in a computer model via the use of the digital twin (Klinc and Turk 2019). It was discussed by Conti et al. (2018) that cognitive computing is replicating (in the cyber world) the way users are understanding and managing data in the physical world.

Cognitive computing is the use of ML algorithms to detect and analyze accumulated data over a period of time. This procedure is aimed to provide the user with a set of related outcomes based on the most probable intended request as determined by the learned data. Because this technology can be applied to many different areas of construction by mimicking the way the human brain functions, it is often capable of performing tasks faster and more accurately than humans. As a result, it has proven to be an invaluable tool in increasing efficiency in the construction industry. Undoubtedly, cognitive computing has the potential to provide tremendous industrial advantages, especially as organizations become more dependent on digitalization to function successfully. It's clear that new computing services play a tremendous role in Industry 4.0 when they have added to the growth of other computing technologies like the edge and the cloud.

1.5 Ecosystem of Cognitive Digital Twins

Once the CDT are in place, it is envisioned that they would be able to form a network among themselves, allowing for completely automated machine-to-machine interaction and decision making, culminating in an ecosystem of cognitive digital twins to emerge. Using edge analytics, communication across digital twins, and domain knowledge, including user experiences, the information gathered will be organized into a unified knowledge graph. This knowledge graph will progressively develop and become a primary source of information inside the CDT ecosystem as it continues to grow and develop (Ali et al. 2021). Figure 1.3 shows an overview of CDT ecosystems from a broad perspective.

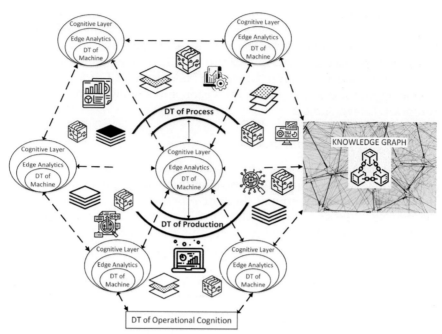

Figure 1.3: Overview of CDT ecosystems from a broad perspective (Adapted from Ali et al. 2021).

1.6 Conclusion

The ultimate objective of Construction 4.0 is to create a digital construction system by integrating industrial production, CPSs, and digital technology. As a result, it is expected that Construction 4.0 will have a significant impact on organizational and project structures, as the framework of Construction 4.0 enables more effective and efficient planning, design, and delivery of built assets, with a focus on physical-to-digital transformation and then digital-to-physical transformation. Artificial intelligence (AI), semantic technologies, ontology engineering, knowledge graphs, cloud/ fog/edge computing, distributed ledger technology, and cognitive computing were recognized as some of the primary enablers for the implementation of the Construction 4.0 concept.

CDT is currently in the early stages of concept development as an emergent concept, and there are numerous challenges and unresolved concerns that must be addressed for it to completely meet its objectives. Knowledge Management (knowledge representation, knowledge acquisition, and knowledge update), Integration of DT models (interoperability at the data level), Standardization (lack of a universal DT standard), and Implementations (project management, data privacy/ security concerns, and intellectual property protection) are the primary challenges for CDT, which can represent potential opportunities for future studies. To further understand these technologies and bridge the gap between their conceptual framework and their commercial implementations, more study is required.

References

Abburu, S., Berre, A., Jacoby, M., Roman, D., Stojanovic, L. and Stojanovic, N. 2020. Cognitive digital twins for the process industry. *Proceedings of the The Twelfth International Conference on Advanced Cognitive Technologies and Applications (COGNITIVE 2020), Nice, France*, 2020: 25–29.

Akinosho, T.D., Oyedele, L.O., Bilal, M., Ajayi, A.O., Delgado, M.D., Akinade, O.O. and Ahmed, A.A. 2020. Deep learning in the construction industry: A review of present status and future innovations. *Journal of Building Engineering*, 32: 101827.

Ali, M.I., Patel, P., Breslin, J.G., Harik, R. and Sheth, A. 2021. Cognitive Digital Twins for smart manufacturing. *IEEE Intelligent Systems*, 36(2): 96–100.

Alizadehsalehi, S. and Yitmen, I. 2021. Digital twin-based progress monitoring management model through reality capture to extended reality technologies (DRX). *Smart and Sustainable Built Environment*.

Alizadehsalehi, S., Hadavi, A. and Huang, J.C. 2020. From BIM to extended reality in AEC industry. *Automation in Construction*, 116: 103254.

Alizadehsalehi, S., Yitmen, I., Celik, T. and Arditi, D. 2018. The effectiveness of an integrated BIM/UAV model in managing safety on construction sites. *International Journal of Occupational Safety and Ergonomics*, 1–16.

Arp, R. and Smith, B. 2008. Function, role, and disposition in basic formal ontology. *Nature Precedings*, 1–1.

Banerjee, A., Dalal, R., Mittal, S. and Joshi, K.P. 2017. Generating digital twin models using knowledge graphs for industrial production lines. *UMBC Information Systems Department 9th International ACM Web Science Conference*, June 25, 2017 in Troy, NY, USA.

Bojc, C., Guerriero, A., Kubicki, S. and Rezgui, Y. 2020. Towards a semantic construction Digital Twin: Directions for future research. *Automation in Construction*, 114: 103179.

Borgo, S., Ferrario, R., Gangemi, A., Guarino, N., Masolo, C., Porello, D., Sanfilippo, E.M. and Vieu, L. 2022. DOLCE: A descriptive ontology for linguistic and cognitive engineering. *Applied Ontology*, 1–25.

Boschert, S., Heinrich, C. and Rosen, R. 2018. Next generation digital twin. *Proc. tmce, 2018. Las Palmas de Gran Canaria, Spain*, 7–11.

Chandra, A., Weissman, J. and Heintz, B. 2013. Decentralized edge clouds. *IEEE Internet Computing*, 17: 70–73.

Chen, J., Cai, T., He, W., Chen, L., Zhao, G., Zou, W. and Guo, L. 2020. A blockchain-driven supply chain finance application for auto retail industry. *Entropy*, 22(1): 95.

Conti, E., Madhavan, V., Petroski Such, F., Lehman, J., Stanley, K. and Clune, J. 2018. Improving exploration in evolution strategies for deep reinforcement learning via a population of novelty-seeking agents. *Advances in Neural Information Processing Systems*, 31.

Craveiroa, F., Duartec, J.P., Bartoloa, H. and Bartolod, P.J. 2019. Additive manufacturing as an enabling technology for digital construction: A perspective on Construction 4.0. *Sustain. Dev.*, 4(6).

Deng, M., Menassa, C.C. and Kamat, V.R. 2021. From BIM to digital twins: A systematic review of the evolution of intelligent building representations in the AEC-FM industry. *Journal of Information Technology in Construction (ITcon)*, 26: 58–83.

Du, J., Zhu, Q., Shi, Y., Wang, Q., Lin, Y. and Zhao, D. 2020. Cognition digital twins for personalized information systems of smart cities: Proof of concept. *Journal of Management in Engineering*, 36: 04019052.

Ehrlinger, L. and Wöß, W. 2016. Towards a definition of knowledge graphs. SEMANTiCS (Posters, Demos, suCCESS). *Metallurgy-Proceedings*, 48.

Eirinakis, P., Kalaboukas, K., Lounis, S., Mourtos, I., Rožanec, J.M., Stojanovic, N. and Zois, G. 2020. Enhancing cognition for digital twins. *2020 IEEE International Conference on Engineering, Technology and Innovation (ICE/ITMC)*, 2020. IEEE, 1–7.

El Kadiri, S. and Kiritsis, D. 2015. Ontologies in the context of product lifecycle management: State of the art literature review. *International Journal of Production Research*, 53: 5657–5668.

Galanos, T. and Chronis, A. 2021. A deep-learning approach to real-time solar radiation prediction. *The Routledge Companion to Artificial Intelligence in Architecture*. Routledge.

Gómez-Berbís, J.M. and Amescua-Seco, A.D. 2019. SEDIT: Semantic digital twin based on industrial IoT data management and knowledge graphs. *International Conference on Technologies and Innovation*. Springer, 178–188.

Gruber, T.R. 1993. A translation approach to portable ontology specifications. *Knowledge Acquisition*, 5: 199–220.

Hartmann, D. and Van der Auweraer, H. 2021. Digital twins. *Progress in Industrial Mathematics: Success Stories*. Springer.

Hou, L., Chen, H., Zhang, G.K. and Wang, X. 2021. Deep learning-based applications for safety management in the AEC industry: A review. *Applied Sciences*, 11: 821.

Irizarry, J. 2020. *Construction 4.0: An Innovation Platform for the Built Environment*, Routledge.

Kalaboukas, K., Rožanec, J., Košmerlj, A., Kiritsis, D. and Arampatzis, G. 2021. Implementation of Cognitive Digital Twins in connected and agile supply networks—An operational model. *Applied Sciences*, 11: 4103.

Khan, F., Jan, M.A., ur Rehman, A., Mastorakis, S., Alazab, M. and Watters, P. 2020. A secured and intelligent communication scheme for IIoT-enabled pervasive edge computing. *IEEE Transactions on Industrial Informatics*, 17: 5128–5137.

Klinc, R. and Turk, Ž. 2019. Construction 4.0–digital transformation of one of the oldest industries. *Economic and Business Review*, 21: 4.

Kor, M., Yitmen, I. and Alizadehsalehi, S. 2022. An investigation for integration of deep learning and digital twins towards Construction 4.0. *Smart and Sustainable Built Environment*.

Liao, Y., Loures, E.d.F.R. and Deschamps, F. 2018. Industrial Internet of Things: A systematic literature review and insights. *IEEE Internet of Things Journal*, 5: 4515–4525.

Lu, J., Zheng, X., Gharaei, A., Kalaboukas, K. and Kiritsis, D. 2020. Cognitive twins for supporting decision-makings of internet of things systems. *Proceedings of 5th International Conference on the Industry 4.0 Model for Advanced Manufacturing*, 2020. Springer, 105–115.

Ma, J.W., Czerniawski, T. and Leite, F. 2020. Semantic segmentation of point clouds of building interiors with deep learning: Augmenting training datasets with synthetic BIM-based point clouds. *Automation in Construction*, 113: 103144.

Mohan, N. and Kangasharju, J. 2016. Edge-fog cloud: A distributed cloud for internet of things computations. *Cloudification of the Internet of Things (CIoT)*, 2016. IEEE, 1–6.

Nguyen, H.L., Vu, D.T. and Jung, J.J. 2020. Knowledge graph fusion for smart systems: A survey. *Information Fusion*, 61: 56–70.

Ordieres-Meré, J., Villalba-Díez, J. and Zheng, X. 2019. Challenges and opportunities for publishing IIoT data in manufacturing as a service business. *Procedia Manufacturing*, 39: 185–193.

Pan, Y. and Zhang, L. 2021. Roles of artificial intelligence in construction engineering and management: A critical review and future trends. *Automation in Construction*, 122: 103517.

Qi, Q. and Tao, F. 2019. A smart manufacturing service system based on edge computing, fog computing, and cloud computing. *IEEE Access*, 7: 86769–86777.

Qi, Q., Tao, F., Zuo, Y. and Zhao, D. 2018. Digital twin service towards smart manufacturing. *Procedia Cirp*, 72: 237–242.

Qiuchen Lu, V., Parlikad, A.K., Woodall, P., Ranasinghe, G.D. and Heaton, J. 2019. Developing a dynamic digital twin at a building level: Using Cambridge campus as case study. *International Conference on Smart Infrastructure and Construction (ICSIC) Driving Data-informed Decision-making*, 2019. ICE Publishing, 67–75.

Rahimian, F., Seyedzadeh, S. and Glesk, I. 2019. OCDMA-based sensor network for monitoring construction sites affected by vibrations. *Journal of Information Technology in Construction*, 24: 299.

Roman, R., Lopez, J. and Mambo, M. 2018. Mobile edge computing, fog et al.: A survey and analysis of security threats and challenges. *Future Generation Computer Systems*, 78: 680–698.

Rozanec, J.M., Jinzhi, L., Kosmerlj, A., Kenda, K., Dimitris, K., Jovanoski, V., Rupnik, J., Karlovcec, M. and Fortuna, B. 2020. Towards actionable Cognitive Digital Twins for manufacturing. SeDiT@ ESWC.

Sacks, R., Brilakis, I., Pikas, E., Xie, H.S. and Girolami, M. 2020. Construction with digital twin information systems. *Data-Centric Engineering*, 1.

Singhal, A. and Rogers, E. 2012. *Entertainment-education: A Communication Strategy for Social Change*, Routledge.

Sun, S., Zheng, X., Villalba-Díez, J. and Ordieres-Meré, J. 2020. Data handling in industry 4.0: Interoperability based on distributed ledger technology. *Sensors*, 20: 3046.

ur Rehman, M.H., Yaqoob, I., Salah, K., Imran, M., Jayaraman, P.P. and Perera, C. 2019. The role of big data analytics in industrial Internet of Things. *Future Generation Computer Systems*, 99: 247–259.

Wang, J., Chen, M., Zhou, J. and Li, P. 2020. Data communication mechanism for greenhouse environment monitoring and control: An agent-based IoT system. *Information Processing in Agriculture*, 7: 444–455.

Yitmen, I. and Alizadehsalehi, S. 2021a. Overview of Cyber-Physical Systems and Enabling Technologies in Cognitive Computing for Smart Built Environment. *BIM-enabled Cognitive Computing for Smart Built Environment*. CRC Press.

Yitmen, I. and Alizadehsalehi, S. 2021b. Towards a Digital Twin-based SMART Built Environment. *BIM-enabled Cognitive Computing for Smart Built Environment*. CRC Press.

Yitmen, I., Alizadehsalehi, S., Akıner, İ. and Akıner, M.E. 2021. An adapted model of cognitive digital twins for building lifecycle management. *Applied Sciences*, 11: 4276.

Zhang, N., Bahsoon, R. and Theodoropoulos, G. 2020. Towards engineering Cognitive Digital Twins with self-awareness. *2020 IEEE International Conference on Systems, Man, and Cybernetics (SMC)*. IEEE, 3891–3891.

Zheng, X., Lu, J. and Kiritsis, D. 2021. The emergence of cognitive digital twin: Vision, challenges and opportunities. *International Journal of Production Research*, 1–23.

Zhong, B., Pan, X., Love, P.E., Sun, J. and Tao, C. 2020. Hazard analysis: A deep learning and text mining framework for accident prevention. *Advanced Engineering Informatics*, 46: 101152.

Chapter 2

Synopsis of Construction 4.0-based Digital Twins to Cognitive Digital Twins

Ibrahim Yitmen[1,]* and *Sepehr Alizadehsalehi*[2]

2.1 Introduction

The Digital Twin (DT) is a key enabling technology for implementing the smart AEC industry paradigm via Industry 4.0 (Alizadehsalehi and Yitmen 2021). A comprehensive physical and virtual description that covers all key properties and behaviors of a component, product, or system is referred to as the DT vision (Kor et al. 2022). At least three elements make up a basic DT model: physical entities in the real world, virtual entities in virtual space, and interactions between physical and virtual entities (Grieves 2014). Some recent research regards DT data and services as independent parts to develop an expanded version of the basic three-dimension DT model (Agrawal et al. 2022). The rapid advancement of information technologies, as well as the widespread deployment of the Internet of Things (IoT), have enabled the extensive applications of DTs across almost all major industries and throughout different lifecycle phases of a project, such as concept development, design, production, and maintenance (Yitmen and Alizadehsalehi 2021, Tao et al. 2018).

Modern AEC projects are getting increasingly complex due to the continuous adoption of advanced technologies (Alizadehsalehi et al.

[1] Department of Construction Engineering and Lighting Science, School of Engineering, Jönköping University, Gjuterigatan 5, 551 11, Jönköping, Sweden.
[2] Project Management Program, Department of Civil and Environmental Engineering, Northwestern University, Evanston, IL, USA.
Email: sepehralizadehsalehi2018@u.northwestern.edu
* Corresponding author: ibrahim.yitmen@ju.se

2020). DTs are considered key digital assets across the entire lifecycle of a project, thus, it is necessary to comprehensively network and integrate all relevant DT models into the system (Tao et al. 2017, Boschert et al. 2018). In addition, a complex system of projects usually contains multiple subsystems and components that can have their own DT models. These DT models might be created by various stakeholders based on different protocols and standards whose data structures are usually heterogeneous in terms of syntax, schema, and semantics (Zheng et al. 2021). This makes the integration of DT models a challenging task. Construction projects are more complex and more expensive than projects in any other industry as they need thousands of pages of documentation to back them up and thousands of functional components and each construction project is unique in its way (Alizadehsalehi and Yitmen 2019, Alizadeh Salehi and Yitmen 2018). Digitalizing construction projects has not been straightforward, and it has required a multi-step process to accomplish. Because DTs are considered essential digital assets throughout the lifecycle of a project, it is vital to connect and incorporate all relevant DT models into the system in a comprehensive manner. Besides that, a complex system of projects typically contains several subsystems and components, each of which may have its own DT model (Zheng et al. 2021). These DT models may be generated by a variety of stakeholders based on a variety of protocols and standards, and their data structures are typically diverse in terms of syntax, schema, and semantics, among other characteristics (Jacoby and Usländer 2020). Therefore, this makes the integration of DT models a challenging task.

A wide range of intelligent systems have made use of semantic technologies as critical enablers to establish semantic interoperability for heterogeneous data and information. It is possible to collect system information in an intuitive manner using semantic models and to offer a clear and coherent description of that information using semantic models. In standardized ontology languages, they characterize the information, allowing for the specification of direct interrelationships between diverse systems and models. The knowledge graph, which is a complex semantic technology, allows one to express model information in the form of entities and connections, which makes it possible to generate new knowledge via the use of a reasoner. Semantic modeling and knowledge graph modeling can be used to connect heterogeneous data-driven models (DT models) from different domains and stages of a complex system.

Recent years have seen a rise in the use of deep learning (DL) technologies in conjunction with advanced semantic modelling technologies in empowering DT with cognition capabilities. The notion of Cognitive Digital Twin (CDT) has emerged in numerous recent research and is regarded to be a potential development trend for the field of DT

(Al Faruque et al. 2021). The purpose of this chapter is to study relevant publications and to examine CDT's vision and characteristics.

2.2 The Rise of "Cognitive Digital Twins"

Previous research has investigated the feasibility of improving the cognitive capabilities of DTs via the use of semantic technologies. On the basis of semantic modeling and ontologies, Kharlamov et al. (Kharlamov et al. 2018) presented the concept of semantically enhanced DTs. It makes it possible to capture the features and state of a system, as well as the manner in which it interacts with other components of a complex system. Gómez-Berbís and Amescua-Seco (2019) developed a Semantic Digital Twin (SEDIT) that relied on IoT data management and knowledge graphs that were used throughout the whole enterprise to generate formal representations of domain specific DTs. It facilitates the finding of data spread throughout complex systems, as well as the provision of dynamic insights in ad-hoc and task-oriented frameworks. Banerjee et al. (2017) created a query language for extracting and inferring information from large-scale production data based on knowledge graphs. It proves that knowledge graph technology can be used to support the development and management of DT in complex systems. Boschert et al. (2018) explored a model for the next generation of DTs, focusing on knowledge graphs as the primary enabler technology for linking and retrieving heterogeneous data, as well as descriptive and simulation models.

These experiments, although not utilizing the terms "cognition" or "cognitive," tried to augment the cognition skills of DTs using semantic technology. The phrase "cognitive digital twins" originally emerged in Adl's (Adl 2016) suggested industry sector. They outlined the cognitive development of IoT technology and introduced the CDT idea, along with its characteristics and categories. It was characterized as a digital representation, augmentation, and intelligent companion of its physical twin in its entirety, including all of its subsystems, throughout all of its life cycles and evolution stages." Later that year, Saracevic (2017) from IBM presented a similar concept, and he tackled this subject from the standpoint of cognitive computing and artificial intelligence, demonstrating cognitive engineering scenarios using IBM Watson as an example. CDT uses real-time data from IoT sensors and other sources to help people make better decisions by learning, reasoning, and making changes automatically. This is a different description from the one that came before.

In addition to the efforts of the industrial sector, academicians are also contributing to the development of the CDT concept. Boschert et al. (2018) developed a model for the next generation of digital twins called nexDT. In their opinion, the existing standalone DT models are unable to satisfy all objectives and functions across the entire lifecycle, and the integration of multiple DT models for diverse business goals is required instead. In order to integrate Product Lifecycle Management (PLM) systems, cloud solutions, and other data artifacts and devices, semantic technologies such as knowledge graphs are potential methods. There is a good fit between the CDT concept and the primary elements of the nextDT definition. For instance, a nextDT is a collection of semantically linked digital artifacts that includes design and engineering data, operational data, and behavioral descriptions. The nextDT is supposed to have all the data and knowledge that has changed over time with the real system.

CDT is a digital representation of a physical system that has been enhanced with certain cognitive capabilities and support to perform autonomous activities; it is made up of a set of semantically interconnected digital models related to different lifecycle phases of the physical system, including its subsystems and components; and it evolves continuously with the physical system throughout its entire life cycle. Fernández et al. (2019) investigate the capabilities of hybrid human-machine cognitive systems and define Symbiotic Autonomous Systems (SAS). CDT was defined by the authors as "a digital expert or copilot who can learn and adapt while integrating various sources of information for the considered purpose." SAS focuses on the interaction and convergence of human and machine augmentation, with growing intelligence and awareness, resulting in a permanent human-machine symbiosis. The authors developed an Associative Cognitive Digital Twin (AC-DT) framework based on the SAS context to improve CDT applications. An AC-DT is a contextually enhanced description of an entity that tries to achieve a certain cognitive outcome and contains all relevant related relationships with other entities.

A formal description of Cognitive Twins as DTs with enhanced semantic capabilities for recognizing the dynamics of virtual model development, boosting comprehension of virtual model interrelationships, and facilitating decision-making was proposed by Lu et al. (2020). They proposed a knowledge graph framework to aid in the generation of CDTs. To facilitate the deployment of CDTs, they established a tool-chain comprised of many available applications and platforms capable of empowering the various components of CDT models. They validated the proposed CDT framework and associated tool-chain using an application case for decision-making assistance during the development of an IoT system.

Abburu et al. (2020) evaluated current DT concepts and proposed a three layer model for categorizing distinct 'twins' into DTs, hybrid twins, and cognitive twins. The definitions are based on the twins' abilities: DTs are isolated models of physical systems; hybrid twins are interconnected models capable of integrative prediction of unusual behaviors; cognitive twins are expanded with expert and problem-solving knowledge and are capable of dealing with unknown situations. According to these criteria, a CDT should contain cognitive capabilities such as perceiving complex and unpredictable behaviors and reasoning about optimization techniques, resulting in a system that is always evolving. In addition, a five-layer implementation architecture incorporating a software toolbox is provided in this research, and it is applied to several relevant use cases in the process sector to determine whether or not it is suitable for implementation.

Ali et al. (2021) advocated extending current DTs with enhanced intelligent capabilities using a three-layer architecture, namely access, analytic, and cognitive, in order to create smart manufacturing systems. Edge computing, domain expertise, and global knowledge bases all contribute to the cognitive layer's functionality. The development of customized communication networks facilitates the integration of many DTs and the ability of these DTs to make decisions on their own. A CDT ecosystem was also envisaged, with a large number of CDTs from various systems and domains being linked together. Table 2.1, as a comprehensive summary, has exhibited diverse CDT applications in various fields of industry based on the latest research (2019–2022).

2.3 Vision of CDT

2.3.1 *Characteristics and Definition of CDT*

As demonstrated in Table 2.2, the CDT concept is described in several existing publications. Even though there is little consensus on what the CDT stands for, there are certain similar elements and features that can be found, as follows:

(i) DT-based: CDT is a more developed or enhanced form of DT. It incorporates at least three of DT's fundamental elements: the physical entity (systems, subsystems, components, etc.), the digital (or virtual) representation or shadows, and the interconnections between the virtual and physical realms. However, the primary distinction is that CDT frequently incorporates many DT models that are all defined using unified semantics and topology specifications (Yitmen et al. 2021). It is projected that a significant number of related digital models would be connected to create extremely complex scenarios.

(ii) Cognition capability: According to Kokar and Endsley (2012), Fernández et al. (2019), and Al Faruque et al. (2021), a CDT should have specific cognition functionality, which means it can perform human-like intelligent functions like attention, perception, comprehension, memory,

Table 2.1: Diverse CDT applications in various fields of industry.

No.	Author(s)	References	Year	Industry	Applications
1.	Shi et al.	(Shi et al. 2022)	2022	Manufacturing	A CDT Framework for mart manufacturing and Human-Robot Collaboration.
2.	Eirinakis et al.	(Eirinakis et al. 2022)	2022	Manufacturing	A CDT Conceptual Framework for Resilience in Production.
3.	Zheng et al.	(Zheng et al. 2021)	2021	Manufacturing	A CDT reference architecture is proposed based on the RAMI4.0.
4.	Rožanec et al.	(Rožanec et al. 2021)	2021	Manufacturing	To capture specific knowledge related to demand forecasting and production planning.
5.	Berlanga et al.	(Berlanga et al. 2021)	2021	Computer Science	Proposed a platform for social networks.
6.	Abburu et al.	(Abburu et al. 2020)	2020	Engineering	Proposed a framework for the implementation of Hybrid and Cognitive Twins as part of the COGNITWIN software toolbox.
7.	Kalaboukas et al.	(Kalaboukas et al. 2021)	2021	Manufacturing	Implementation of CDT in Connected and Agile Supply Networks.
8.	Zhang et al.	(Zhang et al. 2020)	2020	Computer science and Engineering	Discussed how the different levels of self-awareness can be harnessed for the design of CDTs.
9.	Du et al.	(Du et al. 2020)	2020	AEC industry	Established methods and tools for the intelligent information systems of smart cities.
10.	Eirinakis et al.	(Eirinakis et al. 2020)	2020	Management	Proposed enhanced cognitive capabilities to the DT artifact that facilitate decision making.
11.	Albayrak and Ünal	(Albayrak and Ünal 2020)	2020	Engineering	Smart Steel Pipe Production Plant via CDT-based systems.
12.	Abburu et al.	(Abburu et al. 2020)	2020	Engineering	Proposed the CT control system for automation in the process control system.

Table 2.1 contd. ...

...Table 2.1 contd.

No.	Author(s)	References	Year	Industry	Applications
13.	Essa et al.	(Essa et al. 2020)	2020	Computer Science	Introduced the automation of defect detection.
14.	Saracco	(Saracco 2019)	2019	Computer Science	Proposed to bridge Physical Space and Cyberspace.
15.	Fernández et al.	(Fernández et al. 2019)	2019	Engineering	Introduced the concept of Associative CDT, which explicitly includes the associated external relationships of the considered entity for the considered purpose.

reasoning, prediction, decision-making, problem-solving, reaction, and so on. Thus, a CDT is described as a system capable of dynamically recognizing complicated and unpredictable behaviors via the use of optimization strategies. Although this goal is still a long way off, the rapid development of semantic technologies, artificial intelligence, IoT, and ubiquitous sensing technologies, among other things, has made it feasible to actualize cognitive capabilities to some extent.

(iii) Full lifecycle management: A CDT should be composed of digital models that represent various stages of the system's lifecycle, from the start of life, such as design, building, and validation, to the middle of life, such as operation, utilization, and maintenance, and the end of life, such as disassembly, recycling, and remanufacturing. It should also be capable of combining, analyzing, and managing all of the available data, information, and knowledge that is generated at various stages of the product's lifetime (Zheng et al. 2021). Additionally, it will aid in the cognitive processes that were discussed before.

(iv) Autonomy capability: A CDT should be able to operate autonomously or with a minimum of human interaction. This ability is somewhat overlapping and enhanced by a CDT's cognition capabilities (Al Faruque et al. 2021, Eirinakis et al. 2022). For instance, a CDT can autonomously make decisions and respond adaptively to design, production, or operations depending on the findings of perception and prediction.

(v) Continuous evolving: A CDT needs to be able to adapt to the real system throughout its whole lifecycle (Zheng et al. 2021). There are three different levels of evolution. At first, a single digital model updates itself in response to changes in relevant data, information, and knowledge from

Table 2.2: Diverse CDT definitions in various fields of industry.

No.	Author(s)	References	Year	Definition
1.	Eirinakis et al.	(Eirinakis et al. 2022)	2022	An evolution, utilize services and tools towards enabling human-like cognitive capabilities in DTs.
2.	Zheng et al.	(Zheng et al. 2021)	2021	A promising evolution of the current DT concept towards a more intelligent, comprehensive, and full lifecycle representation of complex systems.
3.	Al Faruque et al.	(Al Faruque et al. 2021)	2021	'DTs endowed with the other elements of cognition such as perception, attention, memory, reasoning, problem-solving, etc.'
4.	Ali et al.	(Ali et al. 2021)	2021	'An extension of existing DTs with additional capabilities of communication, analytics, and intelligence in three layers: (i) access, (ii) analytics, and (iii) cognition.'
5.	Abburu et al.	(Abburu et al. 2020)	2020	'An extension of Hybrid DTs incorporating cognitive features that enable sensing complex and unpredicted behavior and reason about dynamic strategies for process optimization, leading to a system that continuously evolve its own digital structure as well as its behavior.'
6.	Fernández et al.	(Fernández et al. 2019)	2019	'A contextual augmented description that explicitly includes the relevant associated relationships, connections or information channels of the considered entity with the other entities, for the considered application and purpose.'
7.	Matthews	(Matthews 2018)	2018	'A digital representation and augmentation of an entity across its lifecycle to optimize cognitive activities.'
8.	Fariz Saracevic	(Saracevic 2017)	2017	'A virtual representation of a physical object or system across its lifecycle (design, build, operate) using real time data from IoT sensors and other sources to enable learning, reasoning and automatically adjusting for improved decision making.'
9.	Adl	(Adl 2016)	2016	'A digital representation, augmentation and intelligent companion of its physical twin as a whole, including its subsystems and across all of its life cycles and evolution phases.'

the real system; then, due to interactions among different digital models contained in the same lifecycle phase, each model evolves dynamically in response to the impact of other models; and finally, due to feedback from other lifecycle phases, the previous two conditions may occur at the same time, and new models and components may be added.

2.3.2 DT vs. CDT

The CDT definition previously discussed makes it clear that there are similarities and differences between a classic DT and a CDT. It is vital to distinguish between their similarities and differences to aid in the growth of both conceptions' respective notions. Figure 2.1 depicts a generic comparison of the two ideas in a broad sense.

The CDT notion is formed on the foundation of the DT concept. As a result, a CDT should have all of the key traits of a DT. The digital representation of physical systems is enabled by DT and CDT, which means that they both contain the three fundamental elements of a physical system: (1) physical entities in real space; (2) virtual entities in virtual space; and (3) the interconnection that connects physical and virtual entities. Furthermore, the virtual entities of both DT and CDT are capable of communicating with their respective physical systems and updating themselves in real time as needed. From this perspective, the CDT concept may be seen as a subset of the DT concept, as shown in Fig. 2.2. It implies that all CDTs are specific types of DTs that have additional characteristics such as cognitive capacities, cross-lifecycle phases, and multiple system levels, among others.

The structural complexity and cognitive capability of the two species are the most significant distinctions between them. First and foremost, a CDT is often more complicated than a DT in terms of design and the

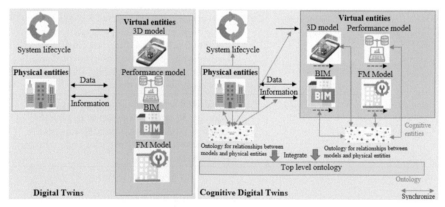

Figure 2.1: Comparison between DTs and CDTs (adapted from (Zheng et al. 2021)).

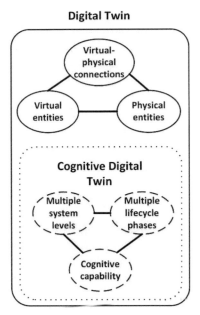

Figure 2.2: Relation between DT and CDT (adapted from (Zheng et al. 2021)).

number of lifecycle stages that are involved. DTs, on the other hand, are typically less complex. The majority of DTs belong to a particular system (or product, subsystem, component, etc.) and are focused on a certain period of the lifecycle. A CDT, on the other hand, should be composed of multiple digital models that correspond to distinct subsystems and components of a complex system, and it should be focused on various lifecycle stages of the system throughout its development. The integration of many related DTs employing ontology definition, semantic modeling, and lifecycle management technologies may result in the development of a CDT in many cases. DTs may correspond to distinct subsystems and components that are mapped to different lifecycle stages, and each DT develops in tandem with the system's overall development and evolution.

Furthermore, cognitive capabilities are required for CDTs, but they are not required for DTs to exhibit such abilities. The majority of current DTs are used for visibility, analytics, and predictability-related services, such as condition monitoring, functional simulation, dynamic scheduling, anomalous detection, and predictive maintenance. Typically, these services are provided using data- and model-based algorithms that use data acquisition from physical reality. Cognitive capability is essential to achieve greater levels of automation and intelligence, such as sensing complex and unpredictable behaviors and autonomously generating dynamic strategies. To accomplish this goal, data- and model-based algorithms are incapable of integrating complex data and models from disparate systems and lifecycle phases, as well as from diverse specifications and standards. To overcome these challenges, various technologies are required, like semantic modeling, systems engineering, and product lifecycle management.

In particular, it is vital to note that the CDT concept is not intended to replace the present DT; rather, it is intended to be an expanded and federated version of the current DT system. Any trade must be made based on the needs of the application scenarios as well as the requirements of the various stakeholders. It is the mission of CDTs to work on complex systems that are composed of several interconnected subsystems or components and that need interactions across various lifecycle phases. It tendens to deliver more advanced and powerful cognitive capabilities, but its implementation will be tougher in terms of technological preparedness, risk level, cost, and time, among other factors. In contrast, the enabling technologies of DT are more established, several successful projects that may be used as examples.

Figure 2.3 (Saracevic 2017) depicts the cognitive engineering journey, which can be used to determine when a DT should be augmented with cognitive skills. A typical DT performs the first three functions, namely, connecting and configuring the physical system, monitoring, and visualizing the system based on acquired data, and analyzing and forecasting the system using model-based or data-driven techniques. These capabilities allow the performance of conventional DT services like process monitoring, abnormal detection, and predictive maintenance, to deal with unpredictable behaviors of dynamic systems, or to perform sensing and reasoning for autonomous decision-making. A DT can accurately represent a system from the standpoint of physical system complexity; however, CDTs are designed to handle more complex scenarios where several systems are involved, particularly when they use various data standards and specifications.

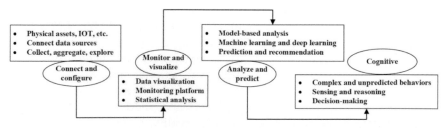

Figure 2.3: Cognitive engineering journey (Adapted from Saracevic 2017).

2.3.3 *CDT Reference Architecture*

Adl (2016) developed a reference architectural framework for CDT in its early development phase, which describes the main architectural building blocks that CDT should have in place. It is proposed that digital representations of physical entities in virtual space are dependent on the Cognitive Digital Twin Core (CDTC), which contains metadata, self-defense mechanisms, and governing rules to support the CDT functions. As indicated in Fig. 2.4, the CDTC is comprised of six layers, and these layers are as follows: anchors (data workers), surrogates (knowledge workers), bots (makers), perspectives (interfaces), self-management [administrators], and defensive systems (guardians). This architectural framework highlights the essential functions and enabling mechanisms that a CDT should support.

In accordance with the standards of the ISO/IEC/IEEE 42010 (Duprez 2019), Zheng et al. (2021) developed a knowledge-graph centric framework for CDT, which is comprised of five main components that cover a wide range of domains, including industrial system dynamic process modeling, ontology-based cross-domain knowledge graphs, CDT construction for dynamic process simulation, CDT-based analysis for process optimization, and a service-oriented interface for data interoperability. This framework aims to enable decision-makers throughout the development of IoT systems that take inputs from business domains and outputs to asset domains. Abburu et al. (2020) presented a five-layer architectural blueprint for CDT that includes a data input and preparation layer, a model management layer, a service management layer, a twin management layer, and a user interaction layer. Additionally, to improve the suggested architecture's standardization, its layers and components are mapped to

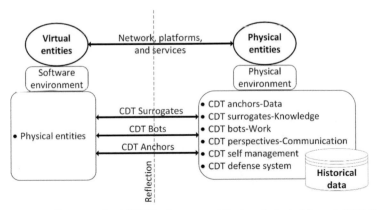

Figure 2.4: Framework of CDTC reference architecture (adapted from Adl 2016).

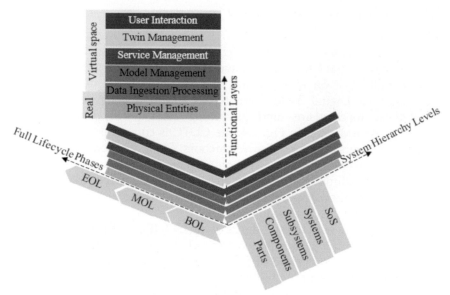

Figure 2.5: Reference architecture of CDT based on RAMI4.0 (Adapted from Zheng et al. 2021).

the Big Data Value Association's (BDVA) reference model and the Artificial Intelligence Public Private Partnership's (AI-PPP) reference model (AI PPP). Furthermore, many use cases are shown to highlight the proposed architecture's capability and adaptability.

Zheng et al. (2021) developed a more detailed CDT reference architecture, intending to address all of its essential elements and characteristics by reusing and complying with current standards and specifications, particularly RAMI4.0 for interoperability. The three dimensions of the proposed reference architecture are shown in Fig. 2.5. They include full lifecycle stages, system hierarchy levels, and six functional layers.

2.4   CDT Applications in Different Industries

CDT is a new concept that has not yet been extensively adopted and validated in the industry. The majority of CDT-related research has either explored the theoretical perspectives of CDT or focused on the vision of CDT. However, there are several ongoing research and studies that are trying to prove the CDT's practicality by applying it to a range of diverse industries and business contexts.

COGNITWIN (Cognitive plants via proactive self-learning hybrid DTs) is a European Union project aiming at increasing the cognitive capabilities of current process control systems, as well as enabling self-organization and solutions to unpredictable behaviors. In another study (Abburu et al. 2020), a cognitive twin toolbox conceptual architecture has been applied to many process industry use cases, including operational optimization of gas treatment centers (GTC) in aluminum production; minimizing health and safety risks while maximizing metallic yield in silicon (Si) production; condition monitoring of assets in steel and related products production; and real-time monitoring of finished products for operational efficiencies. In one of the COGNITWIN project pilots, CDT has been utilized to help with the building of a smart steel pipe manufacturing facility. Albayrak and Ünal (2020) have provided the comprehensive application background, aims, and critical factors, as well as some main findings of this pilot. Another EU project, FACTLOG (Energy-aware Factory Analytics for Process Industries), combines data-driven and model-driven DTs to increase the cognitive capacities of complex process systems. CDT was employed as a semantically improved version of DT to enable autonomous quality in another EU project, QU4LITY (Digital Reality in Zero Defect Manufacturing), which intends to deliver an open, standardized, and transformable zero-defect manufacturing product/service/model. To facilitate ontology creation, a data model called RMPFQ (Resource, Material, Process, Feature/Function, Quality) (Zheng et al. 2020) was adopted. In one of the QU4LITY project pilots, a CDT model for an airplane assembly system is being developed based on these application scenarios. To allow knowledge-based intelligent services for autonomous production, Zhou et al. (2020) linked dynamic knowledge bases with DT models. The intelligent perceiving, simulating, comprehending, anticipating, optimizing, and regulating approach is supported by the knowledge-driven DT. Manufacturing process planning, production scheduling, and production process analysis were three use cases where this system was used. Furthermore, CDTs are used by Yitmen et al. (2021) to facilitate building information management. Throughout the project lifecycle, CDTs primarily help process optimization and decision-making based on knowledge graph modeling and reasoning. Some commercial AI systems also offered industrial solutions that enable CDT applications to move faster. For example, the IBM Watson IoT platform (Saracevic 2017) can facilitate analytics-for-design and design-for-analytics interactions by providing cognitive analytic services. It's a closed-loop framework with features including requirement management, system design, verification, and validation, building and deployment, and operation. The Watson IoT platform offers cognitive manufacturing solutions (IBM 2021), which are made up of four layers: a device layer, an IoT platform layer, an application layer, and an industry solutions layer. These layers serve as a reference for CDT applications in process and quality improvement, resource optimization, and supply chain optimization.

2.5 CDT Framework for Building Lifecycle Management

As discussed in the reference architecture, a CDT should facilitate digital model integration throughout stages of the lifecycle. PLM is crucial in product lifecycle management. In the product lifecycle (BOL, MOL, and EOL), PLM is a strategic approach for managing product information (Kiritsis 2011). In addition to managing product information, it also manages business processes for creating, managing, disseminating, and utilizing information. Currently, PLM is extensively utilized in various industries, particularly in the manufacturing field, as a vital strategy to maintain the long-term sustainability and competitive advantages of businesses (Liu and Liang 2015, Zhang et al. 2017). Many emerging technologies, such as the IoT, data mining, and semantic technologies, among others, have influenced product lifecycle management. Using these technologies, it is feasible to capture hidden knowledge and patterns from huge lifecycle data, enabling the improvement of a wide range of data-driven services (Denkena et al. 2014), which is consistent with the CDT objective. These applications and advancements serve as a solid foundation for the development of CDT technology.

Figure 2.6 illustrates the framework of the CDT for Building Lifecycle Management (CDTsBLM) process flow, which Yitmen et al. (2021) developed to determine the processes and core features of the framework. This research proposes a unique adapted solution that integrates CDT and BLM concepts, allowing all project stakeholders to identify and acquire the proper data sets and appropriately input them into the system to optimize it. In comparison to conventional and existing approaches, the proposed model aims to increase BLM performance.

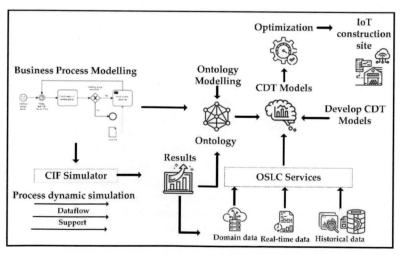

Figure 2.6: Outline of the process flow of CDTsBLM (Yitmen et al. 2021).

Any physical unit can be represented by the CDT in BLM. CDT can be used to virtually model buildings, process phases, total procedures, and ultimately an entire construction operation. CDTs can be elicited at different levels of the hierarchy, with CDTs combining horizontally and vertically to form an aggregated structure. The Cognitive Building Lifecycle Environment (CBLE), which was created by integrating CDTs, distributes a lot of information horizontally. Only critical decision-making information, on the other hand, is conveyed vertically to the top levels. A CDT (monitoring and regulating the status and activities of a mission-critical building) providing information to a specific process phase that feeds the CDT of the building design process is an example. When exchanging data with the different shared data sets and their semantics, these CDTs will act and reply. This research looked at the integration, interoperability, and implementation of CDT in existing BLM practices throughout the life cycle, as well as decision-making skills and AEC industry insights.

2.6 Challenges

CDT is currently in its early stages of development as an emerging technology. To comprehensively accomplish its goal, it must overcome several obstacles. Even though some of the constraints are supposed to be addressed by the aforementioned enabling technologies, still more work will be required in the future. Some of the major issues for CDT are knowledge management, integration of DT models, and implementations of CDT.

Realizing this cognitive capability is the most challenging task for CDT. The basis of this competency is a functioning and comprehensive knowledge base. Abburu et al. (2020) divided the problems of CDT cognition into three categories: knowledge representation, knowledge acquisition, and knowledge updating. The second challenge of CDT is the integration of DT models. Numerous DT models have been developed independently by various stakeholders of a complex system, correlating to the system's various subsystems or components across its entire lifecycle. These existing DT models must be effectively integrated and coordinated into the CDT architecture facilitated by the twin management layer. It is a difficult process in realworld applications since many stakeholders may have chosen varying standards, protocols, and structures for their DT models. This results in interoperability problems at the data level. Additionally, this offers more complex features and services for integration into the DT models. The last major difficulty is implementing CDTs, which is far more challenging than DT. DTs often concentrate their efforts on a single physical system during one of its lifecycle stages. As a result,

DTs may be introduced within enterprises with the assistance of specific technical suppliers as required. Moreover, a CDT may consist of numerous physical systems covering multiple lifecycle stages and including stakeholders from various organizations. Thus, CDT implementation will need both intra- and inter-organizational collaboration. In addition to the above-mentioned interoperability issue, it brings new challenges in terms of project management, data privacy/security concerns, IP protection, etc. The lack of successful demonstrators of CDT implementation further increases its risks.

2.7 Conclusion

This paper proposes a formal definition of CDT based on a systems engineering approach. Moreover, a CDT conceptual architecture is defined based on the systems engineering standard ISO 42010. To facilitate CDT development and implementation, a KG-based framework is developed together with an enabling tool-chain. To verify the proposed framework and tool-chain, a case study of auto-braking system development is conducted. KARMA models and Simulink models are used to define solutions and verify requirements. Based on such models, a multi-layer neural network is trained based on simulation data and ontology models generated from KARMA models, which are then utilized to support decision-making. The case study demonstrated the practicability of the proposed CDT concept, architecture, and reference framework. The simulation results indicate the potential of CDT in promoting decision-making during complex system development. This study bridges the gaps between the theoretical CDT concept and industrial CDT applications. It reveals the great potential of CDT, as the next generation of DT, for complex system development and management.

References

Abburu, S., Berre, A.J., Jacoby, M., Roman, D., Stojanovic, L. and Stojanovic, N. 2020. COGNITWIN–Hybrid and cognitive digital twins for the process industry. *IEEE International Conference on Engineering, Technology and Innovation (ICE/ITMC)*, 2020. IEEE, 1–8.

Adl, A.E. 2016. The Cognitive Digital Twins: Vision, Architecture Framework and Categories.

Agrawal, A., Singh, V., Thiel, R., Pillsbury, M., Knoll, H., Puckett, J. and Fischer, M. 2022. Digital twin in practice: Emergent insights from an ethnographic-action research study. *Construction Research Congress*, 2022: 1253–1260.

Al Faruque, M.A., Muthirayan, D., Yu, S.Y. and Khargonekar, P.P. 2021. Cognitive Digital Twin for manufacturing systems. *Design, Automation & Test in Europe Conference & Exhibition (DATE)*, 2021. IEEE, 440–445.

Albayrak, Ö. and Ünal, P. 2020. Smart steel pipe production plant via Cognitive Digital Twins: A case study on digitalization of spiral welded pipe machinery. *Cybersecurity Workshop by European Steel Technology Platform*, 2020. Springer, 132–143.

Ali, M.I., Patel, P., Breslin, J.G., Harik, R. and Sheth, A. 2021. Cognitive Digital Twins for smart manufacturing. *IEEE Intelligent Systems*, 36(2): 96–100.

Alizadeh Salehi, S. and Yitmen, İ. 2018. Modeling and analysis of the impact of BIM-based field data capturing technologies on automated construction progress monitoring. *International Journal of Civil Engineering*, 16: 1669–1685.

Alizadehsalehi, S. and Yitmen, I. 2019. A concept for automated construction progress monitoring: technologies adoption for benchmarking project performance control. *Arabian Journal for Science and Engineering*, 44: 4993–5008.

Alizadehsalehi, S. and Yitmen, I. 2021. Digital twin-based progress monitoring management model through reality capture to extended reality technologies (DRX). *Smart and Sustainable Built Environment*.

Alizadehsalehi, S., Hadavi, A. and Huang, J.C. 2020. From BIM to extended reality in AEC industry. *Automation in Construction*, 116: 103254.

Banerjee, A., Dalal, R., Mittal, S. and Joshi, K.P. 2017. Generating digital twin models using knowledge graphs for industrial production lines. *UMBC Information Systems Department 9th International ACM Web Science Conference*, June 25, 2017 in Troy, NY, USA.

Berlanga, R., Museros, L., Llidó, D.M., Sanz, I. and Aramburu, M.J. 2021. Towards semantic digital twins for social networks. *Proceedings of the Second International Workshop on Semantic Digital Twins (SeDiT 2021)*, Hersonissos, Greece, June 6, 2021.

Boschert, S., Heinrich, C. and Rosen, R. 2018. Next generation digital twin. *Proc. tmce. Las Palmas de Gran Canaria, Spain*, 7–11.

Du, J., Zhu, Q., Shi, Y., Wang, Q., Lin, Y. and Zhao, D. 2020. Cognition digital twins for personalized information systems of smart cities: Proof of concept. *Journal of Management in Engineering*, 36: 04019052.

Duprez, J. 2019. Approach to structure, formalize and map MBSE meta-models and semantic rules. *INCOSE International Symposium*. Wiley Online Library, 22–36.

Eirinakis, P., Kalaboukas, K., Lounis, S., Mourtos, I., Rožanec, J.M., Stojanovic, N. and Zois, G. 2020. Enhancing cognition for digital twins. *IEEE International Conference on Engineering, Technology and Innovation (ICE/ITMC)*, 2020. IEEE, 1–7.

Eirinakis, P., Lounis, S., Plitsos, S., Arampatzis, G., Kalaboukas, K., Kenda, K., Lu, J., Rožanec, J.M. and Stojanovic, N. 2022. Cognitive Digital Twins for resilience in production: A conceptual framework. *Information*, 13: 33.

Essa, E., Hossain, M.S., Tolba, A.S., Raafat, H.M., Elmogy, S. and Muahmmad, G. 2020. Toward cognitive support for automated defect detection. *Neural Computing and Applications*, 32: 4325–4333.

Fernández, F., Sánchez, Á., Vélez, J.F. and Moreno, A.B. 2019. Symbiotic autonomous systems with consciousness using digital twins. *International Work-Conference on the Interplay Between Natural and Artificial Computation*. Springer, 23–32.

Gómez-Berbís, J.M. and Amescua-Seco, A.d. 2019. SEDIT: semantic digital twin based on industrial IoT data management and knowledge graphs. *International Conference on Technologies and Innovation*. Springer, 178–188.

Grieves, M. 2014. Digital twin: Manufacturing excellence through virtual factory replication. *White paper*, 1: 1–7.

IBM. 2021. *Cognitive Manufacturing: An Overview and Four Applications that are Transforming Manufacturing Today*. Technical Report. https://www.ibm.com/downloads/cas/VDNKMWM6.

Jacoby, M. and Usländer, T. 2020. Digital twin and internet of things—Current standards landscape. *Applied Sciences*, 10: 6519.

Kalaboukas, K., Rožanec, J., Košmerlj, A., Kyritsis, D. and Arampatzis, G. 2021. Implementation of Cognitive Digital Twins in connected and agile supply networks—An operational model. *Applied Sciences*, 11(9): 4103.

Kharlamov, E., Martin-Recuerda, F., Perry, B., Cameron, D., Fjellheim, R. and Waaler, A. 2018. Towards semantically enhanced digital twins. *IEEE International Conference on Big Data (Big Data)*, 2018. IEEE, 4189–4193.

Kiritsis, D. 2011. Closed-loop PLM for intelligent products in the era of the Internet of things. *Computer-Aided Design*, 43(5): 479–501.

Kokar, M.M. and Endsley, M.R. 2012. Situation awareness and cognitive modeling. *IEEE Intelligent Systems*, 27: 91–96.

Kor, M., Yitmen, I. and Alizadehsalehi, S. 2022. An investigation for integration of deep learning and digital twins towards Construction 4.0. *Smart and Sustainable Built Environment*.

Liu, Y. and Liang, L. 2015. Evaluating and developing resource-based operations strategy for competitive advantage: An exploratory study of Finnish high-tech manufacturing industries. *International Journal of Production Research*, 53(4): 1019–1037.

Lu, J., Zheng, X., Gharaei, A., Kalaboukas, K. and Kiritsis, D. 2020. Cognitive twins for supporting decision-makings of internet of things systems. *Proceedings of 5th International Conference on the Industry 4.0 Model for Advanced Manufacturing*. Springer, 105–115.

Matthews, S. 2018. *Designing Better Machines: The Evolution of a Cognitive Digital Twin Explained*. Keynote Delivered at Hannover Messe: Hanover, Germany.

Rožanec, J.M., Lu, J., Rupnik, J., Škrjanc, M., Mladenić, D., Fortuna, B., Zheng, X. and Kiritsis, D. 2021. Actionable cognitive twins for decision making in manufacturing. *arXiv preprint arXiv:2103.12854*.

Saracco, R. 2019. Digital twins: Bridging physical space and cyberspace. *Computer*, 52: 58–64.

Saracevic, F. 2017. Cognitive Digital Twin. IBM.

Shi, Y., Shen, W., Wang, L., Longo, F., Nicoletti, L. and Padovano, A. 2022. A Cognitive Digital Twins framework for human-robot collaboration. *Procedia Computer Science*, 200: 1867–1874.

Tao, F., Zhang, M., Cheng, J. and Qi, Q. 2017. Digital twin workshop: A new paradigm for future workshop. *Computer Integrated Manufacturing Systems*, 23: 1–9.

Tao, F., Zhang, H., Liu, A. and Nee, A.Y. 2018. Digital twin in industry: State-of-the-art. *IEEE Transactions on Industrial Informatics*, 15: 2405–2415.

Yitmen, I. and Alizadehsalehi, S. 2021. Towards a Digital Twin-based SMART Built Environment. *BIM-enabled Cognitive Computing for Smart Built Environment*. CRC Press.

Yitmen, I., Alizadehsalehi, S., Akıner, İ. and Akıner, M.E. 2021. An adapted model of cognitive digital twins for building lifecycle management. *Applied Sciences*, 11: 4276.

Zhang, N., Bahsoon, R. and Theodoropoulos, G. 2020. Towards engineering cognitive digital twins with self-awareness. *IEEE International Conference on Systems, Man, and Cybernetics (SMC)*, 2020. IEEE, 3891–3891.

Zheng, X., Lu, J. and Kiritsis, D. 2021. The emergence of cognitive digital twin: Vision, challenges and opportunities. *International Journal of Production Research*, 1–23.

Zhong, R.Y., Xu, X., Klotz, E. and Newman, S.T. 2017. Intelligent manufacturing in the context of industry 4.0: A review. *Engineering*, 3(5): 616–630.

Chapter 3

Integration of Digital Twins, Blockchain and AI in Metaverse
Enabling Technologies and Challenges

Ibrahim Yitmen,[1,*] *Sepehr Alizadehsalehi,*[2]
Muhammed Ernur Akiner[3] *and Ilknur Akiner*[4]

3.1 Introduction

Metaverse first appeared in Neal Stephenson's novel Snow Crash in 1992 (Joshua 2017). The fast rise of blockchain, the so-called Internet of Things or IoT, Virtual Reality (VR) and Augmented Reality (AR), Artificial Intelligence or AI, cloud and edge computing, and other technologies has led to the term "metaverse" become one of the most prominent buzzwords in the IT sector (Yang et al. 2022). Consider a computer-based or virtual world where you can locate tangible objects, friends, buildings, and universe information. The terms "meta" and "universe" combine to generate the word "metaverse," which refers to a three-dimensional (3D)

[1] Department of Construction Engineering and Lighting Science, School of Engineering, Jönköping University, Gjuterigatan 5, 551 11, Jönköping, Sweden.
[2] Project Management Program, Department of Civil and Environmental Engineering, Northwestern University, Evanston, IL, USA.
[3] Vocational School of Technical Sciences, Akdeniz University, 07058 Antalya, Turkey.
[4] Department of Architecture, Faculty of Architecture, Akdeniz University, 07058 Antalya, Turkey.
Emails: sepehralizadehsalehi2018@u.northwestern.edu; ernurakiner@akdeniz.edu.tr; ilknurakiner@akdeniz.edu.tr
* Corresponding author: ibrahim.yitmen@ju.se

virtual environment that attempts to mirror the actual world as closely as possible (Far and Rad 2022).

Although the metaverse is the successor of the internet, today's edge devices may not meet the high-specification requirements of showing high-definition 3D settings. Users must be able to access the metaverse to succeed as the next-generation internet, much as the internet entertains billions of people daily (Xu et al. 2022). Because the tactile internet, VR, and AR are important parts of 6-G, new communication technologies will be developed to enable the Metaverse (Saad et al. 2019). Furthermore, the current trend away from traditional communication measures such as data rates, and toward co-designing computation and communication systems, such as computation-oriented communication (COC) (Letaief et al. 2021), indicates that the next-generation mobile edge networks would help to distribute the metaverse to mobile users with computational limitations (Xu et al. 2022).

Users are given natural feelings via high-level and realistic simulation, which greatly improves technology and enables designers to foresee future consequences of items and minimize probable difficulties (Thomas 1999). Digital twins (DTs) are the most realistic physical simulations available, accurately signaling and predicting all of the computer's physical output (Tao et al. 2018). Metaverse is projected to connect the actual and virtual worlds by employing DT to create a virtual reproduction of the real environment (Wu et al. 2021). The rigorous sensor, communication, and processor requirements impeded the metaverse's real-time and scalable implementation (Xu et al. 2022). VR and AR headsets are two gadgets; AI and Machine Learning or ML are scientific and technological areas that have significantly advanced the metaverse and virtual worlds in addition to VR and AR (Khurana et al. 2019).

Blockchain technology will be critical in achieving the metaverse at mobile edge networks due to the "Internet of Everything's" paradigm shift from large data to decentralized small data (Saad et al. 2019, Xu et al. 2022). Blockchain is expected to bring up new possibilities in the metaverse, resulting in a new wave of technical innovation and the industrial revolution (Yang et al. 2022). On the other hand, barriers to metaverse development can be overcome through recent AI breakthroughs, big data analytics, AI-powered content creation, and intelligence distribution. As a result, combining AI and metaverse technologies has become a possible trend for promoting the positive growth of the blockchain/AI-powered metaverse ecosystem (Yang et al. 2022).

On the other hand, combining AI and blockchain with the metaverse poses significant research hurdles. Because of the characteristics of digital commodities and marketplaces, transaction volumes in metaverse systems are substantially greater compared to the physical world. Non-fungible

Tokens (NFT) on the Blockchain allow avatars to create content that can be sold for digital certificates (Nadini et al. 2021, Lambert 2021). This chapter discusses the integration of DT, Blockchain, and AI in Metaverse, emphasizing enabling technologies and difficulties.

3.2 Metaverse Enabling Technologies and Ecosystems

As shown in Fig. 3.1, integrating the real world along with its digital counterparts and moving toward the metaverse necessitates the inclusion of technologies like blockchain, computer vision, distributed networks, cloud computing, object identification, as well as ecosystem concerns like avatar, content production, social acceptability, accountability, security, and privacy. Figure 3.1 illustrates an overview of the major subjects in the context of technology and the ecosystem.

The two types' focus zones are shown in Fig. 3.2, where technology permits the metaverse to function as a vast application. Extended reality (XR) and user interaction techniques, which come under the technology

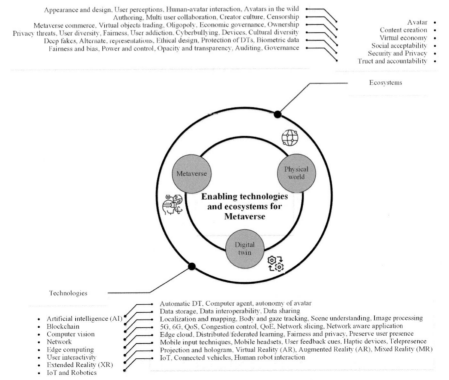

Figure 3.1: Enabling technologies and ecosystems for Metaverse (Adapted from Lee et al. 2021a).

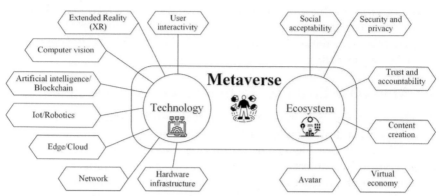

Figure 3.2: The metaverse's primary areas divided into technology and ecosystem (Adapted from Lee et al. 2021a).

side of the eight pillars, may be used to enter the metaverse by humans, such as manipulating virtual objects. User interaction with XR enables the completion of different activities within computer vision or CV, AI, blockchain, robots, IoT, and the metaverse.

The efficiency of latency-sensitive and bandwidth-hungry applications can be enhanced through edge computing. The local data source is operated as preprocessing data by using edge devices. Cloud computing, on the other hand, is known for its highly scalable processing and storage power.

Combining cloud and edge-based services may result in synergies such as increased application performance and user experiences. Consequently, with the right hardware infrastructure, edge devices, and cloud services, CV, AI, robots, and IoT might be enabled, as well as a better mobile network. An ecosystem is a self-contained, meta-sized virtual habitat modeled after reality. In the real world, human users may utilize XR and user interaction techniques to control their avatars for community activities like content creation. These Metaverse activities have naturally led to the creation of a virtual economy. The three main problems we deal with are social acceptability, security and privacy, and trust and accountability. Ownership of virtual economic products, for example, should be kept, and avatars must recognize the impacts of such items; human users exist inside the metaverse and want their behaviors to be free of privacy and security concerns (Lee et al. 2021a). Figure 3.2 displays the major technologies that ignited the 'Digital Big Bang.'

3.3 Metaverse Artificial Intelligence (AI)

AI promises to be able to explain every aspect of learning (Dick 2019). Modern AI research emphasizes ML, deep learning (DL), and reinforcement learning in computer vision, decision-making, and natural language processing (NLP). Individuals are naturally drawn to using artificial intelligence to materialize the metaverse due to real-world developments in AI (Yang et al. 2022).

3.3.1 *Typical AI Algorithms*

Computer learning approaches, such as linear regression (Jammalamadaka 2003), random forest (Oshiro et al. 2012), and decomposition of the singular value (Paige and Saunders 1981), enable machines to learn from experience and data in the same manner that people do. The support vector machine (Vapnik 1999), for example, is a sample machine learning method used for pattern categorization, regression, and learning a ranking function.

Convolutional neural networks (CNNs and also known as ConvNets in Fig. 3.3(b)) are deep neural networks influenced by biological neural networks. Conventional CNNs use a convolution kernel with a shared-weight design to create equivariant translation responses or feature maps. CNN includes convolution, pooling, and fully connected layers (Ketkar and Moolayil 2021). CNN uses a technique known as weight sharing across neurons to achieve a large decrease in size. Consequently, CNNs have supervised learning algorithms that may be used in various computer vision applications, including augmented reality, image search, and face recognition.

Reinforcement learning describes an agent's sequential decision-making problem while interacting with a dynamic environment. Experience is earned via trial and error (Kaebling et al. 1996). Figure 3.3(c) shows the RL schematic. When paired with Markov Decision Processes (MDPs) (Van der Wal 1980) and deep neural networks, deep reinforcement learning has the potential to transform AI. It represents a step toward constructing an autonomous system with an understanding of the visual world, as Arulkumaran et al. (2017) declared. Value functions and policy search are two strategies for RL problem-solving. Asynchronous benefit actor-critic advancements and deep learning-based RL (DRL) algorithm optimization (TRPO) have been found. These DRL algorithms can surpass humans in some fields (Arulkumaran et al. 2017).

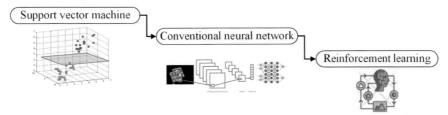

Figure 3.3: Illustration of artificial intelligence technologies (Adapted from Yang et al. 2022).

3.3.2 Metaverse AI-based Activities

Ando et al. (2012) provide a technique for inferring seen exhibits from a Second Life mobility log in a metaverse museum. They must first detect which exhibits the user sees by focusing on the avatar's status to deploy recommendation systems in metaverse museums and complete this job quickly and correctly.

Yampolskiy et al. (2012) describe methods for accurately assessing and recognizing avatar faces. The prototype uses a causal engine based on the unreal tournament gaming engine. This engine bypasses the native physics engine to provide alternate outcomes to competitor actions. Civilization VI, Stellaris, and the research game Prom Week can be examined to evaluate human-centered artificial intelligence-based games through the evaluation technique mentioned by Kreminski et al. (2019). Existing assessment approaches make it difficult to comprehend, such as the normal narrative framework players have in their heads when playing a game. In a game, many subjective experience narratives may occur.

DRL is expected to be a viable solution for automated trading in the open and decentralized metaverse environment since it enables a well-trained agent to make decisions automatically (Puder et al. 1995). According to Liu et al. (2021a, 2021b), the proper use of AI will transform from conventional exchange to a robotized machine learning technique. As a result, Liu et al. (2021a) offer FinRL, a DRL-based system that can effectively design a multi-factor model for ecosystem trade automation to decrease the simulation-to-reality gap and data processing overhead (Liu et al. 2021b).

3.4 Metaverse Blockchain

Blockchain is widely considered to be one of the metaverse's fundamental infrastructures. Blockchain is expected to link disparate small industries and create a stable economic structure, enabling the metaverse to have transparent, open, efficient, and trustworthy rules (Yang et al. 2022). Data traceability and secrecy are provided to metaverse users through hash algorithms and timestamp technologies, for example. The traditional Blockchain architecture comprises network, data, consensus, application, and contract layers. The following is a list of the connections between those levels and the metaverse:

- Data verification and transmission methodologies provide network support for diversified data transfer and metaverse economic system verification.

- The credit issue of metaverse transactions is solved via consensus procedures.
- Blockchain distributed storage assures the protection of virtual assets and metaverse users' identities.
- Smart contract technology ensures that all Metaverse members are in a secure environment. It implements Metaverse value exchange and ensures that system rules specified in contract codes are executed transparently. Smart contracts' codes can't be updated after they've been deployed. The terms of such smart contracts must be followed to the letter.

Metaverse economic systems, as demonstrated in Fig. 3.4, need decentralized exchanges to support cross-chain circulation tokens or NFTs. Based on the decentralized exchange protocol, Tian et al. (2021) propose a decentralized cryptocurrency trading system. This system selects trustworthy people for validation by using two forms of consensus techniques, such as PoW and Proof of Deposit. The number of participants,

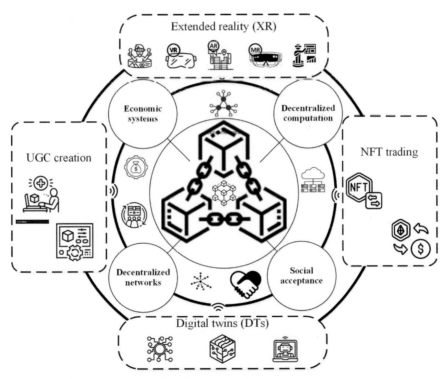

Figure 3.4: Different scenarios of wireless blockchain for virtual and physical services in the Metaverse (Adapted from Xu et al. 2022).

not the number of transactions done by a single participant, determines platform overhead such as provisioning and execution charges.

The economic loop of user-generated digital content is represented, minted as NFTs, and traded for bitcoin. For financial systems, avatar society, and edge resource management, the cooperation of numerous blockchains is depicted.

3.4.1 Metaverse Transaction Characteristics

The metaverse features many financial facts: estate purchases, item rentals, service purchases, and almost anything else that exists in reality. Consequently, Metaverse transactions are not confined to intra-metaverse or token transfers.

On a typical blockchain, when a transaction is started, it is transmitted to miners and kept in localized transaction pools. The miner chooses transactions to agree on and then utilizes hash-based consensus. The first miner that discovers a printing of the puzzle that satisfies the stated difficulty will upload the block to the chain and notify all other miners. Because the metaverse leads trading in the digital world every second while utilizing numerous intraoral inter-metaverse apps, these blockchain nodes are anticipated to handle many transactions. Full blockchain nodes in the metaverse must, as is common, maintain all previous transactions locally, putting huge pressure on the full nodes.

Another problem with metaverse transactions is ensuring that confirmation latency is kept to a minimum. End-to-end latency for Internet apps that cater to human behaviors is measured in milliseconds. Furthermore, metaverse applications based on 3D display and interaction need a 10-millisecond delay to avoid vertigo. Metaverse transactions must have a low confirmation latency for these low-latency applications.

3.4.2 Blockchain-empowered Market in Metaverse

Decentralized finance (DeFi), made possible by modern blockchain technology, has the potential to boost the metaverse's decentralized market and commerce. This section looks at several common studies related to the DeFi market and industry. Daian et al. (2020) investigated the behavior of cryptocurrency arbitrage bots, who may watch transactions in the transaction pool and arbitrage. Daian et al. (2020) also proposed a cooperative strategy for optimizing arbitrage robot profit, as well as the fact that miners can behave as arbitrage robots in certain situations.

The MEV's so-called miner extractable value, on the other hand, may encourage the growth of diverging attacks. A cooperative bidding technique is offered to maximize profit. The monthly MEV supply is also more than 25 times the cost of a 51 percent attack on Ethereum (Daian et al. 2020).

DeFi is a revolutionary approach in the metaverse to construct imaginative economic structures, which are established mainly on smart contracts and fungible tokens or FT. Uniswap, an Ethereum-based decentralized exchange or DEX, offer users cash flows for their tokens (Angeris et al. 2019). DEXs are a new type of exchange that allows for safe peer-to-peer crypto-asset token trading (Dai 2020). The atomic swap is at the heart of a DEX, allowing multiple users to trade tokens or crypto-assets without needing a service provider. A peer-to-peer token trading platform is provided by Cybex (2021), a DEXs-based DApp. Cybex also uses the CYB token.

It should be noted that CYB may only be used to pay for new token exchanges, loan crypto-asset tokens, and Cybex market transaction charges. A network of validator nodes maintains the Diem Blockchain (2021), the payment system's technological backbone. Because blockchain software is open-source, anybody may build on it and expand their financial needs.

3.4.3 *Authentication in the Metaverse Powered by Blockchain*

The sale of virtual assets like land, rare items, valuable real estate, land development, leasing, gaming task rewards, and cryptocurrency investment returns are now the most important economic activities in the metaverse. Consequently, the metaverse presents a new kind of funding influenced by both the physical and virtual worlds.

The non-fungible token, or NFT, has traditionally been utilized to commemorate special anniversaries or amass digital assets. It recently merged with metaverse to launch a contemporary digital content enterprise (Etherium 2021, GDA 2021). NFT can secure the uniqueness of digital assets. The methodology behind this is recording encrypted transaction records on the blockchain. Tokens have a particular and recognizable value that may be used to verify who owns a digital asset. The blockchain-enabled NFT in the metaverse has been utilized to illustrate the unique avatar characteristics. Products are scanned into three-dimensional forms or turned into an avatar (Jeon 2022).

3.5 The Architecture of the Metaverse

Duan et al. (2021) presented the Metaverse design from a macro viewpoint, as illustrated in Fig. 3.5, including ecosystem, interaction, and infrastructure.

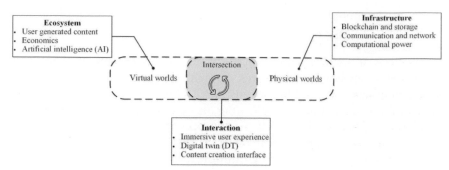

Figure 3.5: The Metaverse's three-layer architecture (Adapted from Duan et al. 2021).

3.5.1 Infrastructure

The infrastructure layer covers processing, communication, blockchain, and storage when operating a virtual environment.

Computation and communication. The metaverse's operation requires significant computational expenses. Communication technologies are important to support since the metaverse should be accessible everywhere. More focus is on how technological advancements in computing and communication might enhance the metaverse's user experience. How specialized computing equipment can be designed to accommodate the metaverse's massive computational usage, how cloud computing can be coordinated with mobile devices to improve the user experience on many terminals, and in the metaverse, the data format or encoding strategy to best transmit and transfer large-scale data are the open research issues for creating computers and communication for the metaverse:

Blockchain and storage. Everyone on the earth is projected to be connected through the metaverse. As a result, big data, maps, and roles will be produced and kept in mass storage. The blockchain must promote decentralization and fairness in the metaverse by facilitating sustainable ecosystem functioning (Berg et al. 2019, Cai et al. 2018). Advanced blockchain systems, such as Ethereum (Buterin 2014), contain a smart contract that might allow DApps to run, greatly increasing the blockchain's application reach and enabling the metaverse (Cai et al. 2018). It creates a decentralized social environment. Blockchain is based on a distributed ledger, it is considered an infrastructure component of the metaverse, and its complete application in the ecosystem layer will be offered. While developing the metaverse, how can the metaverse's massive data be effectively stored and retrieved, what consensus method should the blockchain use to sustain long-term economics, and how mass storage and blockchain can data be distributed and coordinated efficiently are the open research issues to be investigated.

3.5.2 Interaction

The interaction layer that links the actual and virtual worlds is a key component of the immersive user experience, DT, and content development.

Immersive user experience. Two major components must be addressed in user interactions and the metaverse to ensure an immersive user experience. First, data from the real world should be sent to the metaverse so that users may instruct their avatars to do the required actions. Also, real-time three-dimensional rendering technologies like virtual and augmented reality serve as the main interaction interfaces. On the other hand, current methods can only help in particular areas and cannot deliver a fully immersive user experience; hence how we can learn more about our users' preferences and improve our Metaverse interactions, and how we can mix input/output modalities during interactions to provide a comprehensive user experience are the current research problems arise.

Digital twins. Other things or creatures in the actual world may interfere with the virtual metaverse, portrayed as DTs in the simulated space (Essa 2000, El Saddik 2018). Ubiquitous sensing technologies may acquire physical device characteristics to keep them in the same state as their digital counterparts, and this is an interdisciplinary field that should include material science, signal processing, the IoT, and pattern recognition (Paulovich et al. 2018). On the other hand, virtual environment parameters may be returned to physical devices following the operation and processing in the metaverse. The DT generation in the metaverse is in its infancy and needs more investigation about how the physical environment linking to the metaverse should be represented as DTs, and how DTs in the metaverse might be more efficiently utilized to aid the real world.

Interface for creating content. The metaverse is an infinitely scalable and interoperable virtual world always evolving. The operators must construct the core components while users fill the universe with innovative user-generated content (UGC). Consequently, high-efficiency content creation is a crucial aspect of user-Metaverse interactions. 3D reconstruction approaches may be employed in the metaverse to generate DTs of buildings, objects, and environments in the real world (Ma and Liu 2018). 3D modeling software may be used to produce 3D models. On the other hand, these modeling methods depend on experience. How the physical properties of real-world things can be correctly replicated in the virtual world, and how existing interaction modes could be useful for content creation, experience, and functionality are the open research topics.

3.5.3 Ecosystem

The ecosystem may create a parallel living environment that continually benefits every one of the world's populations. Through actions like befriending AI-driven nonplayer individuals, people may have different social experiences than they would in the real world (NPC). UGC, economics, and AI are the three layers that make up the ecosystem layer.

Content created by users. User-generated content (UGC) is material that users develop instead of professionals or site management (Min et al. 2019). UGC in the metaverse is frequently variable and requires ownership (Krum et al. 2008). The blockchain-based NFT is an innovative mechanism for UGC by guaranteeing a digital value that is not interchangeable. UGC is preserved as an NFT on the blockchain. They also use smart contracts to trade them for liquidity. Although the UGCs may encourage individuals, it also poses many research questions about how more UGC based applications can be designed to promote the value of user-generated content, and how a fair mechanism can guarantee that UGCs are unique and prevent deliberate duplication.

Economics. Economic issues are critical in the metaverse's ecology, which may supply rich material and a vibrant community. The metaverse may experiment with new economic models thanks to a decentralized financial system built on smart contracts and the Fungible Token or FT. Existing successful alternatives, such as Uniswap and an Ethereum-based Decentralized Exchange or DEX, provide customers liquidity (Angeris et al. 2019). The auction of virtual items like land, rare things, valuable real estate, leasing, and prizes for accomplishing revenues from cryptocurrency investments are now the most important economic activity in the metaverse. Consequently, the metaverse generates a new kind of funding influenced by both real and virtual worlds. On the other hand, smart contract application development is subject to outside threats. The metaverse smart contract application development is vulnerable to external threats, and the metaverse fails decentralized financial services. As a result, how irreversible and long-lasting smart linkages could be utilized to ensure that the metaverse's economic system is secure, and how effective DeFi models can be created to increase NFT liquidity are the research questions to be formulated.

Artificial intelligence. According to the metaverse's core principle, advanced data analytics for analyzing, regulating, and NPCs are significant aspects of the metaverse. Planning-driven NPCs function as characters such as villains, companions, and plot support by posing challenges that offer aid and giving storyline support. Cutting-edge AI, deep learning (DL), and reinforcement learning (RL) are frequently used, leading to advancements in natural language processing (NLP) and computer vision (CV). How AI technology may enhance the metaverse's user experience by making it easier for users to operate and how AI technology can help NPCs comprehend and communicate more effectively are the research questions to be developed to give users an experience using NPCs.

3.6 Combined Digital Twins, AI, and Blockchain in Metaverse

According to Far and Rad (2022), the relationship between the DTs and the metaverse is depicted as a three-layer architecture supported by blockchain technology and a metaverse interface (see Fig. 3.6). As Yaqoob et al. (2020) state, a blockchain-based NFT is equal to DT and offers several advantages:

- DTs transactions offer immutability and transparency regarding the preceding premise, including purchasing, selling, or ownership transfer. As a result, they may be regarded to be safe against cyber-fraud.
- Since blockchain promotes autonomy, the outcomes of DTs cannot be tampered with by any authority or privileged insider. As a consequence, DT outputs based on the metaverse are trustworthy.
- Due to the decentralized governance of the metaverse, all authorized identities, including DTs, are legal since they are all recognized by a consensus process.
- Blockchain solves many security and resiliency concerns. Metaverse-based DTs are more dependable compared to centralized versions, and they are also more secure.
- Global DT traceability: Blockchain properties such as linking blocks, transparency, and immutability enable global DT and correspondence tracing.
- Product lifecycle management: Any Metaverse-based DT and its corresponding real-world product lifespan can be easily controlled.
- Communication between peers or P2P communications allows machine/user or machine/machine contact across DTs without the intermediate requirement.
- DTs data coordination and access credentials: Blockchain, as a Metaverse infrastructure, allows business coordinators to access DTs data readily.
- Metaverse's leading blockchain capabilities and user-friendly aspects are transparency and accountability for DTs data. Responsibility may

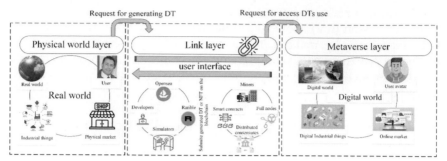

Figure 3.6: The three-layer design of the link between the physical world and the metaverse with the approach of applying DT in Metaverse (Adapted from Far and Rad 2022).

also aid in addressing regulatory issues regarding the legality and usage of DT.

- Decentralized Infrastructure: Metaverse offers DTs decentralized infrastructure that supports all blockchain features. As a result, using DTs in Metaverse is a safe and dependable option.

1. Layer of the Physical/Real World. Users and components in the real-world demand accurate DTs, which are, as previously noted, the best alternative for this need. As the name indicates, people, goods, and services (marketplaces, healthcare facilities, retail, and entertainment) are included in the physical/real-world layer. The requests are sent to the link layer, and the users pay costs referred to as the metaverse to connect to the digital world. DTs may be built on a vast globe, and the planet's largest DT is the world DT. Industrial and commercial DTs are the most common or relevant DTs. Furthermore, in the metaverse, individuals like to have incredibly accurate avatars. As a result, it encourages individuals to utilize DTs in Metaverse.

2. Link (User Interface) Layer. The layer of architecture which connects the real world to the metaverse, along with two sublayers as follows:

i) Simulation/Migration: The Link layer's first sublayer includes NFT generating services such as Opensea and Rarible. Computers such as 3D scanners and developers work together to produce digital representations of real-world items (DTs). Programmers and developers try to create exceptionally realistic and thorough DTs to transmit true experiences to real-world Metaverse users. Consequently, expert developers, affluent businesses, and sophisticated computers compete for new clients at this level. Following the development of the DT, the service/user pays for it by uploading it to the blockchain.

ii) Blockchain: Data, notably DTs, becomes accessible by DApps and other services after being submitted to the blockchain. Blockchain, which contains miners, smart contracts, blockchain nodes, and full nodes, is expected to be part of the Metaverse architecture. Blockchain tracks all Metaverse correspondences and transactions as a distributed ledger. Users in the metaverse may use the blockchain to submit new transactions or material and examine and utilize previously contributed information.

3. Metaverse as a Digital World Layer. The planned building's most attractive layer has a 3D digital environment (Metaverse). In this layer, DTs are combined with blockchain and smart contracts. In the metaverse layer, all people, services, and products may exist as DT or NFT, just as they do in the actual world. The digital world based on DT delivers people's avatars, retail marketplaces, manufacturing facilities, and all high-accuracy industrial items cost-effectively and remotely, digitally servicing the everyday needs of regular people and managers.

3.7 The Change of Business Model and Architecture Engineering and Construction (AEC) Vision in Metaverse

Clients in the conventional architectural and building sector will search for inventive architects, engineers, and contractors to engage in their projects to accomplish a task at the lowest possible cost and in the quickest possible time. Meanwhile, other AEC rivals' ideas will not be employed if they do not win the project contract (Gaffar 2021, Lee et al. 2021b).

Unlike the actual world, the metaverse offers a virtual metropolis full of possibilities. AEC provides several options to produce its unique digital design for everyone who wishes AEC to design art pieces such as architectural design and structural engineering items across the globe. A building project in the actual world takes at least 5 to 7 years from the design stage to the final delivery of the project. AEC provides various ideas, experiences, and technical contributions throughout the process. Thousands of design, structural, MEP, financial, and construction management restrictions are also resolved cooperatively by the AEC. Metaverse provides a platform for AEC to participate and collaborate to bring all knowledge from various disciplines together and virtually stimulate the project, which speeds up the overall coordination process in the digital world (Eno et al. 2009, Lee 2021b, Moneta 2020, Vlavianos and Nagakura 2021). The stimulated project may replicate multiple situations in the metaverse to test and validate other real-life characteristics, and the data gained helps enhance the project's originality, buildability, and sustainability in the actual world (Kit 2022). Unlike the traditional 3D model concept, NFT architecture can be more specifically and precisely described as a form of art even before it is built, allowing AEC to develop ideas that take their profession to new heights and create opportunities for

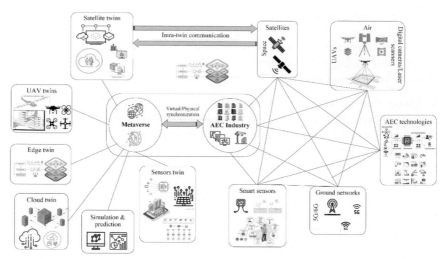

Figure 3.7: The AEC industry achieving real-time physical/virtual synchronization of the Metaverse and intelligent edge networks (Adapted from Xu et al. 2022).

AEC to produce and sell their digital version of the design in the digital economy.

With the growth of AI research, it was about the next-generation virtual world in the AEC business employing artificial intelligence. Users, for example, may use AI to train their avatars to do professional tasks in a virtual environment and Metaverse (Lee 2021b). The issue of labor resources, time, and cost in the actual world is readily substituted and compromised by deploying AI in the metaverse. A tough endeavor will take much work and time in the real world. However, employing AI avatars in the virtual environment and metaverse makes it possible to develop the task quickly and continuously for a long time.

Sensing and actuation need widespread edge devices and servers. The DT (Han et al. 2021) is one possible solution for virtual services, such as city twins and smart factory copies, to virtualize real-world edge networks to improve efficiency. By observing the DTs of edge devices and required infrastructures like UAVs, and space-air-ground integrated networks, users may quickly regulate their physical entities in the real world, which is critical to allocate resources efficiently in secure communications among physical and virtual components within mobile edge networks throughout physical and digital world synchronization to achieve seamless real-time immersion in the metaverse (Cheng et al. 2018, Cheng et al. 2019).

3.8 Challenges for Actualizing Metaverse

Digital twins, digital natives, and the metaverse are the three phases of moving from physical to virtual integration. Technological innovation and ecosystem-building efforts are required for our immersive future in the metaverse. Eternal, shared, contemporaneous, and three-dimensional, the limitless virtual-physical integrated cyberspace will be able to accommodate beyond those on earth. Even other planets may benefit from interplanetary transportation and communication (Alhilal et al. 2021).

Consequently, technology enablers and their technical demands have never been higher. The metaverse also emphasizes bringing virtual worlds together and demanding tasks in large-scale virtual environments. Thus, various socio-economic systems will arise in metacyberspace. Currency, commodity and capital markets, conventions, rules, cultures, and social characteristics are possible examples. Figure 3.8 displays a building and developing cyberspace during the following decade. Autonomous, permanent, united, and infinite cyberspace is made possible by technology enablers and ecosystem drivers. The fourteen major categories described in this chapter are interrelated; for example, Zhang et al. (2021) utilize IoT, network, CV, edge, XR, and user interaction in their design.

All disciplines should be approached holistically by researchers and practitioners. The metaverse, for example, must combine the virtual and real worlds, even if the virtual world is more accurate. It must rely on XR-driven immersive technologies (Lee et al. 2021a). Firstly, edge and cloud produce zero-latency virtual worlds. Secondly, as motion capture and gesture recognition, avatar and user engagement work seamlessly with XR. Thirdly, AI and computer vision are utilized to understand the metaverse and the production of DTs at scale. Finally, edge and AI work together to preserve privacy.

Extended Reality. Virtual worlds act as the metaverse's technical foundation, and it evolves from concept to reality, with VR/AR/MR as a crucial step. It is a virtual space where people can interact in a digital

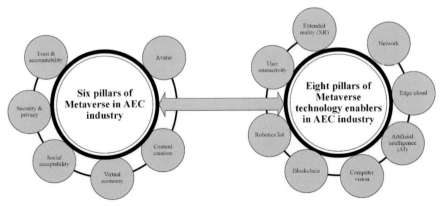

Figure 3.8: A plan for three-stage metaverse growth toward surreality (Adapted from Lee et al. 2021a).

setting. Users dwell in a world made of tangible virtual images as if they were in a parallel reality to ours. Such immersive technology will aid in developing the immersive internet of the future. For a realistic experience in the virtual networked world, the user uses VR to make the virtual world's functioning similar to that of the real world.

AR/MR, on the other hand, has the potential to alter the physical environment, which is becoming more intertwined with the metaverse. Digital entities migrating from virtual (VR) to real (MR) environments should get more design and technology attention. In principle, MR and the Metaverse allow virtual entities to integrate with the real world fully. Consequently, super-realistic virtual creatures combined with real-world surroundings will be shown on large displays, mobile headsets, or holography at any time and place. Users in the metaverse may interact and cooperate with real-world objects through digital entities. Consumers may use XR to access many technologies, including AI, computer vision, and IoT sensors (Lee et al. 2021a).

User Interactivity. Mobile user interaction methods, via the lens of XR, leads users to interact with digital overlays. Invisible computer interfaces allowing ubiquitous human involvement with virtual surroundings in the metaverse may be created through mobile processes that are developed in a body-centric, sensitive manner. Furthermore, multi-modal feedback signals, notably haptic feedback on mobile methods, let users interact with IoT devices and service robots in the metaverse with an improved sense of realism. Virtual worlds (VR/AR/MR), on the other hand, are augmented and complex, giving users a dreamy experience of certain feelings but lacking the ability to share and interact with other senses.

Brain-computer interface (BCI) technology links the human brain and numerous technological devices, enabling people to connect with them without language or limbs. Humanitarian sensations are produced by sending signals toward the brain, and BCI innovation may recreate all sensory experiences by activating the proper brain regions and using a BCI directly linked to the cerebral cortex. Neuralink66 is the best technology for connecting players to the virtual world in the posterity meta-universe age (Lee et al. 2021a).

Robotics and the Internet of Things. IoT devices use XR systems and autonomous automobiles to demonstrate their operations. Also, these systems let people join in decision-making and data management. Meanwhile, excellent XR interface designs will be used to make human-in-the-loop decisions. The user-centric design of immersive and virtual worlds through the design space of user interfaces with different forms of robotics, dark patterns of IoT and robotics, and nuanced controls of new robotic systems are still in their infancy.

Artificial Intelligence. AI, specifically deep learning, has progressed in Metaverse automation for designers, exceeding conventional methods. However, AI is not being used to expedite user operations and improve the immersive experience. Existing AI models are often highly complex and need significant computing power, incompatible with resource-constrained mobile devices. Consequently, it's necessary to create AI models that are both light and efficient.

Blockchain. Proof of work is the consensus process used by blockchain, which encourages users to spend time-solving puzzles regarding data security. Encryption data verification is a slower technique compared to the previous approaches. Consequently, an accelerated method is necessary to improve data scalability and access speed. Furthermore, all users access their data with public blockchains, raising privacy problems. Consequently, solutions for securing privacy in public blockchains may be investigated.

Computer Vision. Computer vision is the ability of computers to understand visual data about users' activities and surroundings. To develop a more trustworthy and realistic three-dimensional virtual world, computer vision algorithms must overcome many challenges. First, an interaction system must be able to grasp more complex settings, such as mixing virtual and real-world objects. Consequently, we expect the metaverse to deploy soon more accurate and computationally efficient spatial and scene understanding algorithms.

Furthermore, since the metaverse is so intertwined with the actual world and its inhabitants, more reliable body and location-tracking algorithms are required. Finally, for creating a realistic 3D environment and engaging with avatars in the metaverse, color correction, texture restoration, blur estimation, and super-resolution are essential. However, more flexible but efficient repair methods for the gap between actual and virtual content and the relationship with avatars should be researched (Lee et al. 2021a).

Edge and Cloud. For a seamless metaverse experience for the user, the last mile latency remains the primary latency bottleneck for both Wi-Fi and cellular networks, particularly for wirelessly connected mobile users. As a result, further edge service latency reduction is dependent on improvements in last-mile transmissions, such as the 1 ms promised by 5G. In addition, suppliers, service providers, and third parties are part of Multi-access edge computing (MEC). Consequently, many adversaries may be able to get access to MEC data and steal or tamper with important knowledge. In terms of security, even a small number of hacked edge devices in a distributed edge environment at various layers might disrupt the edge ecosystem and the metaverse services, such as a feature inference attack in federated learning if any client is compromised.

Network. The main network issues are related to conventional mobile network performance parameters, such as latency, throughput, and jitter, which are critical for a smooth user experience. User movement and embodied senses will add to the confusion. The metaverse will need a two-way connection within layers in contrast to the usual tiered network approach, where only little contact occurs between levels to meet the stringent user experience standards. The gNB will be able to broadcast network measurements to the user equipment connected through 5G and its predecessors, which may subsequently be delivered to the whole protocol stack up to the application to adjust content transport.

The transport layer, which handles congestion management, may send a congestion notification to the application layer. When such data is received, the application reduces requirements for the quantity of data sent to meet the application's throughput, bandwidth, and latency. In the same way, QoE measurements at the application layer are sent down to lower layers to improve content delivery and the user experience (Lee et al. 2021a).

Avatar. Users in virtual environments would rely on avatars as a digital representation to express themselves. The omnipresence of avatars with mobile sensors is inadequate for mobilizing our avatars, despite current technology's ability to record physical appearance features. Further research is required to increase the avatars' micro and nonverbal expressiveness.

It also reveals gaps in our understanding of the avatar design space, user perceptions such as alternating body ownership and super-realism, and their consequences on how avatars interact with a wide range of smart devices such as IoTs, intelligent autos, and robots. Avatar design might extend beyond human avatars. Consider the following scenarios: humans use pets as avatars, or humans and pets coexist and share their metaverse journey. The ethical design of avatars and associated online behaviors/representations would be a difficult task. The metaverse might provide a gray area for distributing undesirable concepts like prejudice, provoking debate, and encouraging a contemporary perspective on identity. In the metaverse, an avatar gives a separate identity to anyone, which may improve dialogue and stimulate new thoughts about human life. The computer clone or anyone's digital identity will live on even if your physical body is destroyed in the actual world (Lee et al. 2021a).

Content Creation. Content development is not only accessible to professional designers; everyone may do it in the metaverse. Different co-design methodologies like Participatory design might enable all Metaverse stakeholders to work together to develop the digital environment. Investigating motivations and incentives would allow the metaverse's content production to be accelerated via participatory design. It's uncertain how automated and decentralized censorship governance should be designed and implemented. Creating creative cultures with a wide range of cultural influences, cross-generational content, and the preservation of phased-out content such as digital heritage should also be considered.

Virtual Economy. The ambiguity in metaverse's currency is how much cryptocurrency can be relied upon to serve as cash and how much innovation is required to adapt it for virtual reality. In addition, since virtual users will be physical-world residents, the digital and real economies will be inextricably linked. Consequently, a holistic approach must be used while determining what the virtual economy means. Individual agent spending patterns in the virtual and real worlds and how economic activities in the two realms may interact are topics that should be investigated holistically. In addition, a virtual environment may be utilized as a virtual assessment tool to evaluate new economic policies before they are implemented in real life. The conversion mechanism optimizes the computer-mediated sandbox's configuration to properly reflect economic actors' motives to capitalize on such potential.

Social Acceptability. The behavior of metaverse users is depicted by social acceptability, which expresses collective assessments and views on acts and policies. Metaverse's long-term viability would decide on social acceptability concerning privacy threats, user diversity, justice, and addiction. Furthermore, appropriate regulations and standards must be implemented since the metaverse will impact both the actual and virtual worlds. On the other hand, it is believed that present societal acceptability norms may be applied. Manually matching such bits to the huge cyberspace, on the other hand, would be time-consuming and costly. Examining such elements on a case-by-case basis takes time as well. Hence autonomous agents in the metaverse rely on the automated adoption of rules.

Consequently, the scalability of such agents in the metaverse would become a major challenge. Procedures and instruments to prevent cybercrime and report abuse must be developed to increase the social acceptability of the huge internet (Lee et al. 2021a).

Security and Privacy. In terms of security, the increasingly digital-physical world will need constant verification of users' identities while accessing certain Metaverse applications and services, XR-mediated IoTs, and everyday mechanical objects. Furthermore, safeguarding the metaverse civilizations at scale requires preserving digital assets.

Requiring textual passwords for metaverse applications is a significant impediment to speeding up authentications along with many objects in these cases. The security specialists would look at establishing new ways for app authentication that use various modalities, such as biometric authentication based on muscle movements, body motions, and eye gazes. Our digital journey may include seamless identification in different physical situations, and this system must securely enhance accurate and fast detection.

The metaverse will store massive data on user behavior and interactions. Due to the accumulated data and traces, long-term privacy breaches would occur. Users will be overwhelmed by existing authorization forms when accessing every website with 2D UIs. Users of virtual 3D settings can't afford to regularly fill out so many authorization forms. Instead, machine learning must be developed to recognize user privacy choices in the metaverse's dynamic yet heterogeneous surroundings. Protecting users against digital copies is a great security issue while creating digital assets, such as avatars and twins. With 'deep-fake' avatars, these duplicates may modify users' metaverse behavior and reveal more sensitive information (Lee et al. 2021a).

Trust and Accountability. The metaverse, which merges XR with the internet, broadens the definition of biometrically inferred personal information. Privacy law cannot be used to define personal data because it cannot keep up with the speed of innovation. Providing a standard framework for categorizing personal data while being attentive to future changes would be a huge task. As human civilization advanced from the past to the future, minorities' rights were acknowledged. It's similar to how the internet's socio-technical systems formed in the early days when standards dictated what was and wasn't acceptable, and the democratic majority chose these norms. As the metaverse ecosystem evolves, minorities' and underprivileged communities' rights must be recognized. Potential abuse would have even more significant implications than typical socio-technical systems, with victims feeling abused as if they were in the real world.

3.9 Conclusion

Along with the inclusion of future technologies and the continual growth and refining of the ecosystem, digital twins will appear quite different in the coming years. Thanks to powerful computing devices and intelligent wearables, our digital future will be more interactive, living, embodied, and multidimensional. Many obstacles must be overcome before the metaverse can fully merge with the physical world and our daily lives. The metaverse, it is believed, will exist as a separate huge entity from our physical world. As a result, it is advocated for a comprehensive development plan.

AI and blockchain technologies play pivotal roles in the ever-expanding metaverse. Metaverse is a digital virtual environment that combines AI with blockchain technology to create a digital virtual environment where people may be incorporated into social/economic activities far beyond the physical world's bounds. Metaverse will speed up the application of cutting-edge AI and Blockchain technologies.

The fundamental components of each layer are described in-depth, as well as a list of promising study fields for each aspect. Infrastructure, interactivity, and ecosystem are all of the metaverse's three-layer design. The metaverse represents a human-centered computer vision that helps society in terms of accessibility, variety, equality, and humanism.

Academic and industry experts review comprehensively by assessing the most relevant works in metaverse components, digital currencies, virtual world AI technologies and applications, and blockchain-enabled technologies. It also anticipated major barriers and unsolved issues in building the metaverse's basic features via the marriage of AI and Blockchain. Academia and industry must collaborate to further exploitation and transdisciplinary research on the metaverse to establish an open, fair, and rational future metaverse.

References

Alhilal, A.Y., Braud, T. and Hui, P. 2021. A roadmap toward a unified space communication architecture. *IEEE Access*, 9: 99633–99650.

Ando, Y., Thawonmas, R. and Rinaldo, F. 2012. Level of interest in observed exhibits in metaverse museums. *Proceedings of the Innovations in Information and Communication Science and Technology IICST*, 62–66.

Angeris, G., Kao, H.T., Chiang, R., Noyes, C. and Chitra, T. 2019. An analysis of Uniswap markets. *arXiv preprint arXiv*:1911.03380.

Arulkumaran, K., Deisenroth, M.P., Brundage, M. and Bharath, A.A. 2017. Deep reinforcement learning: A brief survey. *IEEE Signal Processing Magazine*, 34(6): 26–38.

Berg, C., Davidson, S. and Potts, J. 2019. Blockchain technology as economic infrastructure: Revisiting the electronic markets hypothesis. *Frontiers in Blockchain*, 22.

Buterin, V. 2014. Ethereum: A next-generation smart contract and decentralized application platform. *White Paper*, 3(37): 2–1.

Cai, W., Wang, Z., Ernst, J.B., Hong, Z., Feng, C. and Leung, V.C. 2018. Decentralized applications: The blockchain-empowered software system. *IEEE Access*, 6: 53019–53033.

Cheng, N., Lyu, F., Quan, W., Zhou, C., He, H., Shi, W. and Shen, X. 2019. Space/aerial-assisted computing offloading for IoT applications: A learning-based approach. *IEEE Journal on Selected Areas in Communications*, 37(5): 1117–1129.

Cheng, N., Xu, W., Shi, W., Zhou, Y., Lu, N., Zhou, H. and Shen, X. 2018. Air-ground integrated mobile edge networks: Architecture, challenges, and opportunities. *IEEE Communications Magazine*, 56(8): 26–32.

Cybex. Cybex introduction. https://intro.cybex.io/index_en.html accessed: 2022-01-12.

Dai, C. 2020. DEX: A DApp for the decentralized marketplace. *Blockchain and Crypt Currency*, 95.

Daian, P., Goldfeder, S., Kell, T., Li, Y., Zhao, X., Bentov, I., Breidenbach, L. and Juels, A. 2020, May. Flash boys 2.0: Frontrunning in decentralized exchanges, miner extractable value, and consensus instability. *IEEE Symposium on Security and Privacy (SP)*. IEEE, pp. 910–927.

Dick, S. 2019. Artificial intelligence. *Harvard Data Science Review*, 1(1).

Diem. 2021. How the diem payment system works. https://www.diem.com/en-us/vision/#how_it_works, accessed: 2021-11-22.

Duan, H., Li, J., Fan, S., Lin, Z., Wu, X. and Cai, W. 2021. Metaverse for social good: A university campus prototype. *In Proceedings of the 29th ACM International Conference on Multimedia*, pp. 153–161.

Eno, J., Gauch, S. and Thompson, C. 2009, November. Searching for the Metaverse. *In Proceedings of the 16th ACM Symposium on Virtual Reality Software and Technology*, pp. 223–226.

Essa, I.A. 2000. Ubiquitous sensing for smart and aware environments. *IEEE Personal Communications*, 7(5): 47–49.

Ethereum. Non-fungible tokens (nft). https://ethereum.org/en/nft/#gatsby-focus-wrapper, accessed: 2021-11-11.

Far, S.B. and Rad, A.I. 2022. Applying digital twins in Metaverse: User interface, security and privacy challenges. *Journal of Metaverse*, 2(1): 8–16.

Gaffar, A.A.M. 2021. Using Metaverse to rebuild non-reachable or ruined heritage buildings. *International Journal of Architecture, Arts and Applications*, 7(4): 119–130.

Games, E. (2020). *The World's Most Open and Advanced Real-time 3d Creation Tool*.

GDA Capital. Metaerse property. https://metaverse.properties/buy-in-decentraland/2021-11-11.

Han, Y., Niyato, D., Leung, C., Miao, C. and Kim, D.I. 2021. A Dynamic resource allocation framework for synchronizing metaverse with IoT service and data. *arXiv preprint arXiv*:2111.00431.

Jammalamadaka, S.R. 2003. Introduction to linear regression analysis. *The American Statistician*, 57(1): 67–67.

Jeon, H.J., Youn, H.C., Ko, S.M. and Kim, T.H. 2022. Blockchain and AI meet in the Metaverse. *Advances in the Convergence of Blockchain and Artificial Intelligence*, 73.

Joshua, J. 2017. Information bodies: Computational anxiety in neal stephenson's snow crash. *Interdisciplinary Literary Studies*, 19(1): 17–47.

Kaebling, L.P., Littman, M.L. and Moore, A.W. 1996. Reinforcement learning: A survey. *Journal of Artificial Intelligence Research*, 4: 237–285.

Ketkar, N. and Moolayil, J. 2021. Convolutional neural networks. *In Deep Learning with Python*, pp. 197–242. Apress, Berkeley, CA.

Khurana, A., Lohani, B.P. and Bibhu, V. 2019. AI frame-worked virtual world application-the ramification of virtual world on real world. *International Conference on Automation, Computational and Technology Management (ICACTM)*, pp. 582–585. IEEE.

Kit, K.T. 2022. Sustainable engineering paradigm shift in digital architecture, engineering and construction ecology within Metaverse. *International Journal of Computer and Information Engineering*, 16(4): 112–115.

Kreminski, M., Samuel, B., Melcer, E. and Wardrip-Fruin, N. 2019. Evaluating AI-based games through retellings. *In Proceedings of the AAAI Conference on Artificial Intelligence and Interactive Digital Entertainment*, 15(1): 45–51.

Krumm, J., Davies, N. and Narayanaswami, C. 2008. User-generated content. *IEEE Pervasive Computing*, 7(4): 10–11.

Lambert, N. 2021. Beyond nfts: A possible future for digital art. *ITNOW*, 63(3): 8–10.

Lee, C., Ra, H., Oh, Y. and Lee, C. 2021b. Global Busan City brand image development strategy-SWOT/AHP analysis. *East Asian Journal of Business Economics (EAJBE)*, 9(3): 115–124.

Lee, L.H., Braud, T., Zhou, P., Wang, L., Xu, D., Lin, Z., Kumar A., Bermejo, C. and Hui, P. 2021a. All one needs to know about Metaverse: A complete survey on technological singularity, virtual ecosystem, and research agenda. *arXiv preprint arXiv*:2110.05352.

Letaief, K.B., Shi, Y., Lu, J. and Lu, J. 2021. Edge artificial intelligence for 6G: Vision, enabling technologies, and applications. *IEEE Journal on Selected Areas in Communications*, 40(1): 5–36.

Li, T., Sahu, A.K., Talwalkar, A. and Smith, V. 2020. Federated learning: Challenges, methods, and future directions. *IEEE Signal Processing Magazine*, 37(3): 50–60.

Liu, X.Y., Rui, J., Gao, J., Yang, L., Yang, H., Wang, Z., Wang, C.D. and Guo, J. 2021b. FinRL-Meta: A universe of near-real market environments for data-driven deep reinforcement learning in quantitative finance. *arXiv preprint arXiv*:2112.06753.

Liu, X.Y., Yang, H., Gao, J. and Wang, C.D. 2021a. FinRL: Deep reinforcement learning framework to automate trading in quantitative finance. *arXiv preprint arXiv*:2111.09395.

Ludlow, P. and Wallace, M. 2007. The Second Life Herald: The Virtual Tabloid that Witnessed the Dawn of the Metaverse. MIT Press.

Lugrin, J.L. and Cavazza, M. 2006. AI-based world behaviour for emergent narratives. *In Proceedings of the 2006 ACM SIGCHI International Conference on Advances in Computer Entertainment Technology*, pp. 25-es.

Ma, Z. and Liu, S. 2018. A review of 3D reconstruction techniques in civil engineering and their applications. *Advanced Engineering Informatics*, 37: 163–174.

MacCallum, K. and Parsons, D. 2019. Teacher perspectives on mobile augmented reality: The potential of metaverse for learning. *In World Conference on Mobile and Contextual Learning*, pp. 21–28. Retrieved February 11, 2022 from https://www.learntechlib.org/p/210597/.

Min, T., Wang, H., Guo, Y. and Cai, W. 2019, August. Blockchain games: A survey. *IEEE Conference on Games (CoG)*. IEEE, pp. 1–8.

Moneta, A.N.D.R.E.A. 2020. Architecture, heritage and Metaverse: New approaches and methods for the digital built environment. *Traditional Dwellings and Settlements Review*, 32(2).

Nadini, M., Alessandretti, L., Di Giacinto, F., Martino, M., Aiello, L.M. and Andrea Baronchelli, A. 2021. Mapping the NFT revolution: Market trends, trade networks and visual features. *arXiv preprint arXiv*:2106.00647.

Ning, H., Wang, H., Lin, Y., Wang, W., Dhelim, S., Farha, F., Ding, J. and Daneshmand, M. 2021. A survey on Metaverse: The state-of-the-art, technologies, applications, and challenges. *arXiv preprint arXiv*:2111.09673.

Oshiro, T.M., Perez, P.S. and Baranauskas, J.A. 2012, July. How many trees in a random forest? *In International Workshop on Machine Learning and Data Mining in Pattern Recognition*, pp. 154–168. Springer, Berlin, Heidelberg.

Paige, C.C. and Saunders, M.A. 1981. Towards a generalized singular value decomposition. *SIAM Journal on Numerical Analysis*, 18(3): 398–405.

Paulovich, F.V., De Oliveira, M.C.F. and Oliveira Jr, O.N. 2018. A future with ubiquitous sensing and intelligent systems. *ACS sensors*, 3(8): 1433–1438.

Puder, A., Markwitz, S., Gudermann, F. and Geihs, K. 1995. AI-based trading in open distributed environments. *In Open Distributed Processing*, pp. 157–169. Springer, Boston, MA.

Rieke, N., Hancox, J., Li, W., Milletari, F., Roth, H.R., Albarqouni, S., Bakas, S., Galtier, M.N., Maier-Hein, K., Ourselin, S., Sheller, M., Summers, R.M., Trask, A., Xu, D., Baust, M. and Cardoso, M.J. 2020. The future of digital health with federated learning. *NPJ Digital Medicine*, 3(1): 1–7.

Saad, W., Bennis, M. and Chen, M. 2019. A vision of 6G wireless systems: Applications, trends, technologies, and open research problems. *IEEE Network*, 34(3): 134–142.

Tao, F., Zhang, H., Liu, A. and Nee, A.Y. 2018. Digital twin in industry: State-of-the-art. *IEEE Transactions on Industrial Informatics*, 15(4): 2405–2415.

Thomas, P.J. 1999. *Simulation of Industrial Processes for Control Engineers*. Elsevier.

Tian, H., Xue, K., Luo, X., Li, S., Xu, J., Liu, J., Zhao, J. and Wei, D.S.L. 2021. Enabling cross-chain transactions: A decentralized cryptocurrency exchange protocol. *IEEE Transactions on Information Forensics and Security*, 16: 3928–3941.

Van Der Wal, J. 1980. *Stochastic Dynamic Programming*. PhD Thesis, Methematisch Centrum Amsterdam, The Netherlands.

Vapnik, V. 1999. *The Nature of Statistical Learning Theory*. Springer Science & Business Media.

Vlavianos, N. and Nagakura, T. 2021. An architectural Metaverse that combines dynamic and static 3D data in XR, in CHNT – ICOMOS editorial board. *Proceedings of the 26th International Conference on Cultural Heritage and New Technologies*. Heidelberg: Propylaeum.

Wu, Y., Zhang, K. and Zhang, Y. 2021. Digital twin networks: A survey. *IEEE Internet of Things Journal*, 8(18): 13789–13804.

Xu, M., Ng, W.C., Lim, W.Y.B., Kang, J., Xiong, Z., Niyato, D., Yang, Q., Shen, X.S. and Miao, C. 2022. A full dive into realizing the edge-enabled Metaverse: Visions, enabling technologies, and challenges. *arXiv preprint arXiv*:2203.05471.

Yampolskiy, R.V., Klare, B. and Jain, A.K. 2012, December. Face recognition in the virtual world: recognizing avatar faces. In *2012 11th International Conference on Machine Learning and Applications* (Vol. 1, pp. 40–45). IEEE.

Yang, Q., Zhao, Y., Huang, H., Xiong, Z., Kang, J. and Zheng, Z. 2022. Fusing blockchain and AI with Metaverse: A survey. *arXiv preprint arXiv*:2201.03201.

Yaqoob, I., Salah, K., Uddin, M., Jayaraman, R., Omar, M. and Imran, M. 2020. Blockchain for digital twins: Recent advances and future research challenges. *IEEE Network*, 34(5): 290–298.

Zhang, W., Lin, S., Bijarbooneh, F.H., Cheng, H.F., Braud, T., Zhou, P., Lee, L.H. and Hui, P. 2021. EdgeXAR: A 6-DoF camera multi-target interaction framework for MAR with user-friendly latency compensation. *arXiv preprint arXiv*:2111.05173.

Chapter 4

AI-Driven Digital Twins for Predictive Operation and Maintenance in Building Facilities

Ibrahim Yitmen,[1,*] *Habib Sadri*[1] and *Afshin Taheri*[2]

4.1 Introduction

Maintaining building assets and installation and keeping them in the best condition with the highest efficiency has always been one of the most outstanding challenges in this industry. Due to the degradation of materials and damage produced by many harmful factors, it is almost impossible to keep the equipment in an optimum state all the time, during the operation of a building. So, because of the growing number of deteriorating buildings, maintenance issues have been recognized as a long-term dispute in the life cycle of buildings. Maintenance tasks, such as repairing the breakdowns, replacing the components, and detecting construction problems (and solving them in a timely manner to make sure they are functioning normally and safely) are a vital part of building operation. Typical building operational and maintenance (O&M) patterns have a number of deficiencies, including data management issues, poor measurements, low detection accuracy, reliance on a single technical means, and prohibitive cost. Therefore, experts have undertaken extensive

---
[1] Department of Construction Engineering and Lighting Science, School of Engineering, Jönköping University, Gjuterigatan 5, 551 11, Jönköping, Sweden.
[2] Pythagoras AB, Söder Mälarstrand 27B, 118 25, Stockholm, Sweden.
Emails: habib.sadri@ju.se; afshin.taheri@pythagoras.se
* Corresponding author: ibrahim.yitmen@ju.se

research and investigations on intelligent O&M management in order to overcome these challenges and boost the growth of O&M technology (Zhao et al. 2022).

In order to meet smart building management, specifically in operation and maintenance as a highly complex phase, recording thorough information about the facility's performance, historical records, etc., as well as the implementation of various technologies and devices is inevitable. Although different systems and tools such as Building Automation Systems (BAS) and Computerized Maintenance Management Systems (CMMS) have already been designed and developed to enhance O&M management, the lack of an integrated platform to manage information dispersed in various databases and to support different O&M activities is quite obvious (Lu et al. 2020).

Since its origin in 2002, the Digital Twin (DT) concept has evolved, resulting in a variety of definitions and interpretations, some of which differ dramatically. This concept has been studied extensively in recent years in order to implement it in a more appropriate way and recognize its properties. DT needs to be the most pragmatic virtual replica of physical assets, comprising the digital model and all essential data, synchronized with those assets. In addition, self-evolution is another feature of DT, which implies they must alter and evolve in response to changing circumstances while maintaining the distinction between real and virtual spaces. Self-evolution and interactive feedback are two fundamental properties of DT, and they may achieve intuitive observations and working condition predictions, making O&M activities more efficient, promptly, and smart (Zhao et al. 2022).

The concept of DT evolved as a comprehensive approach to managing, planning, predicting, and demonstrating building assets. DTs integrate their sub-DTs and intelligent functions (e.g., artificial intelligence (AI), machine learning (ML), data analytics, etc.) to create digital models that are able to learn and update from multiple sources, and to represent and predict the current and future condition of their physical counterparts correspondingly and timely. The concept of predictive maintenance relies on processing the operation data accumulated by sensors using ML algorithms and data analytics techniques allowing the detection of abnormal behaviors before the breakdown happens. This approach offers the possibility to address the gap in maintenance practices by supporting the facility management (FM) teams to take early action and avoid unplanned failures without the need for costly intensive site inspections of the installations (Bouabdallaoui et al. 2021, Villa et al. 2021).

This chapter presents a conceptual framework of an AI-driven DT for predictive operation and maintenance in building facilities. As a result of implementing such an AI-driven DT platform, it is anticipated that the unexpected breakdowns of building facilities and the associated costs will be reduced, and their efficiency will be increased. Therefore, this chapter addresses the key characteristics, requirements, and system architecture of the framework for integration of AI-based DT to enable predictive O&M in building facilities, the system applications of the framework to simulate and optimize the predictive cases autonomously and collaboratively for smart asset lifecycle management, and the potential values to be created for the facility operators, real estate practitioners, and end users/inhabitants.

4.2 Smart Asset Operation and Maintenance

Building installations and facilities account for a major portion of the total consumed energy and the associated cost and indeed, improper building installation operations result in considerable waste and a significant increase in this energy consumption and cost. Thus, building maintenance and management practices must be upgraded and optimized in order to meet energy and cost efficiency targets. To execute daily maintenance and deliver correct information to top management, FM specialists should rely on real-time and accurate data. Inspections, maintenance assessments, and data collection, on the other hand, are labor-intensive and time-consuming operations. Furthermore, due to the limits in the budget and resources allotted for building maintenance, the specialists find it insufficient and believe that the resources fall short of their requirements. These challenges have an adverse impact on the quality and relevance of inspections and operations and maintenance activities, resulting in low-quality management policies and poor facility maintenance (Bouabdallaoui et al. 2021).

4.2.1 Different Maintenance Approaches

According to Villa et al. (2021), maintenance is commonly divided into five categories, proactive, predictive, preventive, scheduled, and corrective (run-to-failure). In order to improve system operation, proactive maintenance focuses on the core causes of failure rather than fault symptoms. Predictive maintenance by taking advantage of sensor data and ML algorithms makes it possible to detect asset anomalous behaviors before they happen. Preventive maintenance entails inspecting and controlling a system at predetermined intervals to reduce the risk of unexpected failures. Scheduled maintenance throughout the projected life span of each component allows for their replacement according to specified timetables. Corrective maintenance only takes place in the event of failures and service interruptions.

Today, the procedures for facility management are primarily based on corrective maintenance, which means late actions are taken when something goes wrong, a user complains, or an unforeseen failure takes place. Due to the limitation of resources, preventive maintenance is limited to the minimum mandatory inspections of the most important facilities. On the other hand, the implementation of data analytics tools for processing the operation data captured by sensors forms the basis of predictive maintenance. Such an approach has the potential of bridging the gap in maintenance procedures by assisting facility managers in taking proper and timely actions to prevent unexpected failures with no need for costly and time-consuming site inspections of the facilities (Bouabdallaoui et al. 2021).

Choosing a successful maintenance plan necessitates a thorough understanding of maintenance management concepts and procedures, as well as an in-depth understanding of facility performance. There is no universal formula for selecting a maintenance strategy, and most selection processes include a mix of alternative maintenance methods to suit the facility's individual performance and circumstances. Today, there are a variety of maintenance solutions available that have been tried and proven through time. To reduce maintenance requirements, these solutions vary from optimizing existing maintenance routines to completely removing the core causes of failures. Ultimately, the goal should be to increase equipment dependability while lowering the total cost of ownership, boosting equipment uptime and facility performance while balancing the related resources, and eventually, cost saving is the major yield of an efficient maintenance strategy (Deighton 2016).

The predictive maintenance strategy is one of the most conservative strategies, which reduces the O&M associated risk. Higher reliability and an enhanced life cycle are the results of this method and at the same time, for newer and more advanced technologies, it is the preferred strategy (Farhat 2021). Predictive maintenance approaches are intended to assist in determining the state of in-service equipment so that repair may be scheduled. Therefore, it is viewed as condition-based maintenance that is carried out in accordance with estimates of an item's deterioration status (Medjaher et al. 2016). Data collection and preprocessing, early fault detection, maintenance scheduling, as well as resource optimization are some of the primary components required for adopting predictive maintenance (Amruthnath and Gupta 2018). State-of-the-art technologies with the ability to transmit and process large amounts of data have taken a big step in helping to improve predictive maintenance. Among these technologies that play an important role in the framework proposed in this chapter are Digital Twins, the Internet of Things, Artificial Intelligence, and Machine Learning, which are discussed in the following section.

4.3 Supportive Technologies

Many elements of modern civilization have recently embraced artificial intelligence and data science approaches. Aside from recent developments in machine learning, the introduction of the Internet of Things (IoT) and smart devices made it possible to connect physical assets and broadcast real-time data at a low cost. Consequently, operations and maintenance management are changing, as DTs, IoT, AI, and ML are being used to contribute to the facility management sector and enhance asset management through changing traditional maintenance procedures and quality management systems that were previously all controlled by humans. (Bouabdallaoui et al. 2021).

4.3.1 Digital Twins

The DT is considered a trustworthy auxiliary tool for decision-making help in order to achieve optimal productivity and functionality in its early phases of development. The DT is the appropriate solution for process emulation because of its information-driven nature and ability to replicate the physical asset's behavior. As the industry begins to realize the advantage of applying DT, its concept is expanding and progressively becoming more prevalent. Due to the very complicated structure, DT symbolizes the twin entities' two-way interaction, which is a difficult undertaking to achieve. The DT must be fully integrated into the production line engineering and interact with the surrounding environment and physical processes. The heterogeneity of components and the close interplay between software, platforms/networks, and physical components make this integration even more intricate. Hence, the DT is more than a passive replica of the real system; it is in fact an active and reactive element that can continuously assess the current state of its real twin and make expert recommendations for process optimization, maintenance prediction, scheduling, and design and overall performance. Although this integration necessitates domain knowledge of the physical asset as well as a number of enabling technologies, it is only through the successful implementation of this two-way connection that the DT's capabilities for facility management and maintenance can be deployed to increase production efficiency and prevent equipment failure (Mihai et al. 2021).

4.3.2 Internet of Things

The advent of IoT and the use of wireless sensors to collect data from building systems is a game changer for enhancing FM efficiency. As a result, the new technologies should enable facility managers to visualize and analyze enormous data sets in real time to better control, performance optimization, energy consumption, operating expenses, and user comfort.

In general, research on the implementation of these new technologies during the service life of a building, notably in the FM industry, is currently limited. Even when automated devices/sensors and databases are used, the collected information is often not completely exploited (Villa et al. 2021).

The Internet of Things is defined by Gubbi et al. (2013) as the "interconnection of sensing and actuating devices providing the ability to share information across platforms through a unified framework, developing a common operating picture for enabling innovative applications". IoT enabling technologies consist of recognition and identification, sensing, positioning, networks and communication technologies, and their infrastructure requirements such as hardware, software, and cloud platforms (Čolaković and Hadžialić 2018). IoT devices vary from smart mobile devices and different kinds of actuators and sensors to single board computers (Dehury and Sahoo 2016).

The role of IoT data in the building industry is chiefly to enhance BIM models by providing a complementary set of real-time data and recordable status from the construction process and operation and maintenance phase of the building lifecycle which are collected and organized as time series data streams from single sensor point samples (Tang et al. 2019). Predictive maintenance is an outstanding use case of IoT considered in various contexts, where the data (generally sensor data) is used to update the maintenance activities (Khan 2021). Adopting predictive maintenance requires performance data and service life forecasting models (Hallberg 2009). The integration of IoT with BIM models, boosted by AI algorithms can enable data-driven predictive maintenance and effect significant implications such as early defect detection to prevent failures; future condition prediction to understand when a failure may occur; reducing or avoiding overtime expenditures by pre-planning maintenance supplies and tools (Mannino et al. 2021).

4.3.3 *Artificial Intelligence, Machine Learning, and Deep Learning*

Data analytics and AI technology can be used to understand the repetitive patterns in data from facilities as well as the occupants' behavior to optimize the building's performance, operation, and maintenance. Despite the potential of data analytics technologies in processing massive data effectively, their applicability in building facilities still remains a great challenge. For each data processing approach, a variety of both general purpose and specialized algorithms are available, and in most circumstances, no algorithm is universally superior. The input data cardinality, data distribution, and the analytical end goal are among the factors that influence which method works best. Hence, only skilled IT experts have the competence to manually pick an ideal algorithm, as well as tune its parameters, in order to achieve a suitable trade-off between accuracy and execution time (Capozzoli et al. 2016).

ML as, a subset of AI, refers to a method of extracting knowledge from raw data, covering the topics of statistical learning and predictive analytics. ML produces value from disparate big data sources with the minimum reliance on human intervention. It is well suitable for dealing with a huge variety of variables and complex data sources, and unlike traditional analyses, ML improves on growing datasets. The more data is input into an ML system, the more it would be able to learn and apply the results (Bakshi and Bakshi 2018). Basically, as it is depicted in Fig. 4.1 (adapted from Sarker 2021), ML algorithms in the first of phase the machine learning process are trained through historical data in order to develop a predictive model. Then, in the second phase, the derived predictive model is utilized as a means of interpreting the new data to make eventual predictions as the outcome of the process.

ML algorithms decide based on available data heedless of the algorithm structures. This independency is the most outstanding advantage of ML algorithms (Uçar et al. 2020). Supervised, semi-supervised and unsupervised learning are among the different working structures of ML, which are explained below:

– Supervised ML: this structure implements labeled variables as a means of prediction and classification of an outcome measure. Classification models categorize the input data into specific classes, while regression techniques can predict continuous variables. Due to the complexity

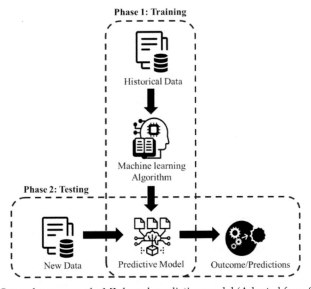

Figure 4.1: General structure of a ML-based predictive model (Adapted from Sarker 2021).

of the ML process, particularly for supervised learning, the speed of training, predictive accuracy, memory usage, and interpretability of the models must be well-considered (Tuena et al. 2022).

- Semi-supervised ML: this approach is an extension of supervised learning. The difference is that here only a limited set of the training dataset is labeled by the designer and labeling the rest of the training data set would be done algorithmically by inductive or transductive approaches, chosen by the designer. This has been proved that semi-supervised ML can improve accuracy overall. The added advantage is that the ML algorithm designer should not necessarily be a subject matter expert to label the entire training dataset. If sufficient accuracy, sensitivity, and specificity are achieved, the ML algorithm would be ready to be implemented, otherwise, the designer should return to the semi-supervision learning methods and attributes for reconsideration (Koff and Doyle 2019).

- Unsupervised ML: this method involves datasets without labeling, while the machine extrapolates the information and recognizes the pattern to perform predictions and generate outputs (Ho et al. 2022). Unsupervised ML allows for addressing problems or circumstances when there is no idea or limited sense regarding how the results will look. Herein, there is no extraction of feedback based on the results of predictions (Kumar et al. 2022). Compared to supervised ML, unsupervised ML only deals with the input data without target variables. Thus, unlike supervised learning, there is no instructor to correct the model. This approach is also beneficial in exploratory data analysis through automatically identifying structure and relationships in the data as well as providing initial insights for testing individual hypotheses. On the other hand, dimensionality reduction, which refers to the methods of representing data with fewer features, is achievable through unsupervised ML. The sparse latent structure with fewer features greatly reduces further data processing and eliminates redundant features (Schneider and Xhafa 2022).

Deep learning, as a sub-field of ML, applies more complex algorithms based on artificial neural networks to make sense of raw data in form of text, pictures, sound, etc., while adapting the same working structures as ML in terms of supervised, semi-supervised, and unsupervised approaches. Deep learning utilizes a cascade of several layers of nonlinear processing units to extract and transform features. The closer layers to the input data at a lower level can learn simple features, while the more intricate features, taken from the lower layers, can be learnt at the higher layers. Such architecture constructs a powerful hierarchical feature representation, which makes deep learning a proper approach for analyzing big data collected from various sources such as IoT sensors and extracting valuable knowledge from them (Shinde and Shah 2018). The adaption of ML and DL to predictive maintenance systems can play a key role in the building industry by offering effective solutions for keeping the facilities operating in optimal condition while reducing the energy consumption level.

4.4 Framework of AI-based Digital Twins for Predictive Maintenance

4.4.1 *The DT-centric Technical Architecture*

A multi-source real-time data flow, adapted from Rozanec et al. (2020), as the technical architecture of the AI-based DT framework for predictive maintenance is represented in Fig. 4.2 this AI-driven DT framework describes decision-making and optimization processes for predictive operation and maintenance for learning, event identification, and providing prediction and reasoning skills through developed algorithms, ontology, and interconnected knowledge graphs.

Four components, introduced by Rozanec et al. (2020), define actionable AI-driven DTs for predictive operation and maintenance decision makings, which are explained below:

– Ontology and Knowledge Graph: representing the background knowledge regarding entities and the relationships between them is captured by ontology in the physical world as well as the digital replica. This is instantiated in a knowledge graph, bringing cognitive capabilities to the AI-driven DT.

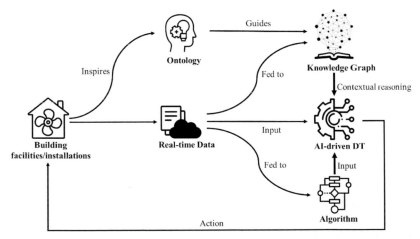

Figure 4.2: Technical architecture of the AI-driven DT framework (Adapted from Rozanec et al. 2020).

– Data: recorded information regarding the building's assets, operations and maintenance (e.g., anomaly detection), actors (suppliers, sub-contractors, etc.).

– Algorithms: the operators that provide the AI-driven DT with particular capabilities.

– Actions: the recommended decision-making opportunities to the users based on the acquired insights through the performed analytics and algorithms on the AI-driven DT.

4.4.2 *The Modular ML Architecture*

A modular ML architecture of the proposed framework, adapted from Bouabdallaoui et al. (2021), is also introduced in Fig. 4.3, which tailors an ML approach to the building context.

The five major steps in this framework are elaborated as follows:

– Data collection: in the first step the required data is collected via sensors and IoT devices from the built environment. For this purpose, the data sources in the building are initially defined and the necessary data is extracted from them.

– Data storage: depending on the users' preference and infrastructure capabilities different storage methods (local, cloud, etc.) may be utilized to store the collected data.

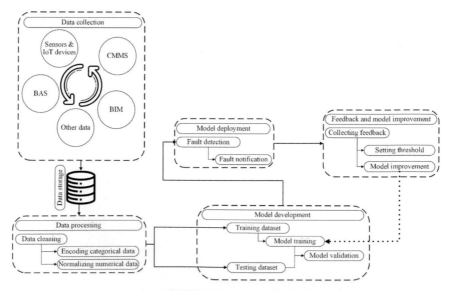

Figure 4.3: Modular ML architecture of the AI-driven DT framework (Adapted from Bouabdallaoui et al. 2021).

- Data processing: in this step, the raw data are cleaned (irrelevant entries are removed, Nan values are replaced, etc.) and transformed into a structured dataset for training processes.
- Model development: the dataset in this framework is divided into a training set (to train the model to recognize anomaly patterns) and a testing set (to validate the model as well as tunie the parameters such as the anomaly threshold). To this end, an unsupervised learning algorithm is implemented for developing the intended machine-learning model.
- Model deployment: after the training and validation step the model is deployed online. This stage consists of fault detection (based on machine ML algorithms) and fault notification containing the equipment name, its location, as well as the alert event time.
- Feedback and continuous improvement: the ML model should be updated regularly to enhance the accuracy of the results. Therefore, collecting feedback after model deployment is critical to improving the fault prediction model. Such feedback is provided by the facility managers/users reporting undetected failures or false alerts, based on which the model is updated through new training data.

4.4.3 *The Framework Implementation*

The overall purpose of implementing such a framework is anomaly detection in building installations and facilities, enhancing their life span and efficiency, avoiding downtime, and ultimately reducing the operation and maintenance cost. Among the practical scenarios in the built environment is an unusual deviation in transmitted data from IoT sensor data such as temperature in HVAC systems, which can be interpreted as a result of some anomalous behaviors in the system. Similar deficiencies in lighting fixtures, elevators, security systems, or other installations may also be recognized through ML algorithm analytics, processing the sensor data, and other values such as energy consumption level. Having the building historical data captured and analyzed in various reference scenarios, the AI-based DT structure can comprehend the real-time status of the asset functioning by monitoring its real-time data and warn about the imminent breakdown/malfunction well before it takes place.

The recognition ability of this system will also improve over time as the ML algorithm is fed more data. Moreover, the system can be taught directly by the users/maintainers defining new thresholds or conditions as exceptions in asset status or to enhancing the decision-making accuracy. Although this framework is well supported by cutting-edge scientific evidence and research, it needs to be implemented in real-world case studies to prove its functionality and reveal possible defects.

4.5 Conclusion

To minimize the building facilities' downtime and to keep them functioning as smoothly as possible a proper maintenance plan is of paramount importance, as it will positively impact the asset efficiency and eventually the operation cost reduction. Predictive maintenance as an effective approach can well fulfill such a demand. Taking advantage of AI and ML algorithms to process the data from IoT sensors, predictive maintenance creates the opportunity to detect anomalous behaviors in the building assets through their DTs, to avoid failures before they happen.

This chapter introduces a conceptual framework of AI-based digital twins for predictive maintenance. The DT-centric technical architecture of this framework elucidates how the real-time data, gathered from the building facilities feed the algorithms empowering the AI-driven DT to optimize the maintenance plan of the asset. Whilst the ontology and knowledge graph provides the AI-driven DT with the required cognitive capabilities. On the other hand, the modular ML architecture sheds light on the procedure in which building facilities' data is collected via different techniques and stored in a database. Then, after the data processing, an ML model is developed and validated to be deployed for fault detection. To improve the developed model, the outcomes in the next stage would be appraised by the users to provide the model with feedback from the real world. This cycle can be repeated continuously to evolve the learning model.

The offered theoretical framework can be implemented in real-world case studies to streamline the maintenance activities in various types of building installations and facilities such as mechanical, electrical, lighting, security, and HVAC system for indoor quality enhancement, energy optimization, and cost reduction.

References

Amruthnath, N. and Gupta, T. 2018. *Fault Class Prediction in Unsupervised Learning Using Model-Based Clustering Approach*, 5–12.

Bakshi, K. and Bakshi, K. 2018. *Considerations for Artificial Intelligence and Machine Learning: Approaches and Use Cases*, 1–9.

Bouabdallaoui, Y., Lafhaj, Z., Yim, P., Ducoulombier, L. and Bennadji, B. 2021. Predictive maintenance in building facilities: A machine learning-based approach. *Sensors*, 21(4): 1044.

Capozzoli, A., Cerquitelli, T. and Piscitelli, M.S. 2016. Chapter 11—Enhancing energy efficiency in buildings through innovative data analytics technologiesa. pp. 353–389. *In*: Dobre, C. and Xhafa, F. (eds.). *Pervasive Computing*. Academic Press. https://doi.org/10.1016/B978-0-12-803663-1.00011-5.

Čolaković, A. and Hadžialić, M. 2018. Internet of Things (IoT): A review of enabling technologies, challenges, and open research issues. *Computer Networks*, 144, 17–39.

Dehury, C.K. and Sahoo, P.K. 2016. Design and implementation of a novel service management framework for IoT devices in cloud. *Journal of Systems and Software*, 119: 149–161. https://doi.org/10.1016/j.jss.2016.06.059.

Deighton, M.G. 2016. Chapter 5—Maintenance management. pp. 87–139. *In*: Deighton, M.G. (ed.). *Facility Integrity Management*. Gulf Professional Publishing. https://doi.org/10.1016/B978-0-12-801764-7.00005-X.

Farhat, H. 2021. Chapter 4—Maintenance: Availability and reliability. pp. 89–106. *In*: Farhat, H. (ed.). *Operation, Maintenance, and Repair of Land-Based Gas Turbines*. Elsevier. https://doi.org/10.1016/B978-0-12-821834-1.00009-5.

Gubbi, J., Buyya, R., Marusic, S. and Palaniswami, M. 2013. Internet of Things (IoT): A vision, architectural elements, and future directions. *Including Special Sections: Cyber-Enabled Distributed Computing for Ubiquitous Cloud and Network Services & Cloud Computing and Scientific Applications — Big Data, Scalable Analytics, and Beyond*, 29(7): 1645–1660. https://doi.org/10.1016/j.future.2013.01.010.

Hallberg, D. 2009. *System for Predictive Life Cycle Management of Buildings and Infrastructures*. Doctoral Dissertation, KTH.

Ho, T.T., Joyce Wang, Y.R. and Daldrup-Link, H. 2022. Chapter 7—Artificial intelligence for bone cancer imaging. pp. 75–90. *In*: Heymann, D. (ed.). *Bone Sarcomas and Bone Metastases—From Bench to Bedside (Third Edition)*. Academic Press. https://doi.org/10.1016/B978-0-12-821666-8.00023-2.

Khan, Z.J. 2021. *Predictive Maintenance and Internet of Things*, 1–5.

Koff, D.A. and Doyle, T.E. 2019. Imaging informatics. pp. 551–560. *In*: Narayan, R. (ed.). *Encyclopedia of Biomedical Engineering*. Elsevier. https://doi.org/10.1016/B978-0-12-801238-3.64123-5.

Kumar, I., Singh, S.P. and Shivam. 2022. Chapter 26—Machine learning in bioinformatics. pp. 443–456. *In*: Singh, D.B. and Pathak, R.K. (eds.). *Bioinformatics*. Academic Press. https://doi.org/10.1016/B978-0-323-89775-4.00020-1.

Lu, Q., Xie, X., Parlikad, A.K. and Schooling, J.M. 2020. Digital twin-enabled anomaly detection for built asset monitoring in operation and maintenance. *Automation in Construction*, 118: 103277. https://doi.org/10.1016/j.autcon.2020.103277.

Mannino, A., Dejaco, M.C. and Re Cecconi, F. 2021. Building information modelling and internet of things integration for facility management—Literature review and future needs. *Applied Sciences*, 11(7): 3062.

Medjaher, K., Zerhouni, N. and Gouriveau, R. 2016. *From Prognostics and Health Systems Management to Predictive Maintenance 1: Monitoring and Prognostics*. John Wiley & Sons.

Mihai, S., Davis, W., Hung, D.V., Trestian, R., Karamanoglu, M., Barn, B., Prasad, R., Venkataraman, H. and Nguyen, H.X. 2021. *A Digital Twin Framework for Predictive Maintenance in Industry 4.0*.

Rozanec, J.M., Jinzhi, L., Kosmerlj, A., Kenda, K., Dimitris, K., Jovanoski, V., Rupnik, J., Karlovcec, M. and Fortuna, B. 2020. *Towards Actionable Cognitive Digital Twins for Manufacturing*. SeDiT@ESWC.

Sarker, I.H. 2021. Machine learning: Algorithms, real-world applications and research directions. *SN Computer Science*, 2(3): 1–21.

Schneider, P. and Xhafa, F. 2022. Chapter 8—Machine learning: ML for eHealth systems. pp. 149–191. *In*: Schneider, P. and Xhafa, F. (eds.). *Anomaly Detection and Complex Event Processing over IoT Data Streams*. Academic Press. https://doi.org/10.1016/B978-0-12-823818-9.00019-5.

Shinde, P.P. and Shah, S. 2018. *A Review of Machine Learning and Deep Learning Applications*, 1–6.

Tang, S., Shelden, D.R., Eastman, C.M., Pishdad-Bozorgi, P. and Gao, X. 2019. A review of building information modeling (BIM) and the internet of things (IoT) devices integration: Present status and future trends. *Automation in Construction*, 101: 127–139.

Tuena, C., Chiappini, M., Repetto, C. and Riva, G. 2022. 10.02—Artificial intelligence in clinical psychology. pp. 10–27. *In*: Asmundson, G.J.G. (ed.). *Comprehensive Clinical Psychology (Second Edition)*. Elsevier. https://doi.org/10.1016/B978-0-12-818697-8.00001-7.

Uçar, M.K., Nour, M., Sindi, H. and Polat, K. 2020. The effect of training and testing process on machine learning in biomedical datasets. *Mathematical Problems in Engineering*, 2020.

Villa, V., Naticchia, B., Bruno, G., Aliev, K., Piantanida, P. and Antonelli, D. 2021. IoT open-source architecture for the maintenance of building facilities. *Applied Sciences-basel*, 11(12). https://doi.org/10.3390/app11125374.

Zhao, Y., Wang, N., Liu, Z. and Mu, E. 2022. Construction theory for a building intelligent operation and maintenance system based on digital twins and machine learning. *Buildings*, 12(2): 87.

Chapter 5

Knowledge Graph-based Approach for Adopting Cognitive Digital Twins in Shop-floor of Modular Production

Ibrahim Yitmen,[1,*] *Sepehr Alizadehsalehi,*[2] *Ilknur Akiner*[3]
and *Muhammed Ernur Akiner*[4]

5.1 Introduction

The custom product's unique specifications affect the whole production process, causing it to proceed more slowly and take a longer time to complete (Liu et al. 2019, Du et al. 2020). The so-called Cyber-physical Production System (CPPS) architecture of the Industrial Internet of Things (IIoT) presents a novel, promising way to solve these challenges (Liu et al. 2021). It uses various sensors and analytical intelligence algorithms to provide a wide range of facilities involving sensing and monitoring identifying information with various qualities of aspects (Sisinni et al. 2018). Digital Twin (DT) technology facilitates Cyber-physical systems

---

[1] Department of Construction Engineering and Lighting Science, School of Engineering, Jönköping University, Gjuterigatan 5, 551 11, Jönköping, Sweden.
[2] Project Management Program, Department of Civil and Environmental Engineering, Northwestern University, Evanston, IL, USA.
[3] Department of Architecture, Faculty of Architecture, Akdeniz University, 07058 Antalya, Turkey.
[4] Vocational School of Technical Sciences, Akdeniz University, 07058 Antalya, Turkey.
Emails: sepehralizadehsalehi2018@u.northwestern.edu; ilknurakiner@akdeniz.edu.tr; ernurakiner@akdeniz.edu.tr
* Corresponding author: ibrahim.yitmen@ju.se

(CPS), and it offers a contemporary implementation path for the achievement of virtual-real fusion (Alizadehsalehi and Yitmen 2021, Kor et al. 2022, Yitmen et al. 2021, Yitmen and Alizadehsalehi 2021a, Yitmen and Alizadehsalehi 2021b, Zhuang et al. 2021). Applying DT in smart production and the smart shop-floor is an important effort by the industry. Models of the shop-floor digital twins (SDTs) are required because they may be set up to monitor existing statuses in real-time, track historical data as needed, and assist in future operational decision-making (Leng et al. 2019, Park et al. 2019). CPPS is an efficient method for enhancing production, optimizing resource allocation, and lowering costs. As a part of the CPPS, academics have typically concentrated on developing and implementing the SDT in the most efficient manner possible. Businesses and academics have worked together to undertake the required theoretical and real-world case studies (Lu et al. 2020a, b). Many recent studies examined the utilization of SDT for human-robot interaction, real-time monitoring, and production (Modoni et al. 2019). A shop-floor's broad and complicated system includes business process, control flow, technical flow, logistics, personnel, machinery, supplies, procedures, and the environment. SDT system creation and maintenance is seldom handled in a hierarchical, organized, modularized way, resulting in poor block reuse, scalability difficulties, and high upgrade and maintenance costs. As a result, SDT construction must be meticulous.

For better integration of CPPS resources' semantic knowledge, a different technology, known as Knowledge Graph (KG), is being used across the whole production process (Li et al. 2021a). Semantics and prediction reasoning may be examined in conjunction with IIoT time series data acquired during a dynamic change in production (Zhou et al. 2022). One may build the industrial brain using these two sorts of enabler technologies and have it respond immediately to anomalies in sensing data and make advanced predictions and projections for long-term trends such as perception and cognition (Li et al. 2021b, Lyu et al. 2022).

Nevertheless, existing data fusion approaches cannot effectively fuse real-time information for data with complex structures in the modular production scenario (Chen et al. 2020). Knowledge graphs in the modular production scenario lack sufficient cognitive ability in terms of reasoning, decision-making, and resource allocation (Zhao et al. 2017). An intelligent, IIoT-enabled, cognitive modular production paradigm has been envisioned and investigated to allow a computer-aided production system with perception and decision-making abilities that allow autonomous system operation, known as cognitive intelligence, to be developed and implemented (Wang et al. 2020). Industrial production systems can decompose the semantic meanings of provided industrial data into manageable components, then reassemble them in a logical sequence that considers available resources and existing restrictions; as a result, they know how to respond to the perceiver (Grossberg 2020, Li et al. 2021c). The cognitive modular production paradigm will incorporate robots with proactive thinking skills into real production, autonomously detect changes quickly in the production process, and greatly enhance production decision-making outputs' interpretability and sustainability using distributed agents or integrated cognitive reasoning engines (Kumar and Jaiswal 2021).

This chapter lays the groundwork for the cognitive modular production paradigm by outlining a data representation approach based on a knowledge graph, which may be used by utilizing the graph embedding approach to achieve reasoning and decision-making. The IIoT data is fused using a built multi-layer knowledge graph. The device's process knowledge is forwarded to the cognitive module for analysis for the whole line, which operates to forecast machine perception and cognition responses. Perception cognition systems are utilized to make these responses possible. The knowledge graph driven by cognition may be utilized for multi-source heterogeneous data of tailored objects to accomplish autonomous data fusion. The present state of DT applications and how to make a shop-floor CDT are covered on the shop-floor.

5.2 Cognition in Modular Production

Perceptual intelligence has been mostly achieved through artificial intelligence (AI) since cognitive intelligence is still in its early phases (Qu et al. 2021, Grossberg 2020). A cognitive modular production system learns the key information from the human brain and uses algorithms as a computational engine, enabling the computer to automatically grasp and make decisions, transforming the computer into an "industrial brain." This industrial brain's cognition outputs include optimization techniques developed by cognition in modular production. The cognitive production system designed by Dumitrache et al. (2019) and Liu et al. (2022) depends on the IIoT and cognitive control; hence the system is capable of controlling the cycle of perception and reasoning to learn through a Knowledge Graph-based data representation technique.

Meanwhile, in a factory environment, cognitive production methods have been deployed (Hu et al. 2019). Bannat et al. (2011) clearly state that in factories, cognitive production is primarily used to keep the system operational and maintainable during urgent situations. Although integrating multi-category tailored product orders remain a challenge, some proposals exist regarding the production system architecture using the IIoT and cognitive control. For instance, Iarovyi et al. (2015) provide mass-personalized product dependability solutions within their study. In customized product development, Maier et al. (2010) successfully build resource scheduling production plans through a model-based approach for personalized product manufacturing.

5.2.1 Knowledge Graph Representation for Cognitive Modular Production

Moving from perceptual to cognitive intelligence will need knowledge graph technology (Zheng et al. 2021, Pan et al. 2017). As a multidisciplinary technical system, a knowledge graph (KG) combines technologies including deep learning, natural language processing (NLP), data mining, information retrieval, cognitive computing, and complex network analysis (Nguyen et al. 2020, Li et al. 2017, 2018 2021, Yoo and Jeong 2020).

Industrial KGs improve the cognitive capacity of the machine. A deep learning-based computation methodology for the nonlinear distribution of IoT data was developed by Wang et al. (2000). The accuracy of data set identification was increased by combining multi-source heterogeneous data. On the other hand, the property of combining redundant and dynamic data flow is unable to attain precise accuracy. Multiple data models were created through real-time analysis using the IoT-supported unstructured and diverse data by Jabbar et al. (2018). Li et al. (2020) used two KGs to express multi-source knowledge, taking into account topological and semantical features in common and providing four concept-knowledge operators to connect nodes and combine relations within graphs semi-automatically.

Chen et al. (2020) developed a reinforcement learning-based ternary data fusion technique to generate a contemporary ontology following a reduced dimensionality of the connected data. Wang et al. (2019, 2021) implemented a graph embedding-based approach for merging data generated through IoT devices with data from social sensors and a random-walk methodology to identify future demands.

5.2.2 Data Representation through the Cognition-driven Knowledge Graph

Cognitive modular production brings cognitive intelligence to the production sector, providing cognitive capabilities to industrial production systems, detecting production process fluctuations, and performing reasoning and decision-making activities, as shown in Fig. 5.1. The IIoT infrastructure will gather different IIoT data throughout the design, production, operation, and maintenance phases. After controlling the primary sensing devices and sensors, valves, pumps, and motors as actuators through the Supervisory control and data acquisition (SCADA) system in the IIoT infrastructure, the data is monitored,

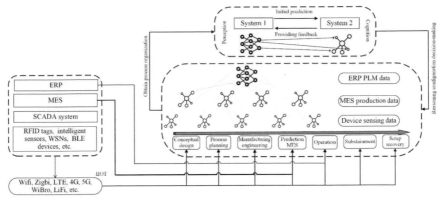

Figure 5.1: Knowledge graph-based IIoT data fusion framework toward cognitive modular production (Adapted from Liu et al. 2022).

collected, and processed using multiple communication protocols (such as WiFi) before being transmitted to MES, ERP as a higher-level industrial information system.

All of the data such as user demands and resource management contained from ERP and data gathered from modular production, such as device business hours and downtime gathered from MES, are integrated into a single digital thread, which is used to incorporate all data such as a maintenance status and logistics orders picked from IIoT infrastructures are represented by blue arrows. After that, the knowledge graph (KG) will be the key facilitator of cognitive intelligence in the production environment, connecting the isolated items obtained in the production process via their intrinsic semantic link.

Cognitive reasoning relies on the KG's multi-hop semantic chains represented by red dash arrows. This new dual system of vision and cognition would tie into the current multi-layer knowledge network represented by black arrows. Intelligent applications and KGs may be implemented to get cognitive reasoning, self-decision, and configuration from observation to cognition.

Industrial data is distributed in a three-level multi-layer knowledge network. Device sensing data, often discrete data, is instantly gathered at the lowest layer from the associated digital thread and reflects the functional status of the device. Manufacturing Execution Systems (MES) provide the intermediate layer data. This layer collects data about the manufacturing process, product status, and loosely related data. ERP and PLM systems, which integrate human resources, business logic, and resource allocation, form the top layer of the data stack in correlation with the manufactured product. As a starting point, ERP and PLM nodes in the multi-layer KG will be used to fuse and integrate the nodes at the MES and device sensing layers.

Based on the proposed paradigm, a dual perceptual cognition system has been created with multi-layered KG integration. Perception-based rationale, the so-called System I, and the so-called System II, the cognition-based rationale, will all be used to reason and make judgments. Based on real-time IIoT data seen through the Digital Thread, the system I would provide an initial assessment and rapid response based on preset rules or basic prediction models, akin to human subconscious reactions. If the real-time status data deviates from typical patterns or exceeds predetermined thresholds, a decision tree or XGBoost algorithms may quickly identify the failure of a particular device. System II will utilize the first judgment to develop a more advanced plan based on cognitive reasoning about the semantics and logic linkages among nodes and links in the KG. KG data will be used to identify whether the production process is in a stable state based on CNN or AutoEncoder models with sliding time frames for the example of a single device. Predictive maintenance plans may also be reasoned by analyzing and synthesizing the probable disruption trend of the device and the available maintenance resources through GNN-based algorithms on the relevant nodes and relations in the KG. Once cognitive reasoning has been completed, some new rules or adjustments to current cases will be stored in the KG so that the system may react more swiftly in future instances of production process variation.

Shallow Content Agents (SCAs) will play various roles in the cognition-driven organization process and generate multi-layer KGs based on CPPS resources. At the Cognition Matching stage, the multi-source heterogeneous data is sorted; also, entities are extracted. During the Cognition Generation step, disambiguation and coreference resolution are carried out; the system connects the recovered things to their knowledge base counterparts, creating an ontology model for formalizing knowledge. A quality review procedure may be performed in a dual-channel manner during the Cognition Update step to ensure database quality. Devices based on the IIoT are thus capable of continually monitoring and acquiring all created data kinds and dynamically updating knowledge maps.

The Deep Cognition Agent (DCA) is primarily used to configure device production processes minimum makespan), as well as self-healing (diagnosing faults and resolving breakdowns) (Qin and Lu 2021). The goal of resource allocation prediction, such as long and short-term predictions, is to respond quickly to disturbance events and improve the timeliness of the allocation process (Zhang et al. 2021a). The long-term prognosis of the energy consumption scenario will consider the ideal total energy spent by all resources (Zhang et al. 2021b). The energy consumption for each processing type is then predicted, and an operating plan and resource allocation for the entire batch of goods is implemented. On the other hand, the short-term prediction is based on IIoT time-series data (Li et al. 2020). When anomalous resource energy consumption is discovered in certain sections, the relevant stations are shut down for repair, and resource reconfiguration is carried out in the case of the linked devices.

CPPS's complete production process is integrated with a multi-layered KG that governs the resources from two levels for flexible production. The resources are optimized and controlled at the macro level. The system will automatically adjust the cluster's resource allocation to improve the overall plan's logic. IIoT data from a single-stage may be used as a library and selection engine for self-organization at the micro-level. The self-organizing components link machines, work pieces, and other production resources in the KG. Self-organization matching for personalized items is performed autonomously by the system based on the inference result. Figure 5.2 depicts the two moduled DCA for cognitive thinking in this process.

An entity-node subgraph will be derived from the multi-layer knowledge graph (KG) based on the requirements of a new order using this module, in essence, a full-entity-node chart. This subgraph's nodes indicate production resources. The relevant module, cognitive reasoning, will combine all relationships between materials and devices and develop a production resource plan. When the actual production scenario differs from the recorded historical or predicted one, real-time device status data is used to guide the planned scheme. Following the disturbance events, the real-time monitoring system will notice changes in data stream resources. The scheme changes appropriately when the system finds a discrepancy

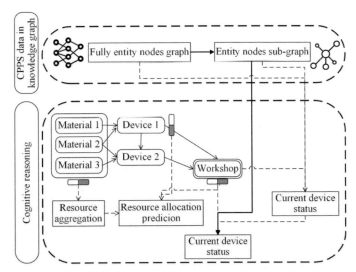

Figure 5.2: Knowledge graph-based cognitive reasoning (Adapted from Liu et al. 2022).

between the anomalous quantity and the recorded values of the KG. The system will then search the cognitive management library for relevant abnormal scenarios to identify the probable range and explanation for unconventional resources. The production network inspection plan is produced from important cognitive outcomes and is based on the places to be maintained and particular procedures.

The system must also rearrange production resources throughout the production process to respond quickly and effectively with an efficient makespan to changes in the whole production line. The system will employ the cognitive engine to think through all possible ways to integrate the activities into the current process plan, particularly for unique goods that need a new machining operation. The different proportions of processing situations create the corresponding assessment indices. The system will automatically choose and reformulate the most efficient resource allocation scheme.

5.3 CDT Applications on the Shop Floor

Culminating in a smart shop-floor increases efficiency and product quality, optimizes resource allocation, shortens the production cycle, and decreases energy usage (Tao et al. 2019). Tao and Zhang (2017) presented the digital twin shop-floor idea, which uses real-time mapping and interaction between real and virtual shop-floors to achieve optimum productivity and management. A DT-driven assembly and commissioning technique were implemented by Sun et al. (2019) for transdisciplinary high-precision products; they also created a framework and completed assembly prediction and process optimization. Leng et al. (2020) employed DT to increase system performance while lowering reconfiguration overhead in automated production systems. Liu et al. (2020) proposed a systematic framework that combines DT modeling, resource registration/binding, event-driven distributed cooperation mechanisms, and web technologies to give instructions for the quick design and runtime of DT-based CPPS. Through the sheet metal assembly station case study, Söderberg et al. (2017) built a DT for real-time geometry and explained how the DT notion supports the shift from mass production to customized production. In their research, a data production approach for supporting DT applications on the shop-floor with efficient and reliable data was proposed by Kong et al. (2021). DT was used to train deep reinforcement learning agents for automating smart manufacturing systems in easily optimized conditions by Xia et al. (2021).

CPPS and digital twin shop-floors can only be achieved with a thorough and precise digital mapping of their physical counterparts, such as SDT (Zhuang et al. 2018). The rules of geometry, physics, and human behavior (Tao et al. 2017). According to Modoni et al. (2019), a wholly synchronized SDT may be achieved via the component logical schema and instances and the historical persisted data. Geometric and logical dimensions are often used to construct the SDT at the application level.

Texture mapping, animation production, and 3D modeling software are often used for model development. Models from this collection are used to create a virtual 3D shop-floor scenario for the real world (Wenzel and Jensen 2001). To assess, synthesize, and optimize the structure and state of the internal shop-floor operation logic, SDT's logic modeling mainly relies on abstracting and documenting it. NC milling and sophisticated product assembly are discrete event dynamic systems on a production shop-floor (DEDS). The most general modeling approaches are fractal and informal. An example of formal modeling is queuing network method (Do 2011), a maximal algebra method, an analysis of disturbances method, and a Petri net (Li et al. 2012).

Informal modeling methods include the activity cycle diagram, flowcharts, and object-oriented techniques (Ning et al. 2006). Images and mathematical expressions may be used to describe Petri nets. Therefore, it is frequently used in production system modeling to explain the concurrency, synchronization, conflict, and various interactions of DEDSs. It is possible to use a hierarchical timed and colored Petri net model in an IoT setting to show the shop-floor's operational state by changing the coloring token, as Zhang et al. (2016) have done in their study.

Scalability, interoperability, expansibility, and accuracy are characteristics of the reference model published by Schleich et al. (2017), based on skin model forms. Simulating products across their entire lifecycles is an essential feature of digital twins (DT) (Boschert et al. 2016). There are three levels of the DT-enhanced Industrial Internet (DT-II) reference framework suggested by Cheng et al. (2020): product lifecycle, intra-enterprise, and inter-enterprise. DTs were also used by Siemens throughout the product lifecycle, including during development, to simulate the production system before investing in physical prototypes and assets, under the three broad headings of "product DT," "production DT," and "performance DT." For wind turbine condition monitoring, predictive maintenance, and operation management, Beckoff (2019) developed the TwinCAT Wind Framework software program. Azure Digital Twins is an IoT platform developed by Microsoft that enables users to create and construct advanced digital models of whole environments, such as DT based on physics and DT for infrastructure.

SDT's online prediction function is critical when optimizing operations on the actual shop-floor. The shop-floor operating state may be estimated using two currently used methods. In the first, a logic model for shop-floor operations is used via offline simulation to examine how various dynamic factors such as processing time, workpiece arrival, and delivery delay cost affect key shop-floor performance indicators (Ghezavati and Saidi-Mehrabad 2011, Sharda and Banerjee 2013). The alternative is to do a thorough data analysis to discover the shop-floor performance progression rules. For example, Ioannou and Dimitrou (2012) suggested that a dynamic prediction and updating approach for accomplishment time for multi-machine, multi-product, order-oriented production shop-floors may be integrated into ERP/MRP.

The iterative decomposition technique is used in one approach, while the most prolonged route problem approach is used in another. Specific cases were utilized to show the effectiveness of the solutions presented (Ioannou and Dimitriou 2012). Berling and Farvid (2014) used the spontaneous demand rate instead of random lead time demand to solve the distributed system delay problem. This study's numerical findings show that the suggested approaches outperform current methods and that batch size and service level substantially influence delay. The researchers might predict a variety of supply networks (Berling and Farvid 2014). In the present study on shop-floor operation prediction, the simulation approach is based on manual initial system design and setting. The findings will never be up to date because of the time lag between the simulation and the real system operation. Predictive models rely heavily on previous data to make accurate predictions. However, compiling large amounts of historical data for many real-world applications. In addition, a steady-state forecast based on extensive data is excellent. Real-time transient prediction is also essential when shop-floor operating conditions unexpectedly change, which is also one of the critical responsibilities of SDT.

5.3.1 *Constructing Shop-floor CDT and Implementation Stage*

Humans, machines, materials, procedures, the environment, and other processes are part of a large shop-floor complex system. This includes business processes, control flow, logistical, and technical flow. Model-based Systems Engineering (MBSE) technique has been used to create and utilize SDT from a system perspective, as has been shown. An SE (Qian 2007) includes text-based SE and MBSE in its organizational management system. A system is described and expressed digitally and graphically using MBSE (Estefan 2007), an extension of standard text-based SE. UML 2.0's subset, SysML, is utilized as an object-oriented paradigm derived from SysML. It's easy to understand and avoids mistakes, so it's a lot more efficient. At any scale, it may be utilized for Systems Engineering (SE) modeling with complex components such as hardware (people

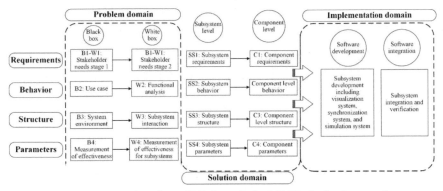

Figure 5.3: Constructing shop-floor CDT through the MBSE: the implementation process (Adapted from Liu et al. 2021).

and equipment), as well as mathematical models (Delligatti 2013). An implementation strategy to construct an SDT using MBSE is shown in Fig. 5.3.

Following creating an SDT issue domain model, the SDT system requirements, the external environment, use cases, and measurement criteria of effectiveness (MoEs) are outlined during the black box stage. A functional study of the SDT at the white box stage involves determining how the display system, synchronization system, and simulation system interact and then tuning the MoEs parameters. Second, the three SDT subsystems give their solution domain model. There are several iterations of the three dimensions of structure, behavior, and parameters for each subsystem, dependent on the needs of the overall project. An existing shop-floor is used to test the MBSE approach by building and implementing an SDT. The visualization system comes with a method for combining commercial software. The synchronization system's technical plan covers all four areas of man, machine, material, and data transmission schemes. A continuous transient simulation based on real-time data is suggested using event-driven DEDS technology. Several interfaces may be used to test the SDT's functionality during the system integration and verification phase. Model completeness and synchronization timings are assessed numerically by the SDT.

The problem and solution domain models explain the links between the requirements, structures, behaviors, parameters, and objects for systems, subsystems, and components. However, the implementation of model components and the technologies employed are not considered. The implementation domain is responsible for writing the logic structure of process components like activity, operation, or reception. The parts of the system model that aren't universally applicable are adapted and implemented depending on specifics. The implementation domain is typically a stage where interdisciplinary teams work jointly since each system block includes varied disciplines and technologies.

5.3.1.1 The Visualization System

Revit is used to create a shop-floor layout for the first time offline. Second, the product was modeled in SolidWorks using the manufacturer's equipment model. Solidworks and SketchUp are used for the model analysis, while 3DS MAX is used for the format conversion. It is then used for non-product items in the production line, whereas Mixamo Fuse is used for human simulations. As a final tool for designing and rendering, the real-time 3D rendering engine Unity3D is used. It's a game engine that can handle the visual demands of a shop-floor CDT.

5.3.1.2 The Synchronization System

In model ontology, three-dimensional models of people are constructed as a part of human ontology and created by modeling the sixty-six fundamental bones of a person's skeleton, then abstracting the frame as a connecting rod to represent their posture. This model consists of the head and neck, neck and upper chest, upper and lower arms, wrist and finger joints, belly and lower legs, and toe and feet joints. Structures of the outward appearance are formed and the muscles that make them up. The last step is to upload your images. The static modeling step is when the 3D model of a person is built. The model ontology is not modified throughout the system operation; only the human positions, rotations, and actions are updated.

In motor function, an improper posture is prevented by adjusting and binding the articulation between the bones of humans and the range of rotation and angle that each joint may rotate in connection. A state machine is utilized to govern human behavior. The design of the state machine and the algorithm for transferring states are two parts of its implementation. According to the state transfer algorithm, real-time data is utilized to drive the state machine, which causes the synchronized operation of the people in the model. Figure 5.4 depicts the human synchronization system and the technological scheme.

According to Fig. 5.5, an Internet of Things (IoT)-based data connection mechanism is used to bring the virtual and physical shop-floors into real-time sync. When the SDT begins operating, the SQL configuration file is produced, the database connection knowledge is extracted from the configuration file, and a connection is made. The datasheet results are then saved once the SQL instructions are delivered to the RFID, UWB, and MES databases. Finally, to send data in real-time, we extract the query results. Because the IoT system uses a MySQL database, the same database is

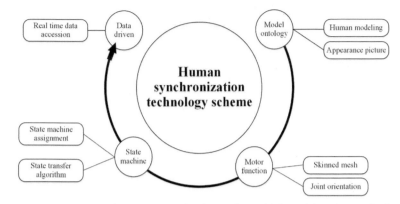

Figure 5.4: Human synchronization technology scheme (Adapted from Liu et al. 2021).

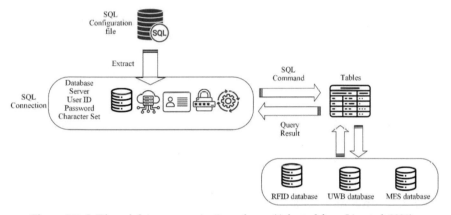

Figure 5.5: IoT-based data communication scheme (Adapted from Liu et al. 2021).

being utilized in the synchronization system to eliminate excessive strain during the integration process.

5.3.1.3 *Realization of the Simulation System*

The event-driven scheduling approach to run a continuous transient simulation is employed. All events must be scheduled following the Future Event List (FEL) when using the event-driven scheduling strategy. In this strategy, random events such as the entrance of a participant and the conclusion of a session aren't planned; they happen. The simulation object's system input characteristics should be documented. For example, arrival, processing end, and departure are specified using abstract models in this scenario that investigate the operation logic. As part of this process, the distribution types of various occurrences are identified, and past shop-floor data are used to estimate the distribution parameters of those

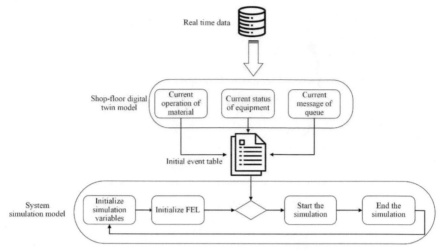

Figure 5.6: Real-time data used to create a continuous transient simulation framework (Adapted from Liu et al. 2021).

events. A screening process is then used to decide which sample input generator is most appropriate for the simulation and shop-floor settings. The production process is used for the simulation process to build the logic for various simulations, which are activated by the simulation clock as it advances. Initialize simulation variables, FEL, start execution policy and terminate simulation are four phases in this method's execution procedure. On the other hand, the approach described above is completely offline and is based only on temporal data. Figure 5.6 depicts a continuous transient simulation using real-time data due to our work.

This is accomplished by using real-time data belonging to the shop-floor CDT to augment and enhance the physical shop-floor's current condition. It is possible to perform a transient simulation using the shop-floor CDT's current state and actual statistics as the initial simulation value. Second, if the normal simulation process runs, it can produce continuous stimulation. The orange lines in the illustration show a continuous transient simulation approach using real-time data.

5.3.1.4 *The System Integration and Verification*

After seeing the shop-floor offline, Revit is used to create the plan. Second, a Solidworks model of the product is made. Solidworks and SketchUp were used for the model analysis, while 3DS MAX was used for the format conversion. Rhino models non-product and non-equipment objects on the shop- floor, whereas Mixamo Fuse models humans. It's now time to import the visual models from SysML into Unity3D and combine them with the model's class library by setting up a data communication mechanism. As

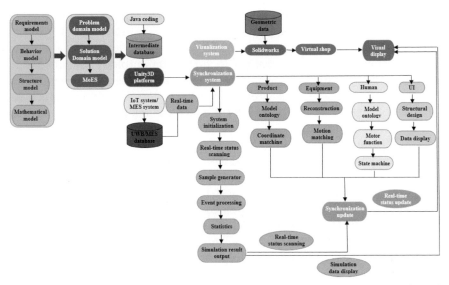

Figure 5.7: Constructing a shop-floor CDT: Implementation process using MBSE (Adapted from Liu et al. 2021).

a result, a separate simulation engine for system integration is created. Protocol stacks, network modules, buses, sample generators, and database read-write modules are among the reusable model elements bundled into a common library by MBSE tools for usage on the shop-floor during the building of top-level systems. These models may be dragged and dropped into future system design and software development to match shop-floor needs.

Figure 5.7 depicts the deployment of a shop-floor CDT. Before investigating the requirements, behavior, structure, and parameters of SDT, the system design of the problem and solution domain models and system MoEs must be accomplished. A communication channel is established between SysML and Unity3D To complete the system integration. To communicate with the intermediate database, use the SysML modeling software; store SysML model data in the intermediate database; facilitate communication between Unity3D and the intermediate database; read information stored in the SysML intermediate database and run the Unity3D program.

The shop-floor CDT scenario in this study includes visualization, synchronization, and simulation systems. The following describes the specific technique used to construct these three Unity3D subsystems. First, a 3D model of the shop-floor is created using commercial modeling tools such as SolidWorks, and then integrate this model into the Unity3D game engine using 3DMAX software. In Unity3D, rendering effects are added to the simulated shop-floor depending on the actual shop-floor production plan. Secondly, a human/equipment/ product/user interface (UI) Kanban model is designed using activity diagrams. When creating a human state machine, adding the motor function to its ontology is considered. Ontology reconstruction, the parent-child link between components for the equipment model, and control over each item's mobility range are all part of this phase of the project. Finally, the shop-floor CDT system is integrated with the IoT/MES system. When the SDT system is started, an EXCEL file containing the EXCEL script setup is read to determine the database connection code. The database, server, user names, and password are all editable in this setup file. The IoT system is subsequently connected to a local area network (LAN), and remote access to its databases is provided through the SDT system's configuration file. At last, scanning the real-time CDT status and cyclically updating the FEL to finish the shop-floor operating online status simulation is conducted through the SysML-created event processing logic and the input characteristic model and sample generator. The simulation findings should be transmitted to the visualization system's Kanban for storage after the simulation.

5.6 Conclusions

Designing, producing, and distributing customized products due to extreme diversity orders must be redeveloped thoroughly. It is important to adapt to the great range of needs without impacting the stability of the present working conditions as much as feasible. IIoT technology may be used to link and interoperate industrial data in CPPS, enabling the interpretation of massive amounts of rapidly changing sensing data with wide-scale and real-time monitoring capabilities. The lack of semantic information analysis still hinders moving from the perception cognition paradigm to the cognitive manufacturing paradigm.

This chapter presented an IIoTs-enabled knowledge graph-based data representation approach for cognitive modular production. The system collects all product data throughout its life cycle using IIoT infrastructures. An SCA and DCA-supported data fusion approach may integrate the data into existing industrial knowledge graphs; the product information is processed using a cognition-driven knowledge graph model. It is then possible to use the IIoT data cognition-driven knowledge graph to predict resource allocation and self-organization. The suggested technique requires reduced dependence on manual processing of complicated interactions between cyber and physical entities to achieve human-like data fusion, opening the way for the era of cognitive modular production.

How Constructing a shop-floor CDT model is required for using CDT technology in the production phase, which is really a focus for academics and businesses. The present SDT creation process concentrates on theory but ignores demand, low system function module reuse, and scalability. This chapter suggests an MBSE-based construction technique for SDT. Shopfloor CDT software development can be easily tracked and traced thanks to this method's clear description of the shop floor CDT's production elements and their relationship. The digital model organizes system function modules and solutions, making software development for the shop floor CDT more manageable, repeatable, reusable, and extendable. The following are the chapter's most important contributions:

The shop floor is characterized by its enormous size, complex structure, and interconnected interactions between many components. Shop-floor operations are nonlinear and dynamic, requiring a great deal of communication, coordination of resources, and interruption of production at all stages. Errors and omissions are easy to make during the creation of shop floor CDT.

This chapter's MBSE-based approach helps designers avoid common pitfalls early in the system's development process and produces a model library that is normalized and standardized using requirements-based modular development and accessible design model diagrams. Modules may be reused and custom-designed according to the real circumstances of various shop floors when developing a CPPS model with comparable functional modules.

It is possible to describe design schemes and data in a more readable format using the method described in this article. As a result, the number of issues that can arise during system development is reduced significantly, which helps developers understand the shop floor's overall status, ensuring that the system can be implemented. The whole building process may be traced to completion, from requirement analysis through system design and test verification. An R&D framework that goes within "function to fulfill requirements" and "requirements-driven design," which can be tracked continuously and confirmed at every stage, has been built using this method. In addition, the technique has become more widespread.

A transient simulation approach is developed depending on real-time data for discrete manufacturing. The research methodology includes real-time data in the discrete event system simulation, allowing for real-time simulation employing the state cycle scanning, cycle execution for simulation sustainability, and event-driven scheduling mode for transient simulation. This technique combines real-time status scanning and offline system modeling to predict more accurately than forecasting based on extensive data. It is very close to the system model and takes into account real-time data. This method also occurs in real-time and offers shop floor production with dynamic real-time decision guidance.

Building shop floor CDT and software development may now be approached from a new angle, thanks to the MBSE method. The CDT prediction model can accurately anticipate the shop floor's operational condition by incorporating the data analysis and mechanism models. Future multi-varieties and variable-batch discrete intricate shop-floor research should employ the MBSE methodology. The connection between the multi-dimensional and multi-level production parameters and multi-source heterogeneous production data can only be revealed through the mutual implementation of the MBSE technique and the complex networks.

References

Alizadehsalehi, S. and Yitmen, I. 2021. Digital twin-based progress monitoring management model through reality capture to extended reality technologies (DRX). *Smart and Sustainable Built Environment*.

Bannat, A., Bautze, T., Beetz, M., Blume, J., Diepold, K., Ertelt, C., Geiger, F., Gmeiner, T., Gyger, T., Knoll, A., Lau, C., Lenz, C., Ostgathe, M., Reinhart, G., Roesel, W., Ruehr, T., Schuboe, A., Shea, K., Stork, I., Wersborg, G., Stork, S., Tekouo, W., Wallhoff, F., Wiesbeck, M. and Zaeh, M.F. 2011. Artificial cognition in production systems. *IEEE Trans. Autom. Sci. Eng.*, 8(1): 148–174.

Beckhoff. 2019. TwinCAT Wind and oversampling technology enable highly efficient condition monitoring. [updated 2019 March]. Available from: https://www.beckhoff.com/media/downloads/applikationsberichte-downloads/2019/pcc_0319_goldwind_e.pdf.

Berling, P. and Farvid, M. 2014. Lead-time investigation and estimation in divergent supply chains. *Int. J. Prod. Econ.*, 157(1): 177–89.

Boschert, S. and Rosen, R. 2016. *Digital Twin—The Simulation Aspect*. Mechatronic Futures. Berlin, Germany: Springer, Cham, pp. 59–74.

Chen, S., Wang, J., Li, H., Wang, Z., Liu, F. and Li, S. 2020. Top-down human-cyber-physical data fusion based on reinforcement learning. *IEEE Access*, 8: 134233–134245. https://doi.org/10.1109/ACCESS.2020.3011254.

Cheng, J., Zhang, H., Tao, F. and Juang, C.F. 2020. DT-II: Digital twin enhanced industrial internet reference framework towards smart manufacturing. *Robot. Comput. Integr. Manuf.*, 62: 101881.

Delligatti, L. 2013. *SysML Distilled: A Brief Guide to the Systems Modeling Language*. Addison-Wesley.

Do, T.V. 2011. A new solution for a queueing model of a manufacturing cell with negative customers under a rotation rule. *Perform Eval.*, 68(4): 330–7.

Du, X., Ge, S.L., Wang, N.X. and Yang, Z. 2020. Personalized product service scheme recommendation based on trust and cloud model. *IEEE Access*, 8: 82581–82591.

Dumitrache, I., Caramihai, S.I., Moisescu, M.A. and Sacala, I.S. 2019. Neuro-inspired framework for cognitive manufacturing control. *IFAC-PapersOnLine*, 52(13): 910–915.

Estefan, J.A. 2007. Survey of model-based systems engineering (MBSE) methodologies. *Incose MBSE Focus Group*, 25(8): 1–12.

Ghezavati, V.R. and Saidi-Mehrabad, M. 2011. An efficient hybrid self-learning method for stochastic cellular manufacturing problem: A queuing-based analysis. *Expert. Syst. Appl.*, 38(3): 1326–35.

Grossberg, S. 2020. A path toward explainable AI and autonomous adaptive intelligence: Deep learning, adaptive resonance, and models of perception, emotion, and action. *Front. Neurorobot.* 14: 36.

Hu, L., Miao, Y., Wu, G., Hassan, M.M. and Humar, I. 2019. iRobot-Factory: An intelligent robot factory based on cognitive manufacturing and edge computing. *Futur. Gener. Comput. Syst.*, 90: 569–577.

Iarovyi, S., Lastra, J.L.M., Haber, R. and Del Toro, R. 2015. From artificial cognitive systems and open architectures to cognitive manufacturing systems. In: *Proceeding – 2015 IEEE Int. Conf. Ind. Informatics*, INDIN 2015, 2015.

Ioannou, G. and Dimitriou, S. 2012. Lead time estimation in MRP/ERP for make-to-order manufacturing systems. *Int. J. Prod. Econ.*, 139(2): 551–63.

Jabbar, S., Malik, K.R., Ahmad, M., Aldabbas, O., Asif, M., Khalid, S., Han, K. and Ahmed, S.H. 2018. A Methodology of real-time data fusion for localized big data analytics. *IEEE Access*, 6: 24510–24520.

Kong, T., Hu, T., Zhou, T. and Ye, Y. 2021. Data construction method for the applications of shop floor digital twin system. *J. Manuf. Syst.*, 58: 323–8.

Kor, M., Yitmen, I. and Alizadehsalehi, S. 2022. An investigation for integration of deep learning and digital twins towards Construction 4.0. *Smart and Sustainable Built Environment.*

Kumar, A. and Jaiswal, A. 2021. A deep swarm-optimized model for leveraging industrial data analytics in cognitive manufacturing. *IEEE Trans. Ind. Informatics*, 17(4): 2938–2946.

Leng, J., Liu, Q., Ye, S., Jing, J., Wang, Y., Zhang, C., Zhang, D. and Chen, X. 2020. Digital twin-driven rapid reconfiguration of the automated manufacturing system via an open architecture model. *Robot. Comput. Integr. Manuf.*, 63: 101895.

Leng, J., Zhang, H., Yan, D., Liu, Q., Chen, X. and Zhang, D. 2019. Digital twin-driven manufacturing cyber-physical system for parallel controlling of smart shop-floor. *J. Ambient. Intell. Humaniz Comput.*, 10(3): 1155–66.

Li, X., Chen, C.H., Zheng, P., Wang, Z., Jiang, Z. and Jiang, Z. 2020. A knowledge graph-aided concept-knowledge approach for evolutionary smart product-service system development. *J. Mech. Des.*, 142(10): 101403.

Li, X., Jiang, Z., Song, B. and Liu, L. 2017. Long-term knowledge evolution modeling for empirical engineering knowledge. *Adv. Eng. Informatics*, 34: 17–35.

Li, X., Jiang, Z., Liu, L. and Song, B. 2018. A novel approach for analysing evolutional motivation of empirical engineering knowledge. *Int. J. Prod. Res.*, 56(8): 2897–2923.

Li, X., Lyu, M., Wang, Z., Chen, C.H. and Zheng, P. 2021a. Exploiting knowledge graphs in industrial products and services: A survey of key aspects, challenges, and future perspectives. *Comput. Ind.*, 129: 103449.

Li, X., Wang, Z., Chen, C.H. and Zheng, P. 2021b. A data-driven reversible framework for achieving sustainable smart product-service systems. *J. Clean. Prod.*, 279: 123618.

Li, X., Zheng, P., Bao, J., Gao, L. and Xu, X. 2021c. Achieving cognitive mass personalization via the self-X cognitive manufacturing network: An industrial-knowledge-graph- and graph-embedding-enabled pathway. *Engineering*. In Press.

Li, J., Zhang, Y., Qian, C., Ma, S. and Zhang, G. 2020. Research on recommendation and interaction strategies based on resource similarity in the manufacturing ecosystem. *Adv. Eng. Informatics*, 46: 101183.

Li, Z., Liu, G., Hanisch, H.M. and Zhou, M. 2012. Deadlock prevention based on structure reuse of Petri net supervisors for flexible manufacturing systems. *IEEE Trans. Syst. Man. Cybern. A Syst. Hum.*, 42(1): 178–91.

Liu, B., Zhang, Y., Zhang, G. and Zheng, P. 2019. Edge-cloud orchestration driven industrial smart product-service systems solution design based on CPS and IIoT. *Adv. Eng. Informatics*, 42: 100984.

Liu, B., Zhang, Y., Lv, J., Majeed, A., Chen, C.H. and Zhang, D. 2021 A cost-effective manufacturing process recognition approach based on deep transfer learning for CPS enabled shop-floor. *Robot. Comput. Integr. Manuf.*, 70: 102128.

Liu, C., Jiang, P. and Jiang, W. 2020. Web-based digital twin modeling and remote control of cyber-physical production systems. *Robot. Comput. Integr. Manuf.*, 64: 101956.

Liu, J., Liu, J., Zhuang, C., Liu, Z. and Miao, T. 2021. Construction method of shop-floor digital twin based on MBSE. *Journal of Manufacturing Systems*, 60: 93–118.

Liu, M., Li, X., Li, J., Liu, Y., Zhou, B. and Bao, J. 2022. A knowledge graph-based data representation approach for IIoT-enabled cognitive manufacturing. *Advanced Engineering Informatics*, 51: 101515.

Lu, Y., Liu, C., Kevin, I., Wang, K., Huang, H. and Xu, X. 2020a. Digital Twin-driven smart manufacturing: Connotation, reference model, applications and research issues. *Robot. Comput. Integr. Manuf.*, 61: 101837.

Lu, Y., Xu, X. and Wang, L. 2020b. Smart manufacturing process and system automation—A critical review of the standards and envisioned scenarios. *J. Manuf. Syst.*, 56: 312–325.

Lyu, M., Li, X. and Chen, C.H. 2022. Achieving knowledge-as-a-service in IIoT-driven smart manufacturing: A crowdsourcing-based continuous enrichment method for industrial knowledge graph. *Adv. Eng. Informatics*, 51: 101494.

Maier, P., Sachenbacher, M., Rühr, T. and Kuhn, L. 2010. Automated plan assessment in cognitive manufacturing. *Adv. Eng. Informatics*, 24(3): 308–319.

Modoni, G.E., Caldarola, E.G., Sacco, M. and Terkaj, W. 2019. Synchronizing physical and digital factory: Benefits and technical challenges. *Procedia Cirp*, 79: 472–477.

Nguyen, H.L., Vu, D.T. and Jung, J.J. 2020. Knowledge graph fusion for smart systems: A survey. *Inf. Fusion*, 61: 56–70.

Ning, R., Liu, J. and Tang, C. 2006. Modeling and simulation technology in digital manufacturing. *Chinese J. Mech. Eng.*, 42(7): 132–7.

Pan, J.Z., Vetere, G., Gomez-Perez, J.M. and Wu, H. 2017. *Exploiting Linked Data and Knowledge Graphs in Large Organisations*, Springer International Publishing, Cham.

Park, K.T., Nam, Y.W., Lee, H.S., Im, S.J., Do Noh, S., Son, J.Y. and Kim, H. 2019. Design and implementation of a digital twin application for a connected micro smart factory. *Int. J. Comput. Integr. Manuf.*, 32: 596–614.

Qian, X. 2007. *System Engineering*. Shanghai: Shanghai Jiao Tong University Press.

Qin, Z. and Lu, Y. 2021. Self-organizing manufacturing network: A paradigm towards smart manufacturing in mass personalization. *J. Manuf. Syst.*, 60: 35–47.

Qu, Y., Pokhrel, S.R., Garg, S., Gao, L. and Xiang, Y. 2021. A blockchained federated learning framework for cognitive computing in industry 4.0 networks. *IEEE Trans. Ind. Informatics*, 17(4): 2964–2973. https://doi.org/10.1109/TII.2020.3007817.

Schleich, B., Anwer, N., Mathieu, L. and Wartzack, S. 2017. Shaping the digital twin for design and production engineering. *CIRP Ann. Manuf. Technol.*, 66(1): 141–4.

Sharda, B. and Banerjee, A. 2013. Robust manufacturing system design using multi objective genetic algorithms, Petri nets and Bayesian uncertainty representation. *J. Manuf. Syst.*, 32(2): 315–24.

Siemens. Digital Twin. Available from: https://www.plm.automation.siemens.com/global/en/our-story/glossary/digital-twin/24465.

Sisinni, E., Saifullah, A., Han, S., Jennehag, U. and Gidlund, M. 2018. Industrial internet of things: Challenges, opportunities, and directions. *IEEE Trans. Ind. Informatics*, 14(11): 4724–4734.

Söderberg, R., Wärmefjord, K., Carlson, J.S. and Lindkvist, L. 2017. Toward a Digital Twin for real-time geometry assurance in individualized production. *CIRP Ann.-Manuf. Tech.*, 66(1): 137–40.

Sun, X., Bao, J., Li, J., Zhang, Y., Liu, S. and Zhou, B. 2019. A digital twin-driven approach for the assembly-commissioning of high precision products. *Robot. Comput. Integr. Manuf.*, 61: 101839.

Tao, F. and Zhang, M. 2017. Digital twin shop-floor: A new shop-floor paradigm towards smart manufacturing. *IEEE Access*, 5: 20418–27.

Tao, F., Cheng, Y., Cheng, J., Zhang, M. and Qi, Q. 2017. Theory and technologies for cyberphysical fusion in digital twin shop-floor. *Comput. Integr. Manuf. Syst.*, 23(8): 1603–11.

Tao, F., Zhang, H., Liu, A. and Nee, A.Y.C. 2019. Digital twin in industry: State-of-the-art. *IEEE. T. Ind. Inform.*, 15(4): 2405–15.

Wang, G., Zhang, G., Guo, X. and Zhang, Y. 2021. Digital twin-driven service model and optimal allocation of manufacturing resources in shared manufacturing. *J. Manuf. Syst.*, 59: 165–179.

Wang, J., Xu, C., Zhang, J., Bao, J. and Zhong, R. 2020. A collaborative architecture of the industrial internet platform for manufacturing systems. *Robot. Comput. Integr. Manuf.*, 61: 101854.

Wang, W. and Zhang, M. 2020. Tensor deep learning model for heterogeneous data fusion in internet of things. *IEEE Trans. Emerg. Top. Comput. Intell.*, 4(1): 32–41.

Wang, Z., Chen, C.H., Zheng, P., Li, X. and Khoo, L.P. 2019. A novel data-driven graph-based requirement elicitation framework in the smart product-service system context. *Adv. Eng. Informatics*, 42: 100983.

Wang, Z., Chen, C.H., Zheng, P., Li, X. and Khoo, L.P. 2021. A graph-based context-aware requirement elicitation approach in smart product-service systems. *Int. J. Prod. Res.*, 59(2): 635–651.

Wenzel, S. and Jessen, U. 2001. The integration of 3D visualization into the simulation-based planning process of logistics systems. *Simulation*, 77(3-4): 114–27.

Xia, K., Sacco, C., Kirkpatrick, M., Saidy, C., Nguyen, L., Kircaliali, A. and Harik, R. 2021. A digital twin to train deep reinforcement learning agent for smart manufacturing plants: Environment, interfaces and intelligence. *J. Manuf. Syst.*, 58: 210–30.

Yitmen, I. and Alizadehsalehi, S. 2021a. Overview of Cyber-Physical Systems and Enabling Technologies in Cognitive Computing for Smart Built Environment. *BIM-enabled Cognitive Computing for Smart Built Environment*. CRC Press.

Yitmen, I. and Alizadehsalehi, S. 2021b. Towards a Digital Twin-based SMART Built Environment. *BIM-enabled Cognitive Computing for Smart Built Environment*. CRC Press.

Yitmen, I., Alizadehsalehi, S., Akıner, İ. and Akıner, M.E. 2021. An adapted model of cognitive digital twins for building lifecycle management. *Applied Sciences*, 11: 4276.

Yoo, S. and Jeong, O. 2020. Automating the expansion of a knowledge graph. *Expert. Syst. Appl.*, 141: 112965.

Zhao, Y., Liu, Q. and Xu, W. 2017. Open industrial knowledge graph development for intelligent manufacturing service matchmaking. *Int. Conf. Ind. Informatics - Comput. Technol. Intell. Technol. Ind. Inf. Integr.* IEEE, 194–198.

Zhang, G., Chen, C.H., Liu, B., Li, X. and Wang, Z. 2021a. Hybrid sensing-based approach for the monitoring and maintenance of shared manufacturing resources. *Int. J. Prod. Res.*, 1–19.

Zhang, G., Wang, G., Chen, C.H., Cao, X., Zhang, Y. and Zheng, P. 2021b. Augmented Lagrangian coordination for energy-optimal allocation of smart manufacturing services. *Robot. Comput. Integr. Manuf.*, 71: 102161.

Zhang, Y., Wang, W., Wu, N. and Qian, C. 2016. IoT-enabled real-time production performance analysis and exception diagnosis model. *IEEE Trans. Autom. Sci. Eng.*, 13(3): 1318–32.

Zheng, P., Xia, L., Li, C., Li, X. and Liu, B. 2021. Towards Self-X cognitive manufacturing network: An industrial knowledge graph-based multi-agent reinforcement learning approach. *J. Manuf. Syst.*, 61: 16–26.

Zhou, B., Shen, X., Lu, Y., Li, X., Hua, B., Liu, T. and Bao, J. 2022. Semantic-aware event link reasoning over industrial knowledge graph embedding time series data. *Int. J. Prod. Res.*, 1–18.

Zhuang, C., Gong, J. and Liu, J. 2021. Digital twin-based assembly data management and process traceability for complex products. *J. Manuf. Syst.*, 58: 118–31.

Zhuang, C., Liu, J. and Xiong, H. 2018. Digital twin-based smart production management and control framework for the complex product assembly shop-floor. *Int. J. Adv. Manuf. Technol.*, 96: 1149–63.

Chapter 6

Improving Sustainability in the Built Environment through a BIM-based Integration of Digital Twin and Blockchain

An Analysis of Prefabricated Modular Construction

Karoline Figueiredo,[1,*] *Ahmed WA Hammad*[2] and *Assed Haddad*[1]

6.1 Introduction

Sustainability can be understood as a development that meets the present needs to reconcile environmental, economic, and social aspects without compromising future generations (Holden et al. 2014). The sustainability of the built environment has been the target of many recent studies in the field. This is related to the ever-increasing nature of the construction industry, with a direct impact on the environment, significant consumption of freshwater resources worldwide (Mannan and Al-Ghamdi 2020),

[1] Programa de Engenharia Ambiental, UFRJ (Universidade Federal do Rio de Janeiro), Brazil.
[2] School of Built Environment, UNSW Sydney (University of New South Wales), Australia.
Emails: a.hammad@unsw.edu.au; assed@poli.ufrj.br
* Corresponding author: karolinefigueiredo@poli.ufrj.br

and is one of the biggest consumers of fossil energy (Ritzen et al. 2016). Furthermore, considering that sustainability is a concept based on three different pillars (i.e., environmental, social, and economic), it is essential to note that construction contributes enormously to the global gross domestic product (GDP) and the global employment of labour (Saka et al. 2021). In this context, a great effort has been applied to find robust methodologies and technologies to benefit the sustainability assessment within the built environment.

A commonly utilised methodology in the construction scenario is Building Information Modelling (BIM). It refers to a working methodology based on a digital representation and information exchange, incorporating all stakeholders and facilitating data access along the project's life cycle (Kubicki et al. 2019). A BIM model thus consists of a three-dimensional digital model containing both geometric and semantic data of building materials and components. BIM guarantees the centralisation of all information and improves decision-making in construction projects (Nowak et al. 2016).

BIM has also been utilised to achieve sustainability in the construction industry. BIM can be used as a powerful tool to compare different construction materials and construction methods regarding the environmental impacts generated (Soust-Verdaguer et al. 2020). Besides, the BIM model can be used to perform simulations to minimise the energy consumed in a building (Gao et al. 2019) and improve indoor thermal comfort for end-users (Seghier et al. 2022). It is also possible to use BIM's analytical and simulation tools to assess schedule performance and achieve life-cycle cost savings (al Hattab 2021).

A challenging problem that arises in this domain is that the current state of BIM only provides static data from the built environment and is not compatible with the Internet of Things (IoT) integration (Boje et al. 2020). The IoT implementation in the built environment is essential to carry out accurate building sustainability assessments since IoT allows the digital building model to be updated in real-time, thus assessing the performance of what-if scenarios (Hunhevicz et al. 2022). However, BIM is generally applied during the early design stages to ensure the facility will satisfy the requirements imposed for the project without updating real-time information. The building static data, representing the time-invariant attributes and parameters, are undoubtedly relevant for sustainability assessment (Yuan et al. 2021). Yet, to comprehensively assess the sustainability of built assets, it is also essential to consider several time-dependent factors, such as impacts of seasonal variation, changes in the users' behaviour, the climate condition, and the evolution of the physical structure over time.

Recently, the use of digital twins has been proposed to solve this problem. Conceptually, a Digital Twin (DT) is a virtual representation of an object or a system, serving as the real-time digital counterpart of the physical asset during its lifecycle (Kuo et al. 2021). By dynamically integrating data and information, a DT can improve the design of new assets and the understanding of existing asset conditions (IET—Institution of Engineering and Technology 2019). This concept is applicable in different industries, including the construction industry. From the construction perspective, DT can be understood as an innovative methodology to enhance existing construction processes by utilising cyber-physical synchronicity (Boje et al. 2020).

Despite having different purposes and characteristics, the BIM and digital twin concepts go hand in hand. BIM is seen by several researchers as the starting point for DT implementation in the built environment, as a BIM model can be a primary source of data for developing a building digital twin (Boje et al. 2020). Therefore, several papers in the literature discuss the application of BIM-based DT to assess a building's lifecycle and its impacts. Different concepts and methods are integrated into the analyses in these studies, such as simulation (Pan and Zhang 2021), process mining (Lin and Wu 2021), IoT (Jiang et al. 2021), and Artificial Intelligence (Rafsanjani and Nabizadeh 2021).

Unfortunately, this data aggregation can generate a security risk since the analysis comprises multiple parties and sources. Therefore, confidentiality, traceability, and security issues may arise as obstacles during a BIM-based digital twin development for an asset/facility. In this context, the blockchain application provides a plausible avenue for dealing with these issues. Blockchain is a Distributed Ledger Technology (DLT) that represents a database with interconnected blocks of data cryptographically protected against tampering (Sanka et al. 2021). Regarding the construction industry, blockchain can offer a tamper-proof solution throughout the information supervision of building processes (Li et al. 2021).

This chapter elaborates on viable ways to integrate a BIM-based digital twin with blockchain technology, focusing on the sustainability assessment of prefabricated modular construction as an example. Modular construction can deliver life-cycle cost benefits and minimise environmental impacts, in addition to reducing health and safety incidents (Hammad et al. 2019). The proposed framework intends to critically discuss how this integration can benefit sustainability in the built environment and contribute to the advancement of research in this field. To achieve this, the book chapter is divided as follows: some background knowledge is presented in Section 2. Section 3 explains the research methods, discussing the proposed framework based on prefabricated modular construction. The discussions of the study are presented in Section 4. Finally, concluding remarks are presented in Section 5.

6.2 Background

Before defining the framework of this study, it is crucial to present a summarised overview of the methodologies and technologies to be used, namely digital twin, BIM, and blockchain. Therefore, this section presents the general concepts associated with these subjects and the role that they can play in the built environment. With these concepts well established, the proposed framework will be presented in Section 3.

6.2.1 Digital Twin

A digital twin can be understood as a set of realistic models that simulates the physical asset with its real-time properties, condition, and behaviour across the entire lifecycle (Haag and Anderl 2018). Utilising a digital twin is a crucial step in representing physical assets in a corresponding virtual environment (Lu and Brilakis 2019). This concept has been used in different sectors and industries, such as manufacturing (Li et al. 2022), healthcare (Thiong'o and Rutka 2022), and retail (Shoji et al. 2022). Regarding the construction industry, the advantages of using a building digital twin range from real-time data visualisation to continuous monitoring of assets and the development of self-learning capabilities (Ramos et al. 2022).

A building digital twin can be used from the beginning of the design project throughout the entire life cycle of the physical building. During the operation phase of the building, physical and digital assets coexist and feed each other with data and information. Figure 6.1 represents the components of a building's digital twin, corresponding to the digital building, the physical building, and the data that connects both assets. The physical building collects real-time data through IoT devices and sensors to be processed in the digital building model. In turn, the digital

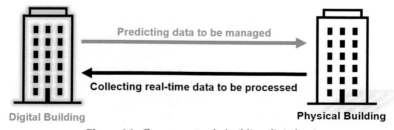

Figure 6.1: Components of a building digital twin.

model is used to predict data that can be used to improve the building's operational efficiency.

Regarding prefabricated modular construction, digital twins can be implemented to guarantee accuracy, completeness, and correctness during assembly (Tran et al. 2021). For example, Jiang et al. (2022) proposed a real-time supervision service to continuously monitor the construction process on a real-time basis, with a robotic testbed demonstration for reengineered on-site assembly in prefabricated construction. However, compared to other assets to be represented via a digital twin, a building requires a high degree of detail since an entire building is composed of different systems and components with an extended lifespan. Many difficulties can arise in analysing the building's life cycles owing to the broad number of data to be considered (Kamali et al. 2018). In this context, this research proposes an integration of concepts to benefit the creation of a building digital twin for sustainability purposes. These concepts will be further explored below.

6.2.2 Building Information Modelling (BIM)

BIM is an effective methodology that centralises building information and can benefit the phases of planning, designing, constructing, managing, and recycling during the life-cycle of buildings (Alirezaei et al. 2016). The advantages of using BIM are numerous, as this methodology can simplify the design process in several ways, upsurging the accessibility of design information to stakeholders and minimising communication failures (Ahmad and Thaheem 2017). Besides, BIM allows the teamwork to efficiently manage their decisions during a project based on a wide range of information about materials, operation, and maintenance instructions (Motalebi et al. 2022).

The 3D model generated in a BIM-based tool is a parametric and data-rich representation of the facility (Gao et al. 2019). With BIM, stakeholders have all the necessary project information centralised, which facilitates performing computer simulations to reduce costs, detect design errors, and track building timelines. Besides, evidence suggests that BIM is a crucial methodology to achieve a smart and sustainable built environment. In the literature, BIM is utilised in several case studies to attain different sustainable goals, such as thermal optimisation (Liu et al. 2020) and the minimisation of energy consumption (El Sayary and Omar 2021), water consumption (Nguyen et al. 2021) and environmental impacts generation (Santos et al. 2020). Therefore, this methodology has been used to enhance the sustainable decision-making process of building projects, especially during the early design stages (Chen and Pan 2016).

6.2.2.1 Level of Development (LOD)

A three-dimensional model generated in a BIM-based tool contains a wide range of information linked to it. In addition to graphical information such as volume, height, width, and length, the digital model also supports non-graphical information such as manufacturer, thermal data, and prices of materials and components. As the amount of data to be inserted depends on the phase and objective of each project, the Level of Development (LOD) concept arises to assist in the classification of a BIM model.

LOD is a classification system based on recognising that the data model evolves progressively throughout the design process (Dupuis et al. 2017). This definition has proved to be very important since a construction project normally involves different parties, and it is essential that everyone understands the building elements' maturity at each particular stage (Abualdenien and Borrmann 2020). The LOD specification works as an agreement on which information is available at each stage, in addition to determining the purpose of the BIM model and its expected deliverables (Beetz et al. 2018). The BIM digital model describes the building geometry approximatively, using an acceptable quality representation based on the specific required LOD (Lu and Brilakis 2019).

To specify and articulate the content and reliability of BIM models at various stages in the design and construction processes, the literature presents five progressively detailed levels from LOD 100 to LOD 500 (Tam et al. 2022). The LOD 100 can be related to the concept design, where the elements are represented only symbolically or schematically (Sanchez et al. 2021). In the following levels, geometric and non-geometric information can be added to the model. It is possible to associate LOD 200 and LOD 300 with the design process, the former being a schematic design and the latter representing a detailed design (BIMForum 2015). In turn, a BIM model with LOD 400 is detailed with enough information for fabrication, assembly, and installation (Sanchez et al. 2021). Finally, LOD 500 refers to a detailed as-built BIM model (D'Angelo et al. 2022).

6.2.2.2 Industry Foundation Classes (IFC)

When using the BIM methodology as a tool to aid in project decision-making, it is often necessary to use different BIM-based computational tools in an integrated manner. In this context, the OpenBIM concept emerges as an initiative from the buildingSMART International (bSI) organisation to disseminate the use of an open data model, allowing interoperability between BIM tools from different owners (buildingSMART International, n.d.). As a manifestation of the openBIM concept, the IFC schema arises.

The Industry Foundation Classes (IFC) data model is a standardised and digital way to describe the built environment's data, including buildings and civil infrastructure (ISO 2018). IFC provides software-agnostic data interoperability in the Architecture, Engineering, and Construction (AEC) industry, since this model data allows sharing and exchange between heterogeneous BIM tools (Oostwegel et al. 2022). The IFC schema codifies the identity, semantics, attributes, and relationships of objects, abstract concepts, processes and people involved in a project.

Although IFC schema has proved to be an excellent solution for BIM data representation and exchange, the growing amount of information relying on semantic web technologies in the construction industry has forced a breakthrough in this domain. Therefore, a connecting point between semantic web technologies and the IFC standard was developed, named ifcOWL. This is a Web Ontology Language (OWL) for IFC that intends to exploit data distribution, extensibility of the data model, querying, and reasoning (Pauwels and Terkaj 2016). While the IFC data is expressed as a schema in the EXPRESS data specification language (ISO 2004), ifcOWL adopts an OWL profile for specifying building information, which brings essential improvements in terms of performance (Pauwels et al. 2017).

Ontology representations of the IFC schema have been a robust backbone for challenging interoperability requirements in the BIM scenario (Venugopal et al. 2015). An ontology can better structure the interoperability of BIM-based tools as it delivers a formal and consistent taxonomy and classification framework. Regarding the use of BIM as the starting point for the DT implementation, it is considered that DT becomes entirely dependent on ifcOWL models, ensuring a robust and knowledge-oriented semantic data storage, which can be exploited by AI technologies (Boje et al. 2020).

6.2.3 Blockchain

Blockchain is an innovative information technology that guarantees decentralisation, security, auditability, and smart execution during its application. A blockchain comprises consecutively linked blocks, each containing a pointer to the previous block, a timestamp, and a compilation of information (Estevam et al. 2021). The way blockchain is structured guarantees that data tampering is easily identified (Saxena et al. 2021). Besides, regarding the decentralisation characteristic, blockchain excludes the need for a trusted third party to validate transactions, creating a delegation of authority among network contributors that improves the service trust (Hewa et al. 2021).

In the blockchain domain, the broadcasts of the transactions are collected into blocks, which are then hashed and receive a timestamp (Lemieux 2016). The name hash is used to identify a cryptographic function intended to encode data to form a unique, fixed-length string (Tsiatsis et al. 2019). The cryptographic functions within a blockchain guarantee the data authenticity and allow the signature of electronic documents (Lemieux 2016), being practically impossible to carry out the opposite process and get the original data from an already formed hash. In turn, the timestamp serves as proof that the data must have existed at that time to get into the specific hash (Nakamoto 2008).

A blockchain can also store a smart contract, representing an agreement between parties in the form of computer code (Wu et al. 2022). A smart contract can automatically self-execute processes based on the satisfaction of preset conditions (Kuhle et al. 2021), and it can be used as a possible solution to the slow, expensive, and fragile transactions associated with the built environment (Chaveesuk et al. 2020). Unfortunately, research shows that the construction sector is classified as one of the sectors that least adopt information technology (McKinsey and Company 2016). The full implementation of blockchain in building projects needs to be increasingly discussed among researchers and professionals. Among the currently existing blockchain platforms in the market, two of them can be applied in the construction domain: Ethereum and Hyperledger Fabric (Yang et al. 2020).

A discussion gaining strength in the literature is about integrating BIM and Blockchain. This integration can overcome several problems associated with the construction project lifecycle since BIM itself is not concerned with confidentiality, traceability, non-repudiation, provenance tracking, and data ownership (Nawari and Ravindran 2019). A blockchain platform can mitigate project delays generated due to discrepancies in the BIM models or conflicts among the interested parties (San et al. 2019). Nevertheless, technical barriers are associated with this integration, such as the need for greater computational power to add a BIM model to a blockchain (Nawari 2021).

6.3 Materials and Methods

The construction sector significantly impacts the three pillars of sustainability (Kamali and Hewage 2017), and therefore, there is a growing search for sustainable practices in this area. Generating a sustainable building involves looking at one that produces less environmental waste, improves societal influences, avoids the utilisation of natural resources indiscriminately, and is economically viable throughout its life cycle.

The use of the prefabricated modular construction method appears to be a viable solution for enhancing the sustainability of the construction industry. It has been reported that prefabricated construction reduces the construction time and the generation of environmental impacts during the construction phase (Navaratnam et al. 2021), in addition to being considered an economical construction approach (Navaratnam et al. 2019). However, for this method to effectively achieve sustainability, it is necessary to carefully optimise building material choices and improve design, manufacturing, logistics, and assembly processes (Bertram et al. 2019).

The framework proposed here addresses the integration of a BIM-based digital twin and blockchain technology to ensure sustainability goals. Modular construction is used as the case example to demonstrate the framework's applicability. In this proposal, BIM serves as the primary data source for developing the building digital twin, while blockchain ensures transparency and security in transactions involving multiple stakeholders. Also, the purpose of the framework proposed is to consider the impacts generated throughout the whole life cycle of a building. It is believed that only by adopting a life-cycle perspective would it be possible to meet the requirements of a sustainable built environment, given that a life-cycle approach comprehensively addresses the impacts of materials and components used, fabrication and construction practices, and waste management.

6.3.1 Building Life Cycle

The building digital twin concept is mainly related to using devices and sensors to collect real-time data, thus especially considering the operational phase of the building. Nonetheless, when the life-cycle approach is inserted into the assessment, the practitioners must consider the design, construction, operation, demolition, and waste treatment stages. In this context, the building digital twin evolves according to the complexity and sophistication required for each stage. With the aid of information technologies, it becomes doable to consider data from the extraction of the raw materials to the waste treatment stage to evaluate all the significant impacts generated by building materials and components. Figure 6.2 presents the entire life cycle of a building that could benefit from integrating BIM, digital twin, and blockchain technology.

Regarding the development of new building projects, the design phase must be used to compare different materials and construction methods so that design choices are conscious and efficient to achieve sustainable goals. In this context, integrating an information technology like blockchain improves the tracking of materials and their impacts throughout their life cycles. Besides, blockchain has proven to positively influence waste management, placing accountability on every member of the chain rather than just on the manufacturer (Gopalakrishnan et al. 2021).

Figure 6.2: Stages of the building life cycle.

6.3.2 *Integrated Framework for the Project Design Stage*

Based on what has been mentioned so far, it is suggested that the building digital twin be generated from a BIM model with LOD 300. With this level of detail of the construction components and already known information about the climate and the position of the building on the ground, it is possible to carry out different types of sustainability assessments. As this study focuses on the prefabricated construction method, it is essential to point out that a large part of the prefabricated components worldwide uses high carbon-intensive construction materials such as concrete and steel (Navaratnam et al. 2021). Therefore, the first step of the proposed integration serves as a possibility for finding alternative sustainable building materials.

During the project design stage, the building digital twin can be used as a descriptive tool, for collecting and visualising data, and as an informative tool, for converting data into information for generating project insights (Seaton et al. 2022). Ideally, a comprehensive digital twin could be developed at this stage, using real-time data about impacts caused by raw materials extraction and transportation, for example, to improve the choice of materials and components and achieve better sustainability outcomes.

With the help of the IFC format and the ifcOWL ontology, it is possible to export the building models to different computational tools to perform various building analyses. With a building model, it is possible to benefit the decision-making process in several ways: testing different materials regarding their environmental, social, and economic impacts, thus improving the building materials choice (Figueiredo et al. 2021); evaluating the annual energy consumption to achieve energy-efficient buildings (González et al. 2021); and analysing adequate interior thermal comfort of the building, minimising the cooling load rate (Seghier et al. 2022). The proposal here is to use a BIM-based digital twin during the early design phases to benefit the decision-making process by focusing on sustainability.

From the simulation results, possible changes will be suggested to the 3D digital model. The idea is to use blockchain to record all these design changes since there is no chronological record of the modifications done in a traditional BIM model. Without the aid of information technology, the revision of the project would occur by updating and replacing the existing data (Kiu et al. 2020). Therefore, the synchronisation of design records through blockchain seems very beneficial. Besides, as this design phase can involve several professionals, it is suggested to use blockchain technology through its smart contracts to ensure transparency and security in transactions. In turn, to not oblige all stakeholders to significantly change their work processes or have extensive knowledge about blockchain, the proposal is to use a blockchain platform as a robust backbone system behind the interface layer of commonly used applications (Yang et al. 2020).

Figure 6.3 illustrates the integration proposal between a building digital twin and blockchain. It is also worth mentioning the importance of considering data on the life cycle of construction materials in the sustainability assessments carried out. Blockchain can be used directly in this task, as this technology can reduce data uncertainty, decrease the data collection time and ensure perfect traceability of data sources (Kouhizadeh and Sarkis 2018).

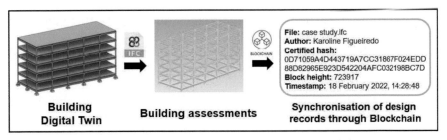

Figure 6.3: First steps to integrate Digital Twin and Blockchain.

6.3.3 *Proposal for the Fabrication and Assembly Stages*

Blockchain utilisation is again encouraged in the fabrication and assembly stages. The difference is that, from the fabrication and assembly stages, it becomes necessary to increase the level of development of the digital building model, now corresponding to LOD 400. Traditionally, stakeholders raised concerns about the absence of systematic records of inspection and operations during the fabrication stage (Wu et al. 2022). Utilising a digital fabrication drawing production with the synchronisation of data records will enable higher transparency and better collaboration opportunities.

Using information from the factory, it is possible to develop a digital fabrication model in real-time. The idea here is to include data about the materials' quality inspection into the digital model so that the digital prototype could be used to ensure minimal chances of flaws during the assembly stage. This whole process becomes accessible due to the BIM characteristic of centralising information in the 3D digital model, in addition to the parametric modelling. Therefore, using the BIM methodology as a preliminary step in developing a building digital twin makes the process more effective, given that BIM is currently considered the best tool for authoring static data for construction specifications and documentation.

The use of DTs during fabrication and assembly stages is still little discussed in the literature since the current state of the art of digital twinning in construction relies on as-built data collection (Rausch et al. 2021). Nevertheless, DTs offer great promise as quality control tools throughout fabrication and assembly, and this idea can be used to improve sustainability in the processes. A DT can be fed with scan data from the building components, which will assist professionals during the building assembly to match parts, find clamp positions and select the optimal joining sequence (Söderberg et al. 2017). But it is also possible to conduct construction simulation, safety planning, and virtual job site planning from the digital twin model, which can guarantee worker safety and minimise material waste, directly affecting the three pillars of sustainability.

On the other hand, the inherent characteristics of the prefabricated modular construction method suggest the involvement of more participants than in conventional construction since manufacturers represent additional parties (Yin et al. 2019). The literature shows that blockchain can enable the establishment of more efficient connections with partners and stakeholders and provide innovative solutions for the challenges faced by external professionals through a dynamic perspective on value creation (Wan et al. 2022). Based on the above, the benefits of the proposed integration are summarised in Fig. 6.4.

6.3.4 *Framework for the Operational and Maintenance Stages*

After the assembly stage, the digital BIM model can be updated based on LOD 500. With the help of IoT and using devices and sensors to collect real-time data, the building digital twin can be updated with dynamic and static data from multiple sources. Therefore, the dynamic digital model updates will provide a better understanding of the building's

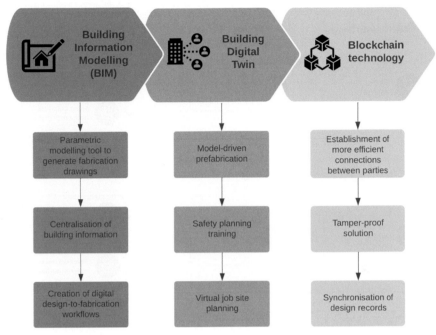

Figure 6.4: Advantages of integrating concepts during the fabrication and assembly stages.

performance, enabling the decision-makers to achieve a sustainable smart building. The sustainability certification experts can also make good use of the building twin, updating the digital model following established procedures (Tagliabue et al. 2021).

Indeed, this process also needs to be a tamper-proof solution, ensuring security and transparency between the parties involved. Then, it is recommended that blockchain technology be applied throughout the entire process. Figure 6.5 presents the idea of dividing the framework into three steps, corresponding to the different levels of development (LOD) used during the integration process.

6.3.5 *Proposal for Designing a Semantic BIM-based Digital Twin Integrated with Blockchain*

From all that has been exposed so far, it is suggested the creation of a platform for integrating BIM, DT, and blockchain regarding the application in building projects. Figure 6.6 presents the semantic architecture for the integrated framework. Three different layers are created (i.e., the database layer, the logic layer, and the user interface) for the platform to be operable. Simulation data will be generated from the BIM-based digital twin

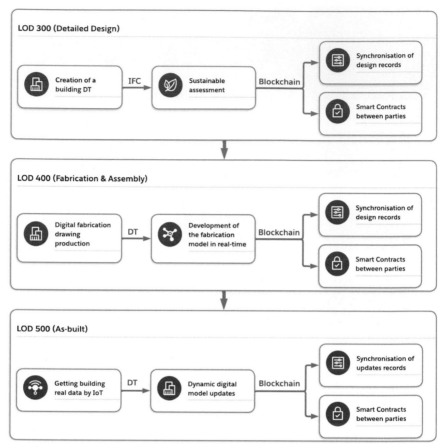

Figure 6.5: Framework to integrate BIM, digital twin and blockchain across various stages of the building life cycle.

models. Then, these three-dimensional models need to be fed back with information with every change, while everything must be recorded on a blockchain. During the design, fabrication and assembly, and operation stages, all documentation generated must be stored on the blockchain so that data reliability and traceability are guaranteed.

The database layer consists of the 3-D BIM models and all data to be inserted and generated. Simulations can be developed throughout the entire project lifecycle, either to benefit decision-making of which materials and methods should be used to achieve sustainable standards or to optimise the use of building systems throughout the operation phase. During the operation phase, sensors and devices collect real-time data from the physical asset. The building digital twin can be calibrated

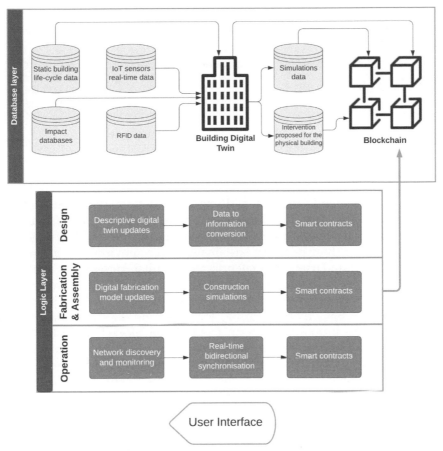

Figure 6.6: Proposed semantic architecture for the integrated framework.

to accept data from numerous data streams, such as video devices, accelerometers, laser scanners, Radio Frequency Identification (RFID) devices, and displacement sensors (Seaton et al. 2022). Therefore, new simulations can be performed based on real-time data, and all information generated must be recorded in a blockchain.

The logic layer needs to be divided into the three project phases as the permissions of each entity will be different in each step. For example, the manufacturer does not need permission to modify any files (i.e., digital model, drawings, and documentation) generated during the design and operation stages. However, this entity needs some permission during fabrication and assembly when the BIM-based digital twin is based on LOD 400. In this context, it is necessary to precisely define a role mapping with permissions defined for each entity. It is illustrated in Figure 6.7.

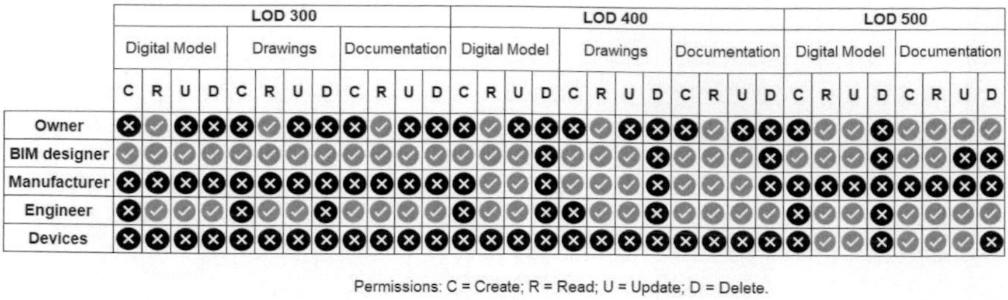

	LOD 300												LOD 400												LOD 500							
	Digital Model				Drawings				Documentation				Digital Model				Drawings				Documentation				Digital Model				Documentation			
	C	R	U	D	C	R	U	D	C	R	U	D	C	R	U	D	C	R	U	D	C	R	U	D	C	R	U	D	C	R	U	D
Owner	✗	✓	✗	✗	✗	✓	✗	✗	✓	✗	✗	✗	✗	✓	✗	✗	✗	✓	✗	✗	✓	✗	✗	✗	✗	✓	✗	✗	✓	✓	✓	✓
BIM designer	✓	✓	✓	✓	✓	✓	✓	✓	✓	✓	✓	✓	✓	✓	✗	✓	✓	✓	✓	✓	✓	✓	✓	✗	✓	✓	✓	✗	✓	✓	✗	✗
Manufacturer	✗	✗	✗	✗	✗	✗	✗	✗	✗	✗	✗	✗	✗	✗	✗	✗	✓	✗	✓	✓	✗	✓	✓	✗	✗	✗	✗	✗	✗	✗	✗	✗
Engineer	✗	✓	✓	✓	✗	✓	✓	✗	✓	✓	✓	✓	✗	✓	✓	✗	✗	✓	✓	✓	✗	✓	✓	✓	✗	✓	✓	✗	✓	✗	✓	✓
Devices	✗	✗	✗	✗	✗	✗	✗	✗	✗	✗	✗	✗	✗	✗	✗	✗	✗	✗	✗	✗	✗	✗	✗	✗	✗	✓	✓	✗	✓	✓	✓	✗

Permissions: C = Create; R = Read; U = Update; D = Delete.

Figure 6.7: An example of a role mapping with permissions defined for each entity.

6.4 Discussion

This chapter intends to start a discussion on how digital twin and blockchain technology can be integrated to assist designers, manufacturers, engineers, and architects in developing more sustainable building projects, considering the three pillars of sustainability (i.e., environmental, social, and economic), and using the prefabricated modular construction method. The main achievements, including contributions to the field, are related to the proposal for designing a semantic BIM-based digital twin platform to improve design, manufacturing, logistics, and assembly processes. Besides, as the proposed platform is based on blockchain technology, it will consist of a tamper-proof solution for a building sustainability assessment. Thus, this research sheds light on the sustainable benefits that building assessment tools offer to the built environment, also assisting in analysing the entire building life cycle.

Unfortunately, as the framework is proposed, considerable manual effort is required for practitioners to manually update the digital model during the design and fabrication stages. This problem will persist as long as the three-dimensional modelling is done in BIM tools currently available on the market since they do not use domain ontology. Indeed, some BIM applications support the IFC standard but do not adequately export the IoT information, focusing on the physical object and not considering its behaviour.

Another critical issue to be pointed out is that building models may require greater computational power to be added to a blockchain, which can create technical barriers to the implementation of the proposed framework. Besides, the performance of this integrative framework can face many cultural and organisational challenges, given that the construction industry delays the adoption of process and technology advancements. Therefore, the application in real projects of what has been discussed so far and the dissemination of this integration directly depend on advances in research in this regard.

The following steps of this research refer to the practical development of this platform, with the validation of its use through application in a case study. However, it is worth mentioning that the platform in its current state already represents an advance for research in this area, as it presents a feasible solution to minimise errors and achieve greater sustainability in prefabricated modular construction.

6.5 Conclusion

A semantic architecture for the integrated framework was proposed in this chapter, with an example of how practitioners could develop a role mapping with permissions defined for each entity. The proposal uses the Building Information Modelling (BIM) methodology as a primary data source to establish a building digital twin, focusing on the sustainability assessment of prefabricated modular construction. The digital twin is examined for its benefits in sustainability decision-making throughout the construction lifecycle, ensuring that the evaluation is not tampered with due to blockchain application.

Several challenges are associated with the proposal discussed. It is essential to note that a life-cycle sustainability assessment of a built asset, considering the three pillars of sustainability jointly, is very challenging as it requires a comprehensive understanding of uncertainties and processing a large amount of data. As such, several technical barriers can appear during the integration of digital twins and blockchain and the development of the proposed platform. Nonetheless, more research needs to be conducted to explore the links between environment, society, and economy, realistically quantifying the impacts generated by the construction industry and encouraging the creation of a more sustainable and smarter built environment.

Future studies will focus on three main aspects:

1. The practical development of this platform, with the validation of its use through application in a building case study;
2. Improvement of the platform to minimise manual and repetitive work related to 3D-BIM models;
3. Investigation about the integration of the Life Cycle Sustainability Assessment (LCSA) methodology into this platform, so that it will be possible to analyse environmental, social, and economic impacts based on the whole life-cycle of the building.

Acknowledgement

This study was financed in part by the Coordenação de Aperfeiçoamento de Pessoal de Nível Superior - Brasil (CAPES) - Finance Code 001.

References

Abualdenien, J. and Borrmann, A. 2020. Vagueness visualization in building models across different design stages. *Advanced Engineering Informatics*, 45: 101107. https://doi.org/10.1016/J.AEI.2020.101107.

Ahmad, T. and Thaheem, M.J. 2017. Developing a residential building-related social sustainability assessment framework and its implications for BIM. *Sustainable Cities and Society*, 28: 1–15. https://doi.org/10.1016/j.scs.2016.08.002.

al Hattab, M. 2021. The dynamic evolution of synergies between BIM and sustainability: A text mining and network theory approach. *Journal of Building Engineering*, 37: 102159. https://doi.org/10.1016/J.JOBE.2021.102159.

Alirezaei, M., Noori, M., Tatari, O., Mackie, K.R. and Elgamal, A. 2016. BIM-based damage estimation of buildings under earthquake loading condition. *Procedia Engineering*, 145: 1051–1058. https://doi.org/10.1016/j.proeng.2016.04.136.

Beetz, J., Borrmann, A. and Weise, M. 2018. Process-based definition of model content. *In*: *Building Information Modeling: Technology Foundations and Industry Practice*. Springer, Cham, pp. 127–138. https://doi.org/10.1007/978-3-319-92862-3_6.

Bertram, N., Fuchs, S., Mischke, J., Palter, R., Strube, G. and Woetzel, J. 2019. Modular construction: From projects to products. *McKinsey & Company: Capital Projects & Infrastructure*, 1–34.

BIMForum. 2015. Level of Development Specification.

Boje, C., Guerriero, A., Kubicki, S. and Rezgui, Y. 2020. Towards a semantic construction digital twin: Directions for future research. *Automation in Construction*, 114: 103179. https://doi.org/10.1016/J.AUTCON.2020.103179.

buildingSMART International. n.d. The International Home of openBIM [WWW Document]. URL https://www.buildingsmart.org/about/openbim/ (accessed 2.9.22).

Chaveesuk, S., Khalid, B. and Chaiyasoonthorn, W. 2020. Understanding stakeholders needs for using blockchain based smart contracts in construction industry of thailand: Extended tam framework. *In*: International Conference on Human System Interaction, HSI. IEEE Computer Society, pp. 137–141. https://doi.org/10.1109/HSI49210.2020.9142675.

Chen, L. and Pan, W. 2016. BIM-aided variable fuzzy multi-criteria decision making of low-carbon building measures selection. *Sustainable Cities and Society*, 27: 222–232. https://doi.org/10.1016/j.scs.2016.04.008.

D'Angelo, L., Hajdukiewicz, M., Seri, F. and Keane, M.M. 2022. A novel BIM-based process workflow for building retrofit. *Journal of Building Engineering*, 50: 104163. https://doi.org/10.1016/J.JOBE.2022.104163.

Dupuis, M., April, A., Lesage, P. and Forgues, D. 2017. Method to enable LCA analysis through each level of development of a BIM model. *Procedia Engineering*, 196: 857–863. https://doi.org/10.1016/J.PROENG.2017.08.017.

El Sayary, S. and Omar, O. 2021. Designing a BIM energy-consumption template to calculate and achieve a net-zero-energy house. *Solar Energy*, 216: 315–320. https://doi.org/10.1016/j.solener.2021.01.003.

Estevam, G., Palma, L.M., Silva, L.R., Martina, J.E. and Vigil, M. 2021. Accurate and decentralized time stamping using smart contracts on the Ethereum blockchain. *Information Processing and Management*, 58. https://doi.org/10.1016/j.ipm.2020.102471.

Figueiredo, K., Pierott, R., Hammad, A.W.A. and Haddad, A. 2021. Sustainable material choice for construction projects: A life cycle sustainability assessment framework based on BIM and Fuzzy-AHP. *Building and Environment*, 196: 107805. https://doi.org/10.1016/J.BUILDENV.2021.107805.

Gao, H., Koch, C. and Wu, Y. 2019. Building information modelling based building energy modelling: A review. *Applied Energy*, 238: 320–343. https://doi.org/10.1016/J.APENERGY.2019.01.032.

González, J., Soares, C.A.P., Najjar, M. and Haddad, A.N. 2021. BIM and BEM methodologies integration in energy-efficient buildings using experimental design. *Buildings*, 11: 491. https://doi.org/10.3390/BUILDINGS11100491.

Gopalakrishnan, P.K., Hall, J. and Behdad, S. 2021. Cost analysis and optimization of Blockchain-based solid waste management traceability system. *Waste Management*, 120: 594–607. https://doi.org/10.1016/j.wasman.2020.10.027.

Haag, S. and Anderl, R. 2018. Digital twin – Proof of concept. *Manufacturing Letters*, 15: 64–66. https://doi.org/10.1016/J.MFGLET.2018.02.006.

Hammad, A.W., Akbarnezhad, A., Wu, P., Wang, X. and Haddad, A. 2019. Building information modelling-based framework to contrast conventional and modular construction methods through selected sustainability factors. *Journal of Cleaner Production*, 228: 1264–1281. https://doi.org/10.1016/J.JCLEPRO.2019.04.150.

Hewa, T., Ylianttila, M. and Liyanage, M. 2021. Survey on blockchain based smart contracts: Applications, opportunities and challenges. *Journal of Network and Computer Applications*. https://doi.org/10.1016/j.jnca.2020.102857.

Holden, E., Linnerud, K. and Banister, D. 2014. Sustainable development: Our common future revisited. *Global Environmental Change*, 26: 130–139. https://doi.org/10.1016/J.GLOENVCHA.2014.04.006.

Hunhevicz, J.J., Motie, M. and Hall, D.M. 2022. Digital building twins and blockchain for performance-based (smart) contracts. *Automation in Construction*, 133: 103981. https://doi.org/10.1016/J.AUTCON.2021.103981.

IET - Institution of Engineering and Technology. 2019. Digital Twin for the Built Environment: An introduction to the opportunities, benefts, challenges and risks.

ISO. 2018. Industry Foundation Classes (IFC) for data sharing in the construction and facility management industries — Part 1: Data schema.

ISO. 2004. ISO 10303-11 - Industrial automation systems and integration — Product data representation and exchange — Part 11: Description methods: The EXPRESS language reference manual.

Jiang, F., Ma, L., Broyd, T. and Chen, K. 2021. Digital twin and its implementations in the civil engineering sector. *Automation in Construction*, 130: 103838. https://doi.org/10.1016/J.AUTCON.2021.103838.

Jiang, Y., Li, M., Guo, D., Wu, W., Zhong, R.Y. and Huang, G.Q. 2022. Digital twin-enabled smart modular integrated construction system for on-site assembly. *Computers in Industry*, 136: 103594. https://doi.org/10.1016/J.COMPIND.2021.103594.

Kamali, M. and Hewage, K. 2017. Development of performance criteria for sustainability evaluation of modular versus conventional construction methods. *Journal of Cleaner Production*. https://doi.org/10.1016/j.jclepro.2016.10.108.

Kamali, M., Hewage, K. and Milani, A.S. 2018. Life cycle sustainability performance assessment framework for residential modular buildings: Aggregated sustainability indices. *Building and Environment*, 138: 21–41. https://doi.org/10.1016/j.buildenv.2018.04.019.

Kiu, M.S., Chia, F.C. and Wong, P.F. 2020. Exploring the potentials of blockchain application in construction industry: A systematic review. *International Journal of Construction Management*. https://doi.org/10.1080/15623599.2020.1833436.

Kouhizadeh, M. and Sarkis, J. 2018. Blockchain practices, potentials, and perspectives in greening supply chains. *Sustainability (Switzerland)*, 10. https://doi.org/10.3390/su10103652.

Kubicki, S., Guerriero, A., Schwartz, L., Daher, E. and Idris, B. 2019. Assessment of synchronous interactive devices for BIM project coordination: Prospective ergonomics approach. *Automation in Construction*, 101: 160–178. https://doi.org/10.1016/J.AUTCON.2018.12.009.

Kuhle, P., Arroyo, D. and Schuster, E. 2021. Building A blockchain-based decentralized digital asset management system for commercial aircraft leasing. *Computers in Industry*, 126: 103393. https://doi.org/10.1016/J.COMPIND.2020.103393.

Kuo, Y.H., Pilati, F., Qu, T. and Huang, G.Q. 2021. Digital twin-enabled smart industrial systems: recent developments and future perspectives. *International Journal of Computer Integrated Manufacturing*, 34: 685–689. https://doi.org/10.1080/0951192X.2021.1959710.

Lemieux, V.L. 2016. Trusting records: Is blockchain technology the answer? *Records Management Journal*, 26: 110–139. https://doi.org/10.1108/RMJ-12-2015-0042/FULL/PDF.

Li, L., Lei, B. and Mao, C. 2022. Digital twin in smart manufacturing. *J. Ind. Inf. Integr.*, 26: 100289. https://doi.org/10.1016/J.JII.2021.100289.

Li, X., Wu, L., Zhao, R., Lu, W. and Xue, F. 2021. Two-layer adaptive blockchain-based supervision model for off-site modular housing production. *Computers in Industry*, 128. https://doi.org/10.1016/j.compind.2021.103437.

Lin, J.R. and Wu, D.P. 2021. An approach to twinning and mining collaborative network of construction projects. *Automation in Construction*, 125: 103643. https://doi.org/10.1016/J.AUTCON.2021.103643.

Liu, Z., Wang, Q., Gan, V.J.L. and Peh, L. 2020. Envelope thermal performance analysis based on building information model (BIM) cloud platform - Proposed green mark collaboration environment. *Energies (Basel)*, 13: 586. https://doi.org/10.3390/en13030586.

Lu, R. and Brilakis, I. 2019. Digital twinning of existing reinforced concrete bridges from labelled point clusters. *Automation in Construction*, 105: 102837. https://doi.org/10.1016/J.AUTCON.2019.102837.

Mannan, M. and Al-Ghamdi, S.G. 2020. Environmental impact of water-use in buildings: Latest developments from a life-cycle assessment perspective. *Journal of Environmental Management*, 261: 110198. https://doi.org/10.1016/J.JENVMAN.2020.110198.

McKinsey and Company. 2016. Imagining construction's digital future | McKinsey [WWW Document]. URL https://www.mckinsey.com/business-functions/operations/our-insights/imagining-constructions-digital-future# (accessed 3.29.21).

Motalebi, M., Rashidi, A. and Nasiri, M.M. 2022. Optimization and BIM-based lifecycle assessment integration for energy efficiency retrofit of buildings. *Journal of Building Engineering*, 49: 104022. https://doi.org/10.1016/J.JOBE.2022.104022.

Nakamoto, S. 2008. Bitcoin: A Peer-to-Peer Electronic Cash System [WWW Document]. URL https://git.dhimmel.com/bitcoin-whitepaper/ (accessed 3.16.21).

Navaratnam, S., Ngo, T., Gunawardena, T. and Henderson, D. 2019. Performance review of prefabricated building systems and future research in Australia. *Buildings*, 9: 38. https://doi.org/10.3390/BUILDINGS9020038.

Navaratnam, S., Widdowfield Small, D., Gatheeshgar, P., Poologanathan, K., Thamboo, J., Higgins, C. and Mendis, P. 2021. Development of cross laminated timber-cold-formed steel composite beam for floor system to sustainable modular building construction. *Structures*, 32: 681–690. https://doi.org/10.1016/J.ISTRUC.2021.03.051.

Nawari, N.O. 2021. Blockchain technologies: Hyperledger fabric in BIM work processes. *In*: *Lecture Notes in Civil Engineering*. Springer, pp. 813–823. https://doi.org/10.1007/978-3-030-51295-8_56.

Nawari, N.O. and Ravindran, S. 2019. Blockchain and the built environment: Potentials and limitations. *Journal of Building Engineering*. https://doi.org/10.1016/j.jobe.2019.100832.

Nguyen, T.P., Nguyen, V.A., Pham, D.D. and Do, H.Q. 2021. Intergrating Building Information Modelling (BIM) and Tools with green building certification system in designing and evaluating water efficiency of green building for sustainable buildings. *IOP Conference Series: Materials Science and Engineering*, 1079. https://doi.org/10.1088/1757-899x/1079/3/032063.

Nowak, P., Książek, M., Draps, M. and Zawistowski, J. 2016. Decision making with use of building information modeling. *Procedia Engineering*, 153: 519–526. https://doi.org/10.1016/J.PROENG.2016.08.177.

Oostwegel, L.J.N., Jaud, Š., Muhič, S. and Malovrh Rebec, K. 2022. Digitalization of culturally significant buildings: Ensuring high-quality data exchanges in the heritage domain using OpenBIM. *Heritage Science*, 10: 1–14. https://doi.org/10.1186/S40494-021-00640-Y/TABLES/3.

Pan, Y. and Zhang, L. 2021. A BIM-data mining integrated digital twin framework for advanced project management. *Automation in Construction*, 124: 103564. https://doi.org/10.1016/J.AUTCON.2021.103564.

Pauwels, P. and Terkaj, W. 2016. EXPRESS to OWL for construction industry: Towards a recommendable and usable ifcOWL ontology. *Automation in Construction*, 63: 100–133. https://doi.org/10.1016/J.AUTCON.2015.12.003.

Pauwels, P., Zhang, S. and Lee, Y.C. 2017. Semantic web technologies in AEC industry: A literature overview. *Automation in Construction*, 73: 145–165. https://doi.org/10.1016/J.AUTCON.2016.10.003.

Rafsanjani, H.N. and Nabizadeh, A.H. 2021. Towards digital architecture, engineering, and construction (AEC) industry through virtual design and construction (VDC) and digital twin. *Energy and Built Environment*. https://doi.org/10.1016/J.ENBENV.2021.10.004.

Ramos, M., Pereira, P., Joe Opoku, D.G., Perera, S., Osei-Kyei, R., Rashidi, M., Famakinwa, T. and Bamdad, K. 2022. Drivers for digital twin adoption in the construction industry: A systematic literature review. *Buildings*, 12: 113. https://doi.org/10.3390/BUILDINGS12020113.

Rausch, C., Lu, R., Talebi, S. and Haas, C. 2021. Deploying 3D scanning based geometric digital twins during fabrication and assembly in offsite manufacturing. *International Journal of Construction Management*, 1. https://doi.org/10.1080/15623599.2021.1896942.

Ritzen, M.J., Haagen, T., Rovers, R., Vroon, Z.A.E.P. and Geurts, C.P.W. 2016. Environmental impact evaluation of energy saving and energy generation: Case study for two Dutch dwelling types. *Building and Environment*, 108: 73–84. https://doi.org/10.1016/J.BUILDENV.2016.07.020.

Saka, N., Saka, A.B., Akinradewo, O. and Aigbavboa, C.O. 2021. Impact assessment of political administrations on the performance of the construction sector: a time series analysis. *Journal of Engineering, Design and Technology*. https://doi.org/10.1108/JEDT-08-2021-0423/FULL/PDF.

San, K.M., Choy, C.F. and Fung, W.P. 2019. The potentials and impacts of blockchain technology in construction industry: A literature review. *In*: IOP Conference Series: Materials Science and Engineering. https://doi.org/10.1088/1757-899X/495/1/012005.

Sanchez, B., Rausch, C., Haas, C. and Hartmann, T. 2021. A framework for BIM-based disassembly models to support reuse of building components. *Resources, Conservation and Recycling*, 175: 105825. https://doi.org/10.1016/J.RESCONREC.2021.105825.

Sanka, A.I., Irfan, M., Huang, I. and Cheung, R.C.C. 2021. A survey of breakthrough in blockchain technology: Adoptions, applications, challenges and future research. *Computer Communications*. https://doi.org/10.1016/j.comcom.2020.12.028.

Santos, R., Costa, A.A., Silvestre, J.D., Vandenbergh, T. and Pyl, L. 2020. BIM-based life cycle assessment and life cycle costing of an office building in Western Europe. *Building and Environment*, 169. https://doi.org/10.1016/j.buildenv.2019.106568.

Saxena, S., Bhushan, B. and Ahad, M.A. 2021. Blockchain based solutions to secure IoT: Background, integration trends and a way forward. *Journal of Network and Computer Applications*. https://doi.org/10.1016/j.jnca.2021.103050.

Seaton, H., Savian, C., Sepasgozar, S. and Sawhney, A. 2022. *Digital Twins from Design to Handover of Constructed Assets*. London.

Seghier, T.E., Lim, Y.W., Harun, M.F., Ahmad, M.H., Samah, A.A. and Majid, H.A. 2022. BIM-based retrofit method (RBIM) for building envelope thermal performance optimization. *Energy and Buildings*, 256: 111693. https://doi.org/10.1016/J.ENBUILD.2021.111693.

Shoji, K., Schudel, S., Onwude, D., Shrivastava, C. and Defraeye, T. 2022. Mapping the postharvest life of imported fruits from packhouse to retail stores using physics-based digital twins. *Resources, Conservation and Recycling*, 176: 105914. https://doi.org/10.1016/J.RESCONREC.2021.105914.

Söderberg, R., Wärmefjord, K., Carlson, J.S. and Lindkvist, L. 2017. Toward a digital twin for real-time geometry assurance in individualized production. *CIRP Annals*, 66: 137–140. https://doi.org/10.1016/J.CIRP.2017.04.038.

Soust-Verdaguer, B., Llatas, C. and Moya, L. 2020. Comparative BIM-based life cycle assessment of Uruguayan timber and concrete-masonry single-family houses in design stage. *Journal of Cleaner Production*, 277: 121958. https://doi.org/10.1016/J.JCLEPRO.2020.121958.

Tagliabue, L.C., Cecconi, F.R., Maltese, S., Rinaldi, S., Ciribini, A.L.C. and Flammini, A. 2021. Leveraging digital twin for sustainability assessment of an educational building. *Sustainability*, 13: 480. https://doi.org/10.3390/SU13020480.

Tam, V.WY., Zhou, Y., Illankoon, C. and Le, K.N. 2022. A critical review on BIM and LCA integration using the ISO 14040 framework. *Building and Environment*, 213: 108865. https://doi.org/10.1016/J.BUILDENV.2022.108865.

Thiong'o, G.M. and Rutka, J.T. 2022. Digital Twin technology: The future of predicting neurological complications of pediatric cancers and their treatment. *Frontiers in Oncology*, 11: 5920. https://doi.org/10.3389/FONC.2021.781499/BIBTEX.

Tran, H., Nguyen, T.N., Christopher, P., Bui, D.K., Khoshelham, K. and Ngo, T.D. 2021. A digital twin approach for geometric quality assessment of as-built prefabricated façades. *Journal of Building Engineering*, 41: 102377. https://doi.org/10.1016/J.JOBE.2021.102377.

Tsiatsis, V., Karnouskos, S., Höller, J., Boyle, D. and Mulligan, C. 2019. Chapter 6 - Security. *In: Internet of Things (Second Edition)*. Academic Press, pp. 127–142. https://doi.org/10.1016/B978-0-12-814435-0.00018-3.

Venugopal, M., Eastman, C.M. and Teizer, J. 2015. An ontology-based analysis of the industry foundation class schema for building information model exchanges. *Advanced Engineering Informatics*, 29: 940–957. https://doi.org/10.1016/J.AEI.2015.09.006.

Wan, Y., Gao, Y. and Hu, Y. 2022. Blockchain application and collaborative innovation in the manufacturing industry: Based on the perspective of social trust. *Technological Forecasting and Social Change*, 177: 121540. https://doi.org/10.1016/J.TECHFORE.2022.121540.

Wu, L., Lu, W., Xue, F., Li, X., Zhao, R. and Tang, M. 2022. Linking permissioned blockchain to Internet of Things (IoT)-BIM platform for off-site production management in modular construction. *Computers in Industry*, 135: 103573. https://doi.org/10.1016/J.COMPIND.2021.103573.

Yang, R., Wakefield, R., Lyu, S., Jayasuriya, S., Han, F., Yi, X., Yang, X., Amarasinghe, G. and Chen, S. 2020. Public and private blockchain in construction business process and information integration. *Automation in Construction*, 118: 103276. https://doi.org/10.1016/J.AUTCON.2020.103276.

Yin, X., Liu, H., Chen, Y. and Al-Hussein, M. 2019. Building information modelling for off-site construction: Review and future directions. *Automation in Construction*, 101: 72–91. https://doi.org/10.1016/J.AUTCON.2019.01.010.

Yuan Shuang, Hu, Z.Z., Lin, J.R., Zhang Yun-Yi, Yuan, S., Hu, Z.Z., Lin, J.R. and Zhang, Y.Y. 2021. A framework for the automatic integration and diagnosis of building energy consumption data. *Sensors*, 21: 1395. https://doi.org/10.3390/S21041395.

Chapter 7

Digital ID Framework for Human-Centric Smart Management of the Indoor Environment

*Min Deng, Carol C Menassa** and *Vineet R Kamat*

7.1 Introduction

A good indoor environment is essential for the occupants in many aspects. It has a significant impact on their well-being and leads to the improvement of their productivity (Huizenga et al. 2006, Humanyze 2018, MIRVAC 2019). To have better management of the indoor environment, many studies have focused on developing smart building control platforms (Tang et al. 2019). The rapid growth of high-speed commercial internet (Rathore et al. 2016), advances in building management systems (BMSs) (Zhan et al. 2021), as well as personal electronic devices such as smartphones (Li et al. 2017) have supported the concept of a smart building (Dong et al. 2019, Deng et al. 2022). A smart building is equipped to automatically control the building systems to address energy waste and improve the indoor environment quality based on smart sensors (Deng et al. 2021b). The sensors are installed in different locations in the building to collect environmental data such as temperature and humidity (Nakama et al. 2015, Riaz et al. 2015, Lee et al. 2016, Pasini et al. 2016, Chang et al. 2018, Ioannou et al. 2018, Pasini 2018, Machado et al. 2019, Rafsanjani and

Department of Civil and Environmental Engineering, University of Michigan, MI 48109.
Emails: mindeng@umich.edu; vkamat@umich.edu
* Corresponding author: menassa@umich.edu

Ghahramani 2020). In addition, technologies such as Wi-Fi, WSN, 5G, and LP-WAN (Lu et al. 2019, Marzouk and Abdelaty 2014, Tang et al. 2019) have been applied to allow for seamless data communication.

Even with such efforts to improve the indoor environment, a survey involving more than 52,000 people in 351 office buildings showed that only half of the occupants are satisfied with their indoor environments (Frontczak et al. 2012). One major reason behind this is that the conventional methods for indoor environment control rely on adaptive comfort models and standards (ASHRAE 2017, Gan et al. 2019), which adopt one-size-fits-all approaches that assume all the occupants have similar preferences (Sood et al. 2020) resulting in an indoor environment that can only satisfy a small proportion of occupants (Frontczak et al. 2012). However, it is well established that different people have distinct preferences for indoor environments resulting from differences in age, gender, and physiological features to name a few (Földváry Ličina et al. 2018, Cheung et al. 2019).

To meet occupants' diverse preferences for the indoor environment, previous studies have focused on approaches regarding individual indoor experiences. To allow employees to choose their workplaces and their settings based on the nature of their work, the idea of activity-based workplaces (ABWs) (Stone and Luchetti 1985) was proposed. The utilization of ABWs aims to provide flexible workplaces for the occupants depending on their personal preferences (e.g., the location and microclimate of the workplace) (Appel-Meulenbroek et al. 2011). For example, some occupants might prefer cooler environments while others enjoy warmer places, the ABWs allow the occupants to stay at workplaces that fit their preferences. Similar principles could be applied to lighting, odor, ventilation, etc. Therefore, the ABWs have shown an advantage in improving people's indoor experience (Engelen et al. 2019). An experiment conducted by Arundell et al. (2018) showed that ABW could lead to a meaningful improvement in people's physical activity, job satisfaction, and relationship with co-workers. In addition, a robust system named OccuSpace was developed by Rahaman et al. (2019) for workplace management. The system allowed the occupants to use the statistical features of the Received Signal Strength Indicator (RSSI) of Bluetooth card beacons to predict the utilization of the shared workplace. However, the application of ABW needs precise control of the indoor environment, as a poor indoor space management strategy may lead to extra energy consumption (Masoso and Grobler 2010) and insufficient indoor comfort improvement for the occupants (Deng et al. 2021a). Therefore, to maximize the gains from ABW, a human-centric smart decision-making system is required. To achieve this, real-time estimation of the occupants' state (e.g., comfort level and work engagement) is the key to mapping personal behavior patterns and performance to improve the comfort level and well-being of each individual (Humanyze 2018).

Prediction models for human comfort as references for the decision-making of the indoor environment have been investigated in several studies. For example, Ho et al. (2015) developed a platform that could connect real-time indoor air quality to a personal health reporting system through a mobile app. The system was able to analyze the data and give alerts to the occupants once the concentration of air pollution exceeded a certain threshold. Moreover, after collecting subjects' thermal comfort feedback and physiological data under different environmental conditions, Li et al. (2017, 2018, 2019) developed different approaches including smartphone applications and thermal camera-based frameworks to estimate the occupants' thermal comfort. Based on the developed personal thermal comfort models, a dynamic determination of the optimum room condition mode was achieved.

Based on the existing technologies and the needs of an integrated system, this chapter proposes a novel DID framework as the fundamental idea for future human-centric smart buildings. More details of the framework are discussed in the following sections. In addition, several case studies are given to help demonstrate the framework.

7.2 Digital ID Framework for Human-Centric Monitoring and Control of Smart Buildings

A new concept of human Digital ID (DID) is the core of the real-time human-centric monitoring framework. By our definition, the concept of DID refers to a digital replica of human biographic data, environment preferences, and personal prediction models that can be used to help with the evaluation of their indoor experience. The systems and information flow of the framework are shown in Fig. 7.1. The DID supports interactions in different connected systems that are important for the decision-making

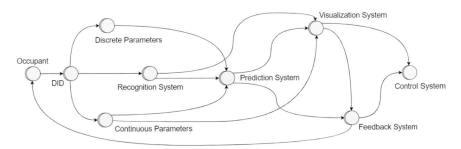

Figure 7.1: Components and information flow of the DID-based system.

and control of indoor spaces. These systems include (1) a recognition system; (2) a prediction system; (3) a visualization system; (4) a feedback system; and (5) a control system. The information stored in DID serves as the personal prediction model to estimate the personal comfort or indoor environment preference of the occupant. After the occupant is recognized by the recognition system, the profile for the specific individual is obtained. In the prediction system, the personal DID combines with real-time environmental data to estimate the human state (e.g., thermal comfort, visual comfort, mental state). In addition, to sufficiently represent the collected and predicted information, a virtualization platform is implemented as a tool for real-time monitoring and decision-making. The details of each system are discussed in the following sections.

7.2.1 Digital ID (DID)

7.2.1.1 DID Data Components

The information contained in DID for an individual is shown in Fig. 7.2. Human information can be categorized into two major categories: (1) dynamic parameters; and (2) static parameters. Dynamic parameters include the parameters that continuously change over time such as clothing type, location, activity intensity, and physiological data (e.g., galvanic skin response (GSR), skin temperature (ST), and heart rate (HR)), when available. In contrast, the static parameters do not change significantly within a short period, such as human physical parameters

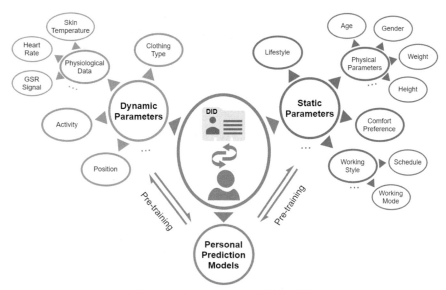

Figure 7.2: Components of Digital ID.

(e.g., age, gender, height, and weight), general environmental perceptions (e.g., preference for temperature, humidity, and lighting level), lifestyle (e.g., level of physical activity), and long-term working style (e.g., sedentary or long-standing). In practice, the dynamic parameters can be obtained through wearable or non-intrusive sensors (Li et al. 2017, Li et al. 2018). The static parameters are used to categorize the profiles of different people and do not need to be collected continuously. In addition, personal prediction models are also considered a part of DID. They refer to the mathematical models (e.g., standardized equations and learned models from machine learning) that are capable of predicting the occupants' state such as thermal comfort, visual comfort, and work engagement. The prediction models use static or dynamic parameters, sometimes combined with environmental parameters, to make the estimation. For example, human activity level and clothing type associated with room temperature and humidity are generally considered good features for predicting thermal comfort (Ma et al. 2019, Gan et al. 2021).

7.2.1.2 *A Framework to Establish and Update the DID Database*

A framework for the establishment and update of the prediction models is proposed as shown in Fig. 7.3. Based on the functionalities of the building, a target group of people is determined. For example, for an educational building with study rooms, the target group of people is students while for an office building the target group of people should be the employees. An initial database is established by collecting the data from the target group. For this chapter, the educational building is used in the case study, thus the data is mostly collected from students. The static parameters of the people including age, gender, weight, height, thermal preference, and lighting preference are collected. Based on the collected information, a further process of the data is conducted to establish the personal prediction models for occupants' states (e.g., thermal comfort, visual comfort, sound comfort, odor comfort, and work engagement).

However, the existence of personal models for all the occupants cannot be guaranteed, due to the lack of data or because someone is a new occupant. Therefore, for the new occupants without existing DID databases, public databases will be applied to give the initial guess of their state. Public databases usually contain a large number of datasets collected from different studies. Based on the databases, general prediction models can also be well-trained, thus they serve as potential sources to initialize the system for new occupants. A good example of a public general database being used in this chapter is the ASHRAE Global Thermal Comfort Database II (Földváry Ličina et al. 2018), which will be described in detail in the case study. While the initial guess of the human

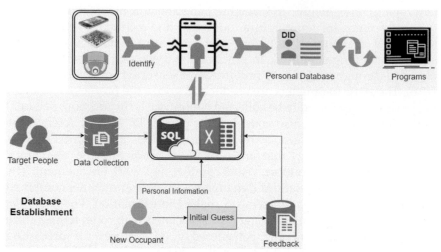

Figure 7.3: The schematic diagram for the establishment, access, and update of the database.

state is conducted, the occupants will give feedback to the system and allow the establishment of their personal database. An example approach to collecting feedback is through a mobile app developed in previous studies (Gupta et al. 2016, Li et al. 2017, Sood et al. 2020). The collection of feedback can not only apply to new occupants but also be feasible for existing occupants to update their existing databases.

7.2.1.3 DID Data Storage and Exchange

All data of the DID is stored in a local or cloud database. In this chapter, a text file on the local disk is used to store the personal information of any occupant, while there is no restriction on the data storage and other approaches such as SQL database are also feasible to keep the database in the cloud. The database is dynamic as the information of humans changes over time. When the database is needed by the system, it is accessed by scripts that are based on computer programs developed in languages such as python, java, C++, and MATLAB (depending on the program platforms). In this chapter, the back-end programs are mostly written in python. For example, when the system needs to estimate the thermal comfort of the occupants using the environmental parameters (e.g., temperature and humidity), the specific thermal comfort prediction model is accessed and applied to make the estimations. Note that there can be multiple models to estimate the same human state, and they take different input features. For instance, temperature and humidity are often used as the input features for thermal comfort (Li et al. 2017, André et al. 2020) while personal physiological data such as skin temperature and heart rate are also useful predictors of thermal comfort (Li et al. 2017). The required information from the database thus depends on real-world scenarios.

7.2.2 *Recognition System based on DID*

To track the human state, a recognition system based on DID is proposed as shown in Fig. 3. Once a person enters the building, the system will recognize the occupant to match him/her with the corresponding DID database (if it exists). One example of the identification method is the QR code. If the QR code is attached to a phone or an identity card, the occupants only need to swipe the card or an identifiable marker on the phone, which they would typically have to do at the entrance of office buildings. Alternatively, computer vision techniques can be another method to recognize occupants through indoor surveillance cameras (Adjabi et al. 2020). Once the DID of the occupant is recognized, the database becomes an open resource for the systems. However, for the new occupants, recognition is considered to fail, and a new database will be generated at the back end of the systems, and newly collected data from the specific occupants will be allocated to the database.

7.2.3 *Prediction System*

The proposed system can deal with the different scenarios: (1) existing occupants with their DID databases well established; and (2) new occupants without DID databases or without enough data to deliver accurate personal prediction models. For the first scenario, assume there is enough data collected from the occupants and have established the mathematical models. Therefore, the existing personal database is used for the estimation of the occupants' states.

However, for the second scenario, there is no personal database for the programs to access. Therefore, it is proposed to conduct the initial guess based on the public open-source database. The process of the model training is shown in Fig. 7.4. For an existing public database with occupants' information, corresponding environment parameters, and associated comfort feedback (e.g., ASHRAE Global Thermal Comfort Database II), a general prediction model can be established using machine learning. Take the thermal sensation as an example, the input includes personal information such as age, gender, weight, height, and clothing level. The environmental parameters include temperature and humidity, while the outputs are the thermal sensation indices (e.g., integer numbers ranging from 3 to 3). Here, it is considered the baseline prediction model. Another approach is to assign human profiles into different categories according to their static parameters such as age, gender, weight, and height,

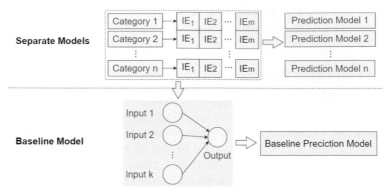

Figure 7.4: The proposed method for model training.

which tend to reduce the number of data points for training as people with similar profiles tend to have similar perceptions and preferences of the environment.

7.2.4 Human-centric Visualization System

Different from indoor environment monitoring, the visualization platform required for DID needs to be human-centric. It should be able to show the state of individuals, such as their location in the building, comfort levels, and preferences of the indoor environment. It can help the building manager to provide a better strategy for indoor environment control. To keep the privacy of the occupants, the visualization system contains no identifiable personal information (e.g., name, age, gender, height, weight) and only the building managers can access it. A comprehensive comparison of existing platforms that allow real-time visualization of the built environment is provided. BIM platforms such as Revit are commonly used in previous studies (Lee et al. 2016, Deng et al. 2021b). The developed interactive interfaces achieved through the Application Programming Interfaces (APIs) using C# programming can show the status quo of the indoor environment such as temperature and humidity (Teizer et al. 2017, Ferreira et al. 2018, Kang et al. 2018, Pasini 2018, Machado et al. 2019). However, due to the model updating mechanism, most of the BIM platforms are not suitable for real-time visualization of moving components such as human subjects, because it requires the model to update from time to time, which may crash the models. To be specific, any modifications of BIM models in Revit will cause a reload of the entire model. In contrast, game engines such as Unity can not only be efficiently connected to BIM models but also provide functionalities that allow human models to update their locations with high frequencies (e.g., > 100 Hz). In addition, data connection and visualization interfaces can also be achieved using C# scripts. The game engine is thus considered the most practical platform.

7.2.5 Feedback System

The feedback system includes recommendations for the occupants based on the DID. With a variety of smart sensors installed in different locations of the buildings, real-time environmental data such as temperature and humidity are readily available. In this chapter, the real-time environmental data is collected and stored in the text files, which are not only connected to the Unity visualization platform but are also being used to provide feedback based on the results from the prediction system. After processing the obtained information, recommendations are sent to the occupants or the building managers. The notifications regarding the recommendation are delivered through a mobile app to the occupant, thus they can know the most suitable places for them to visit.

    With the capability of estimating the comfort levels of the occupants in different aspects, a recommendation system regarding the best-fit room for the occupants is proposed. A composite index is designed to represent the overall comfort score of each room. The indoor environment comfort metric for an occupant includes different aspects such as thermal comfort (TC), lighting comfort (LC), sound comfort (SC), and odor comfort (OC). The score for each aspect can be predicted using a method that is similar to the estimation of thermal sensation (i.e., range from 3 to 3). To evaluate the environment of the room more straightforwardly, a linear method is proposed to evaluate the overall comfort index. A schematic diagram of the linear method is shown in Fig. 7.5. Based on the preference of the

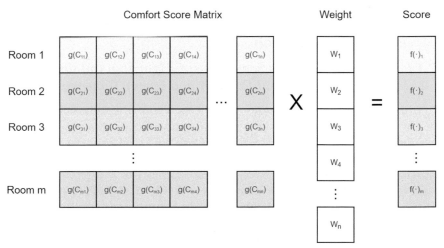

Figure 7.5: Computation of the scores for building rooms.

occupants, different weights are assigned to each type of indoor comfort. The weights could be obtained by questionnaires or learning approaches. However, a higher final score does not necessarily mean the IEQ for a specific room is good in every aspect. Based on the strategy, the best-match rooms will be assigned to the occupants based on DID.

In addition to the indoor experience of the occupants, energy consumption should also be considered. Therefore, the room comfort index could be integrated with energy-saving strategies. In this case, joint optimization of the occupants' comfort and energy consumption is required. Section 3 illustrates a case study of the optimization algorithm that considers both thermal comfort and energy consumption.

7.2.6 Control System

The feedback system provides a valid reference for the building control system. On one hand, the predicted human state of the occupants is used as a signal sent to the control terminal regarding the adjustment of the indoor systems. For example, given the occupants are feeling warm, the corresponding signal will be a trigger to lower the temperature setpoint. The final decision can be transferred to a smart thermostat (e.g., NEST) to control the indoor environment. Similarly, a signal that reflects that the occupants feel the room is too bright can drive the dimming of the lighting systems. On the other hand, the real-time monitoring of the occupants' state provides more insights into the interaction between the occupants and the building. A more flexible control strategy can then be applied by the building manager based on the results of the systems and the visualization platform.

7.3 Room Match to Optimize Thermal Comfort and Energy Consumption

7.3.1 Large Neighborhood Search-based Algorithm to Jointly Optimize the Thermal Comfort and Energy Consumption

In this section, an optimization problem where the thermal comfort of the occupants and the energy consumption are jointly considered is formulated. Binary variables x_{ij} is firstly added to indicate the occupant-room assignment: if occupant $i(1 \leq i \leq m)$ is in room $j(1 \leq j \leq n)$, $x_{ij} = 1$; otherwise, $x_{ij} = 0$. The index of thermal comfort is a discrete number following a standard 7-scale metric (i.e., –3, –2, –1, 0, 1, 2, 3) (ASHRAE 2017). For a specific occupant, it is a non-linear function of multiple indoor environmental parameters, including room temperature (RT), relative humidity (RH), and air velocity (AV). Suppose occupant $i(1 \leq i \leq m)$ is in room $j (1 \leq j \leq n)$, it is assumed that its thermal comfort, TC_i can be computed as follows:

$$TC_i = \sum_{j=1}^{n} g_i(T_j, H_j, V_j) x_{ij} \qquad (1)$$

$g_i(\cdot)$ is the thermal comfort function of occupant i that returns $\{-3, -2, -1, 0, 1, 2, 3\}$, while T_j, H_j, and V_j are the RT, RH, and AV of room j, respectively.

A separate $g_i(\cdot)$ is used to capture the personality of each occupant. Rather than an analytic function, $g_i(\cdot)$ is learned from data. From the perspective of the optimization process, a differentiable model $g_i(\cdot)$ is preferred, such as Support Vector Machines (SVM) and Artificial Neural Networks (ANN). Here, it is assumed that all of the input indoor environmental parameters (T_j, H_j, V_j) are continuous and controllable within a fixed range, and the thermal comfort for all occupants should be optimized. Therefore, the sum deviation is penalized, F_C, in Eq. (3) based on the individual deviation shown in Eq. (2). Note that c_i is a weight on occupant i.

$$f_i(T_j, H_j, V_j) = |g_i(T_j, H_j, V_j) - 0| \qquad (2)$$

$$F_C = \sum_{i=1}^{m} c_i \sum_{j=1}^{n} f_i(T_j, H_j, V_j) x_{ij} \qquad (3)$$

In addition, suppose the outdoor environment temperature is T_0, the cooling/heating load (Q_j) of the room j can be computed according to Eq. (4), where U is the overall heat transfer coefficient of the surface, and A refers to the area of the surface.

$$Q_j = UA_j \Delta T_j = UA_j |T_j - T_0| = k_j |T_j - T_0| \qquad (4)$$

Without considering the efficiency of the pre-designed heating, ventilation, and air conditioning systems (HVAC), the $|T_j - T_0|$ could be used as an indicator of the building energy consumption and should be minimized.

The objective function (5) jointly optimizes the thermal comfort of the occupants and energy consumption. The left part is copied from Eq. (3). The decision variables are x_{ij}, c_i, and T_j, H_j, $V_j (1 \leq i \leq m, 1 \leq j \leq n)$. α is used to adjust the weight between thermal comfort and energy consumption during the optimization. Constraint (6.1) limits the number of minimum and maximum occupant numbers in a room. The constraint (6.2) indicates that a person can only be in one room (6.3), (6.4), (6.5), and (6.6) set up the variable ranges. T_j^{min} and T_j^{max} defines the allowable range of the room temperature, H_j^{min} and H_j^{max} defines the allowable range of the relative humidity, V_j^{max} and V_j^{max} defines the allowable range of the air velocity.

$$\min_{x_{ij},T_j,H_j,V_j} \alpha \sum_{j=1}^{n}\sum_{i=1}^{m} c_i f_i(T_j,H_j,V_j)x_{ij} + (1-\alpha)\sum_{j=1}^{n} k_j \mid T_j - T_0 \mid \tag{5}$$

subject to

$$0 \le \sum_{i=1}^{m} x_{ij} \le 15 \tag{6.1}$$

$$\sum_{j=1}^{n} x_{ij} = 1 \tag{6.2}$$

$$x_{ij} \in \{0, 1\} \tag{6.3}$$

$$T_j^{min} \le T_j \le T_j^{max} \tag{6.4}$$

$$H_j^{min} \le H_j \le H_j^{max} \tag{6.5}$$

$$V_j^{min} \le V_j \le V_j^{max} \tag{6.6}$$

The schematic diagram of the optimization problem is shown in Fig. 7.6. The circles with different colors represent different individuals with distinct characteristics and the cuboids represent different rooms with specific environmental settings. The results should be able to maximize the overall thermal comfort of all occupants in the building. Therefore, the indoor environment parameters T_j, H_j, V_j and the room assignments x_{ij} are simultaneously perturbed and optimized.

The Large Neighborhood Search (LNS) algorithm has proven to be very efficient in solving scheduling problems (Pisinger and Ropke 2010), it explores complex neighborhoods using heuristics. Here, based on the idea of LNS, the optimization process is divided into two separate steps, and the pseudocode is shown in Algorithm 1.

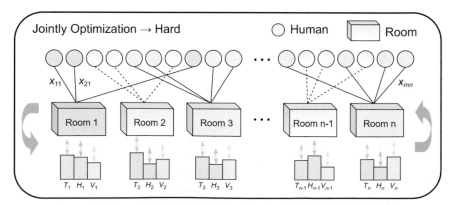

Figure 7.6: The schematic diagram for the original optimization problem.

Algorithm 1: Large Neighborhood Search for Thermal Comfort

Input: initial room parameters T_j^0, H_j^0, V_j^0 $\forall j = 1, ..., n$

           initial room assignment x_{ij}^0 $\forall i = 1, ..., m, \forall j = 1, ..., n$

Output: optimal room parameters T_j^*, H_j^*, V_j^* $\forall j = 1, ..., n$

           optimal room assignment x_{ij}^* $\forall i = 1, ..., m, \forall j = 1, ..., n$

$F^* = +\infty$

for $l = 1, \cdots, l_{\max}$ **do**

   // Step1: optimize x_{ij}, while T_j, H_j, V_j are fixed

   // Simplex-based algorithm

   Solve the linear program: $\min\limits_{x_{ij}^l} \sum_{j=1}^n \sum_{i=1}^m c_i f_i(T_j^{l-1}, H_j^{l-1}, V_j^{l-1}) x_{ij}^l$

   Update x_{ij}^l

   // Step2: optimize T_j, H_j, V_j, while x_{ij} are fixed. Rooms are decoupled

   for $j = 1, \cdots, n$ **do**

     // Trust-region algorithm

     Solve the nonlinear program:

$$\min_{T_j^l, H_j^l, V_j^l} \alpha \sum_{i=1}^m c_i f_i(T_j^l, H_j^l, V_j^l) x_{ij}^l + (1-\alpha) k_j \left| T_j^l - T_0 \right|$$

   Update T_j, H_j, V_j

   end for

$$F^l = \alpha \sum_{j=1}^n \sum_{i=1}^m c_i f_i(T_j^l, H_j^l, V_j^l) x_{ij}^l + (1-\alpha) \sum_{j=1}^n k_j \left| T_j^l - T_0 \right|$$

   if $F^l < F^*$ **then**

     $F^* = F^l, T_j^* = T_j^l, H_j^* = H_j^l, V_j^* = V_j^l, x_{ij}^* = x_{ij}^l$ $\forall i = 1, ..., m, \forall j = 1, ..., n$

   end if

   if the Termination condition is reached **then**

     return T_j^*, H_j^*, V_j^*, while x_{ij}^*

   end if

end for

7.3.2 *Personal Thermal Comfort Models and Loss Function*

To obtain as the prediction model for different occupants, ASHRAE Global Thermal Comfort Database II is used to establish representative personal models. The database contains approximately 76,000 datasets, which allows end-users to export the data with specific parameters through a web-based tool (Földváry Ličina et al. 2018). Figure 7.7 shows the schematic diagram of obtaining $g_i(\cdot)$. Regarding the index for thermal comfort, thermal sensation is used as it is a subjective thermal metric that

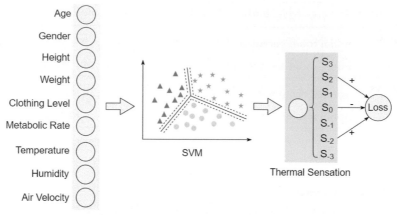

Figure 7.7: Computation of function loss.

has been most widely used (Wang et al. 2020). It evaluates the feeling of the occupants within a 7-scale metric, which uses discrete numbers from –3 to 3 to indicate that people feel cold, cool, slightly cool, neutral, slightly warm, warm, and hot, respectively. Besides thermal sensation, the database is selectively filtered based on the required input data. The filtered data includes the human profiles (i.e., gender, age, height, weight, clothing level, and metabolic rate) and the environmental parameters (i.e., RT, RH, and AV). The details of the data samples are summarized in Table 7.1. Based on the example dataset, the computation of the $f_i(T_j, H_j, V_j)$ of the optimization problem is shown in Fig 7.2. Two most typical differentiable algorithms: support vector machine (SVM), and artificial neural network (ANN) are applied to build the prediction models.

Note that this actual $f_i(\cdot)$ is slightly different from the one defined in Eq. (2). The one in Eq. (2) is conceptual and indicates that there is a penalty for the situation when the thermal comfort is not zero. However, since the $f_i(\cdot)$ in Eq. (2) is discrete, which introduces challenges to the optimization

Table 7.1: Details of the example database.

Count	5339
Age range	16 ~ 70
Gender	Male/Female
Height (cm)	122 ~ 206
Weight (kg)	35 ~ 116
Clothing Level (Clo)	0.04 ~ 1.49
Air Temperature (°C)	13.9 ~ 37.9
Relative Humidity (%)	10.4 ~ 95.3

process, it is replaced with the definition in Fig 7.2. As the goal is to achieve the distribution as close to 0 as possible, the sign of the weight corresponding to 0 is set to be negative while others are set to be positive. For example, the "+" and "−" in Fig. 7.2 indicate that a predicted result of "0" will reduce the function loss while others will increase the function loss. In addition, each predicted thermal sensation value is assigned a weight indicated by S_i with i represented the corresponding value. In this case, the final function loss will be the weighted sum of the probabilities of each possible predicted output (−3 to 3). Therefore, the function becomes continuous and also penalizes the non-zero thermal comfort index while rewarding the thermal comfort index of 0 the SVM is selected to be $g_i(\cdot)$ for the optimization process. The SVM algorithm applies the radial basis function (RBF) kernel, and the accuracy is around 0.706.

7.3.3 Illustrative Example

To evaluate the performance of the optimization results with a suitable trade-off for thermal comfort and energy consumption, a case study with a ratio of 0.9 is evaluated. In this section, it is assumed that there are 12 rooms with a maximum capacity of 15 for each. The total number of people is assumed to be 120. In the following sections, details regarding the changes in the indoor environments as well as the improvement of thermal comfort are discussed. In addition, a figure is given to illustrate the match of occupants and rooms.

7.3.3.1 Trade-off Between Thermal Comfort and Energy Consumption

The proposed algorithm not only concerns the thermal comfort of the occupants but also tries to achieve energy savings. Based on Eq. (5), there is a trade-off between the thermal comfort of the occupants and the energy consumption of the building, represented by α. When α is set to be 1, all effort is paid to optimize the thermal comfort of the occupants without considering the energy consumption. In contrast, if α is set to be 0, all effort is paid into the optimization of the energy consumption without considering the thermal comfort of the occupants. In practice, the weight assigned to thermal comfort and energy consumption might require wise decision-making. Therefore, the trade-off between the thermal comfort of the occupants and the energy consumption of the building is investigated. The algorithm is tested with different ratios of the weights so as to provide more insights regarding the trade-off.

The results are plotted as shown in Fig. 7.8. At the ratio of 0, the cost of the objective function is high for thermal comfort while very low for energy consumption, which indicates that the optimization is done for energy consumption without concerning the thermal comfort of the

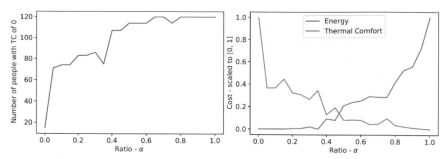

Figure 7.8: The trade-off between thermal comfort and energy consumption.

occupants. In the meanwhile, the number of occupants with a thermal comfort of 0 is relatively low. With the increase in the ratio, the cost of energy consumption goes up while the cost of thermal comfort drops quickly. As a result, when the ratio is 1, the relative values of the cost for thermal comfort and energy consumption are reversed, indicating that the algorithm only optimizes the thermal comfort of the occupants without considering the energy consumption. The plot shows that the number of occupants with a thermal comfort index of 0 increases along with the ratio before reaching 120 at the ratio of 1, indicating that a better thermal comfort result is normally associated with relatively higher energy consumption. As an example, a good trade-off can be obtained by setting the ratio to 0.9 as implied in the plot. As a result, all of the occupants can be thermally comfortable while a significant amount of energy can also be saved. Assume the proportion of the energy-saving (ES) based on Eq. (11), where the temperature difference is used to roughly estimate the energy consumption difference. The results show that around 54.4% of energy is saved with a ratio of 0.9.

$$ES = \frac{\sum_{j=1}^{n}\left|T_j^1 - T_0\right| - \sum_{j=1}^{n}\left|T_j^r - T_0\right|}{\sum_{j=1}^{n}\left|T_j^1 - T_0\right|} \tag{11}$$

where r refers to the ratio and T_0 is set to be 10°C as an example of the outdoor temperature.

7.3.3.2 Distribution of Thermal Comfort

The general comparison of the thermal comfort distribution of the occupants before and after the optimization is shown in Fig. 7.9. As indicated in the plot, the original thermal comfort indices are distributed over the range from –3 to 3. Among the 120 occupants, only 54 of the occupants consider the indoor environments as comfortable. A significant amount of people (41) feel slightly cool, 4 of them feel cool, and 2 feel cold. In contrast, 17 of them feel slightly warm, and 2 of them feel

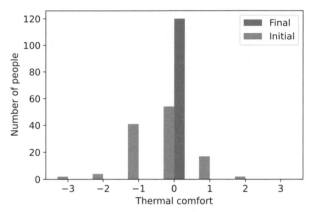

Figure 7.9: Comparison between the initial and optimized thermal comfort distribution.

warm. However, the thermal comfort is significantly improved after the optimization. Results show that all 120 occupants will consider the indoor environments as comfortable (with a thermal comfort index of 0). No one will consider the indoor environments as slightly cool, cool, cold, slightly warm, warm, or hot. Therefore, even with almost 54.4% of energy being saved, the algorithm still shapes the distribution of the thermal comfort indices of the occupants to optimal.

7.3.3.3 Matches Between Occupants and Rooms

The allocation of occupants in different rooms before and after the optimization is shown in Fig. 7.10. The boxes with double borders are used to represent the rooms and the circles refer to the occupants/people. Blue colors are used to represent cool environments and people with negative thermal comfort indices while orange/brown colors are used to represent the warm environments and people with positive thermal comfort indices. In addition, deeper colors represent cooler/warmer, and the white color indicates the neutral cases. Moreover, to track the allocation of the occupants, each individual is assigned a number tag from 1 to 120. Being identical to Fig 7.8, it can be seen from Fig. 7.10 that with an initial random allocation of occupants and indoor environments, most of the occupants are rendered blue or orange, indicating that most of them feel cool or warm. However, the results of the room match and room settings change significantly after the optimization. All of the occupants are in white after the optimization. As for rooms 1, 3, 4, 5, 7, 9, and 11, the number of occupants reaches the maximum capacity (15) of the room. In addition, the energy consumption saving penalty can be reflected in rooms 2, 10, and 12. These three rooms are set as empty with the same temperature as the outdoor environment, indicating that no heating is required in these empty rooms.

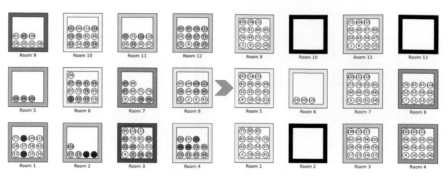

Figure 7.10: Match of occupants and rooms before (left) and after optimization (right).

Table 7.2 shows the indoor environmental conditions (i.e., RT, RH, and AV) before and after the optimization.

Table 7.2: Room environments before and after optimization.

Room	Before Optimization			After Optimization		
	RT (°C)	RH (%)	AV (m/s)	RT (°C)	RH (%)	AV (m/s)
1	31.0	39.7	0.5	24.1	40.6	1.1
2	13.7	50.8	1.3	10.0	61.4	0.3
3	37.0	24.0	2.1	28.7	25.9	1.2
4	20.0	36.6	2.2	10.6	31.8	0.0
5	30.2	90.8	1.0	22.1	74.7	0.0
6	21.6	48.7	2.1	20.2	51.7	2.0
7	32.7	13.9	2.9	20.0	21.6	1.7
8	19.7	13.0	0.3	10.0	32.1	0.0
9	35.5	56.7	2.1	26.1	58.6	2.4
10	22.3	50.8	0.3	10.0	61.4	0.3
11	28.1	72.9	1.9	26.7	66.6	1.1
12	15.0	36.2	1.8	10.0	61.4	0.3

7.4 Establishment of Personal Prediction Models for Work Engagement

In the current challenging business environment, the employee is a key asset to the organization (Saxena and Srivastava 2015), and it is worth spending extra costs to improve the productivity of the employees (Djukanovic et al. 2002, Seppanen and Fisk 2004). Work engagement commonly defined as the "positive, fulfilling, work-related state characterized by vigor, dedication, and absorption" (Schaufeli et al. 2002) in the task being performed, is one of the most important factors that directly relate to employee performance (Brad Shuck et al. 2011) and has a significant positive effect on employee productivity (Echols 2005, Abraham 2012, Anitha 2014, Hanaysha 2016). Work engagement is commonly estimated using indirect methods such as questionnaires and experiments (Kuh 2001, Schaufeli et al. 2002, Ahlfeldt et al. 2005, Schaufeli et al. 2006, Astolfi et al. 2008, Vecchiato et al. 2012). However, these approaches rely on extra feedback (i.e., questionnaires and experimental results) from human subjects to make the estimations, which are not the ground truth indicators measured by the brain. Moreover, they are not practical enough as they are not able to provide real-time measurements.

As indicated in related studies, positive feelings, engagement, and motivation are typically associated with a higher alpha power in the right frontal cortex when compared to alpha power measured in the left frontal cortex (Schaffer et al. 1983, Davidson 2004, Papousek et al. 2014, Harmon-Jones and Gable 2018, Chen et al. 2019). The frontal asymmetry index (FAI), often measured as alpha power in the right relative to the alpha power in the left cortex, is used in this chapter as an indicator of work engagement (Coan and Allen 2004, Jaworska et al. 2012, Sun et al. 2017, Fischer et al. 2018, Schmid et al. 2018, Chen et al. 2019, iMotions 2019, Morys et al. 2020). An electroencephalogram (EEG) is used to measure the brain activities of the subjects, thereby calculating the engagement in a direct way by processing the related brain waves. Although the brain waves of people can be directly measured and processed to obtain the FAI as an indicator of work engagement, EEG headsets may not be practical enough in a real office environment. For example, wearing a headset may cause discomfort (e.g., headache) to the subjects while they are performing tasks. In addition, data collection from the EEG headsets requires the subjects to stay still to avoid intensive artifacts. Previous studies have measured human brain waves under different lighting conditions. Several of them have shown that lighting levels could somehow affect brain activity (Smolders et al. 2012, Chang et al. 2013, Min et al. 2013, Smolders et al. 2016, Kakitsuba 2020), including the frontal region (Medithe and Nelakuditi 2016). Therefore, this study explores the feasibility of using other easily measurable physiological parameters (i.e., GSR, HR, and ST) associated with lighting levels to predict the engagement level. The details of this effort are described in the following sections.

7.4.1 Research Methodology

In this chapter, a comprehensive framework for predicting work engagement using other physiological data was established, as shown in Fig. 7.11. The lighting level was used as the only environmental variable. Brain waves of the subjects were measured using an EEG to calculate the

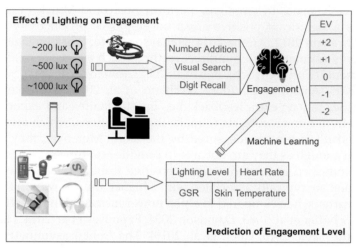

Figure 7.11: Framework for measurement and prediction of work engagement under different lighting levels.

ground truth work engagement under three tasks: (1) number addition, (2) visual search, and (3) digit recall. FAI was then calculated as the indication of engagement based on the raw EEG data. The FAIs were divided into several levels with each level associated with an EV. At the same time, other physiological data of the subjects, including GSR signal, HR, and ST, were collected. After synchronizing the data collected from different sensors, machine learning (ML) techniques were used to explore if easily measurable physiological data and lighting levels could serve as predictors of occupants' EVs. More details of the methodology are described in the following sections.

7.4.1.1 Experimental Design

Each subject participated in a three-day data collection experiment where EEG signal, GSR signal, HR, and ST data were collected while he/she was performing three different cognitive tasks under different lighting levels. Figure 7.12 shows the setup of the experiment. The experiment was designed to reflect real-world scenarios. As in a real office environment, people normally use a computer with a constant backlight to conduct their daily work. At the same time, the lighting conditions of the environment are changeable through a light switch with a dimmer or other building automation system devices. In this experiment, the lighting levels were controlled by the central lighting system with two auxiliary portable lamps as shown in Fig. 7.12, which allowed a flexible control of the lighting level. The consistency of lighting levels surrounding the subjects was ensured by a lighting sensor in the room. Illuminances of 200 lux, 500 lux, and 1000 lux, with a light color of 5000 K, were selected in our study, representing

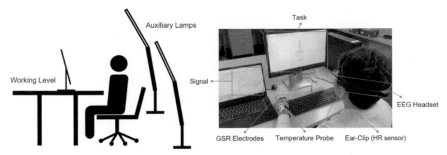

Figure 7.12: Experimental setup.

the suggested levels for performing basic work, normal office work, and normal drawing work, respectively. The selection of lighting levels in each session was randomized.

7.4.1.2 Experimental Procedures and Time Setting

12 subjects who were identified as both physically and mentally healthy participated in the experiment. All of them were graduate students at the University of Michigan between the age of 20 and 30. Details of the experimental procedures for each session are shown in Fig. 7.13. Before starting the experiment, each subject was given 30 min to settle down and relax, at the same time, a short introduction (less than 5 min) of the task rules was provided. To avoid the unexpected effect of fatigue, primary studies were conducted to investigate the reasonable time duration for cognitive tasks. It was found that the engagement level of the subjects was highly likely to decrease after performing the tasks for a long period, and thus 10 min was chosen to be the experiment time for each task. In addition, 10 min of rest time was given to the subjects, which allowed them to recover from the last task and start the new task with a fresh mind.

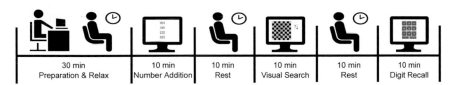

Figure 7.13: Experimental procedures for each session.

7.4.2 EEG Data Processing for Engagement

7.4.2.1 Calculation of Engagement Level (FAI)

Previous studies have investigated and summarized the response of FAI (i.e., alpha power in the right relative to the left cortex) to different external situations. Harmon-Jones and Gable (2018) conducted a

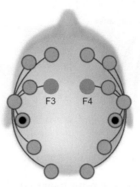

Figure 7.14: Locations of F3 and F4 electrodes.

comprehensive review of research that measured the frontal asymmetry in response to manipulated situations related to motivation and emotion. They concluded that higher FAI was associated with higher approach motivation. Therefore, FAI is reasonably used as an indicator of the ground truth engagement of the human subjects in this chapter. The mathematical representation of FAI is shown in Eq. (12) (Coan and Allen 2004, Jaworska et al. 2012). F3 and F4 indicate the signal from two specific electrodes in the headset and their positions are shown in Fig. 7.14.

$$FAI = ln\left(\frac{Alpha\ power\ of\ F4}{Alpha\ power\ of\ F3}\right) \tag{12}$$

7.4.2.2 Self-defined Engagement Vote (EV)

The raw values of FAI calculated using Eq. (12) are continuous numbers, which may not be straightforward for people to understand and cannot represent the relative engagement levels. A more systematic way to represent the engagement of the occupants can be very helpful. Appropriate representative discrete values can be used to indicate different engagement levels of people. Therefore, a new indication system for work engagement is proposed. The general idea of the approach was to divide the FAI values into different levels, and each level should be represented by a discrete number (e.g., –1, 0, and 1) named "engagement vote" (EV). As the required resolution (number of engagement levels) of the indication system may vary with its application, different scales of the system can be developed. For example, when people only want to know the rough engagement level, a lower resolution should be applied, and vice versa. A 5-scale system is proposed as an example. the FAI values were divided into five levels as shown in Fig. 7.15, the votes for the five levels were –2, –1, 0, 1, and 2, representing engagement levels of very low, low, neutral, high, and very high, respectively.

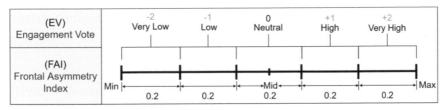

Figure 7.15: Indication system of work engagement for 5-scale.

7.4.3 Prediction of EV using Machine Learning Techniques

Figure 7.16 shows the framework to conduct the ML analysis. Regarding the accuracy of the different traditional ML algorithms, RF was proven to have the highest accuracy in similar studies (Kim et al. 2018). Therefore, RF was chosen to be the baseline ML algorithm for classification in this chapter. In addition, a basic ANN was chosen to be another ML algorithm for data training. The purpose of using an ANN was to compare its performance with traditional ML (i.e., RF) and see whether it could potentially improve the accuracy, as ANN was also proven successful in signal-processing problems (Abraham 2005). In this chapter, the designed ANN contains three hidden layers, the first layer contains 4 neurons, while the second and third layers contain 8 neurons. SoftMax Activation and Categorical Cross-Entropy Loss as shown in Eq. (13) were set for ANN.

$$L = \frac{1}{N}\sum_i -logP(Y = k \mid X = x_i) = \frac{1}{N}\sum_i -log\left(\frac{e^{s_i}}{\Sigma_j e^{s_j}}\right) \qquad (13)$$

After collecting the denoised data, the dataset was built for each potential occupant as shown in Fig. 7.16. With a total of 12 files from different lighting levels and tasks, the total duration of the dataset was around 120 min for each occupant. Based on the time window of 8 seconds, EV and its corresponding physiological data were paired. For the training

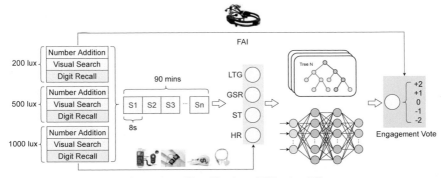

Figure 7.16: Classification of EV using ML.

process, 70% of randomly selected data was used as the training dataset and the rest 30% of the data was used as the test dataset.

7.4.4 The Performance of EV Classification

The overall accuracies of the classification and the confusion matrix for each class were obtained and compared. The overall accuracy was indicated by the fraction of the predictions our model got right. The accuracies of RF and ANN for each subject are listed and compared to give a more comprehensive understanding of the possible results as different algorithms might be suitable for specific characteristics of the datasets. In general, it was found that although ANN was able to give slightly higher accuracies for a few subjects, RF outperforms ANN in most of the cases. Table 7.3 shows the overall accuracies of the classification. The classification accuracy was 62.2% on average. The final accuracies for more than half of the subjects were higher than 60%, and 2 of them were higher than 70%. The highest classification accuracy was found in Subject 6, which reached 74.1%, while the lowest accuracy among all the subjects was found in Subject 12, which was only 48.3%. The final classification accuracies vary across subjects, possible reasons could be individual differences or errors during the data collection and analysis. The findings emphasized the importance of personal characteristics in establishing prediction models. These models could be integrated into the DID framework to help with the prediction of work engagement of the occupants to help with the improvement of their productivity.

Table 7.3: Overall classification accuracies.

Subject	RF (%)	ANN (%)	Final (%)
1	56.3	63.4	63.4
2	57.8	51.0	57.8
3	70.6	54.0	70.6
4	69.8	50.8	69.8
5	57.9	47.2	57.9
6	74.1	61.9	74.1
7	57.1	52.2	57.1
8	51.3	48.1	51.3
9	67.0	51.1	67.0
10	64.1	57.5	64.1
11	55.9	65.1	65.1
12	46.1	48.3	48.3
Avg.	60.7	54.2	**62.2**

7.5 Real-Time Feedback of Indoor Environment Based on Physiological Sensing

7.5.1 Description of the Scene

Three rooms (Fig. 7.17) in the GG Brown Building at the University of Michigan are used as scenes to demonstrate the DID system, all the rooms are student labs. Figure 7.18 shows the floor layout of the basement of GGB, and the locations of these rooms are highlighted. The areas of rooms 1006, 1140, and 1105 are around 40, 30, and 75 square meters, respectively. These rooms do not have any windows, thus there is no natural ventilation, and the indoor environments are fully controlled by the central heating, ventilation, and air conditioning (HVAC) system through thermostats, which allows the occupants to directly control the indoor temperature. Corresponding environment sensors (i.e., COZIR) are selected and installed in the three rooms to obtain real-time temperature and humidity data.

Figure 7.17: Example rooms (1006, 1140, and 1105).

Figure 7.18: The layout of the GGB basement.

7.5.2 Feedback Strategy Based on Physiological Responses

In the real world, there may not necessarily be a room that provides the perfect indoor environment for them. Therefore, adjustment of the indoor environment may be required. For occupants with an existing DID database, the system can not only establish the personal thermal sensation prediction models based on static parameters but also use dynamic parameters to obtain the personal prediction models for thermal sensation and work engagement. Assuming the physiology is accessible, it can be used to estimate the real-time state of the occupants. Therefore, real-time recommendations regarding the set points for thermal environments and lighting levels can be given to maximize the occupants' thermal sensation and work engagement, respectively. In the DID database, the GSR, ST, and HR are used as the dynamic parameters to estimate the thermal sensation and work engagement of the subjects The overall idea of using physiological responses is to leverage the real-time physiological responses to provide a dynamic estimation of the human state, which will be used to help with indoor environment control.

Figure 7.19 shows the schematic diagram regarding the estimation of thermal sensation and work engagement based on physiological responses (and lighting level for work engagement). Different algorithms such as RF and neural network (NN) could potentially be used to establish the prediction models. For the thermal sensation models, they take these physiological data (e.g., GSR, HR, and ST) as the input features, while the thermal sensation values are the output. Therefore, given the GSR, HR, and ST data, the models can output estimations of people's thermal sensations. Based on the previous study (Deng et al. 2021c), lighting level is selected to be the environmental parameter associated with GSR, HR, and ST values to establish the prediction models for work engagement.

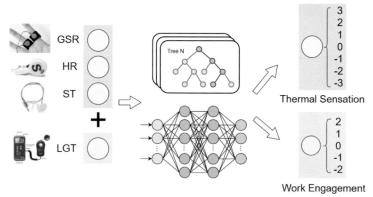

Figure 7.19: Estimation of thermal sensation and work engagement using physiological responses.

As for the outputs, the discrete indices range from –2 to 2. The value –2 is for very low engagement, –1 for low engagement, 0 for a neutral level of engagement, 1 for high engagement, and 2 for very high work engagement, respectively. The designed NN contains three hidden layers, the first layer contains 4 neurons, the second and third layers contain 8 neurons, and it implements SoftMax Activation and Categorical Cross-Entropy Loss. The RF and NN algorithms are used for the example datasets, and the results show that RF outperforms NN for our datasets. However, the accuracies of the prediction models may vary when different datasets are applied, thus the NN is kept here as another potential algorithm as it might be a better option for other datasets. For people in group #1, these prediction models are pre-trained and can be directly used to estimate the thermal sensation and work engagement. Table 7.4 shows the detailed information on these two types of models (accuracies are the average of people in group #1). Please note that there could be many different input features to build the prediction models for either thermal sensation or work engagement, two existing models are used as illustrative examples.

Therefore, corresponding room environment recommendations are made based on the results from the physiological responses. If the model predicts the thermal sensation of –3, –2, and –1 for the occupant, it is recommended to increase the indoor temperature of the room where he/ she stays, while for the value of 1, 2, and 3, it is recommended to decrease the indoor temperature. Similarly, the model for work engagement can also be used to help with the setting of the indoor lighting level. For the existing database, several common lighting levels (i.e., 200 lux, 500 lux, and 1000 lux) are used to see which one gives the highest work engagement. Therefore, a suitable lighting level can be recommended to the occupant. For example, if the lighting level of 500 lux gives the predicted work engagement higher than 1000 lux or 200 lux, then the lighting level is chosen to be 500 lux. However, these models are used for demonstration, in the real-world system, there can be a higher resolution of lighting levels in the models.

Table 7.4: Details of the personal prediction model for thermal sensation and work engagement.

Input Data	Thermal Sensation	Work Engagement
GSR	√	√
HR	√	√
ST	√	√
Lighting Level	×	√
Data Points	370	680
Accuracy (RF)	89.2%	79.3%

7.5.3 Example Feedback

The different models mentioned in the previous section indicate that the framework is compatible with any form of prediction model or any related human database. For example, based on either the physiological responses or the public open source database, corresponding feedback for the room can be given. To demonstrate the feedback from the occupant explicitly, an example of the feedback (shown in Table 7.5 and Table 7.6) is based on the given physiological responses. The strategy here is to only give feedback to the rooms that are recommended for the occupants. Take the thermal sensation as an example, assume the occupants follow the room recommendations, the thermal sensation of occupants 1, 2, 3, 4, 5, 6, 9, 10, and 11 will be 0. Therefore, there is no feedback from them. However, for occupants 7, 8, and 12, no perfect rooms are found for them. By following the recommendations, occupants 7 and 12 are suggested to stay in room 1 or 2, and occupant 8 is recommended to stay in room 1. In this case, corresponding feedback will be given to their assigned rooms. As shown in Table 7.5, considering the feedback from all the occupants, the final feedback is that both room 1 and room 2 are suggested to have a higher temperature.

Table 7.5: Example of the feedback regarding the thermal environment of different rooms.

Occupant	1	2	3	4	5	6	7	8	9	10	11	12
Room 1							↑	↑				↑
Room 2							↑					↑
Room 3												

Note: ↑ indicates feedback for increasing the temperature, ↓ indicates feedback for decreasing the temperature.

Table 7.6: Example of the feedback regarding the lighting levels of different rooms.

Occupant	1	2	3	4	5	6	7	8	9	10	11	12
					Lighting Level							
Room 1		200				500	200	500	500	1000		1000
Room 2	500		500	200	1000		200		500		200	1000
Room 3				200								

7.5.4 Real-time Visualization in Unity

Unity is used to develop a real-time visualization platform because it is compatible with BIM models and allows a real-time update of the human models. A BIM model is generated and imported into Unity

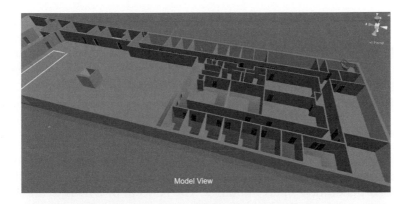

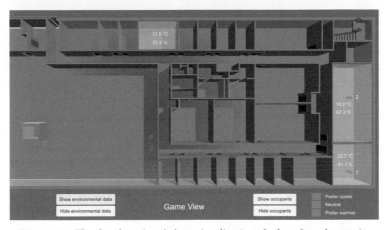

Figure 7.20: The developed real-time visualization platform based on unity.

for the virtual environment. As shown in Fig. 7.20, the building model is a basement described. COZIR sensors are connected to the computer and the environmental data are read and saved in local .csv files. A C# script is generated in Unity to read the imported data in .csv files. It can be seen that the indoor environmental parameters (i.e., temperature and humidity) can be visualized explicitly, and there are two buttons to display or hide the texts of sensing data. In addition, two human models are created to demonstrate how different occupants can be represented, and distinct rendering colors are assigned to them based on the estimated thermal preferences. In this example, blue indicates that the occupant is feeling cool or cold (with the thermal sensation of –3, –2, and –1), and prefer a warmer environment, while red means the occupant feels warm or hot (with the thermal sensation of 1, 2, and 3) and prefers a cooler environment, green implies a neutral feeling of the occupant. Once the corresponding occupants change their locations (e.g., shift to another room), the new thermal comfort preferences will be given based on the new environmental parameters. Similarly, two buttons for displaying and hiding the occupant models are given, and in this way, the user can have better control of the visualization interface. In general, the platform can provide real-time information about the indoor environment and occupants' comfort levels.

7.6 Conclusion

This chapter proposes a novel concept of DID for human-centric monitoring and control of the indoor environment, which provides valuable insights into next-generation smart buildings. The concept of DID is defined and explicitly explained. Based on the DID, the interaction between different systems in the framework is presented, and possible approaches and algorithms for specific systems are discussed. To better demonstrate the proposed framework. Case studies regarding the room assignment approaches and establishment of the personal prediction models are given. Furthermore, example feedback for the building systems is also demonstrated based on previous results. In general, DID-based indoor environment monitoring and control allows efficient human-centric management of the indoor environment. It is scalable and considered a valuable framework for future smart buildings. To make the framework comprehensive, more advanced technologies could be incorporated. For example, to simplify the case study, the temperature difference is used to represent the energy savings in percentage. The energy consumption in real buildings, however, is more complicated and extra parameters such as the design criteria of the HVAC systems could be considered in the future. In addition, rather than thermal comfort and work engagement, the prediction models for other human states could be established and integrated into the framework in future research.

7.7 Acknowledgment

The authors would like to acknowledge the financial support for this research received from the U.S. National Science Foundation (NSF) CBET 1804321. Any opinions and findings in this book chapter are those of the authors and do not necessarily represent those of the NSF.

References

Abraham, A. 2005. Artificial Neural Networks. *Handbook of Measuring System Design.*

Abraham, S. 2012. Job satisfaction as an antecedent to employee engagement. *SIES Journal of Management,* 8(2).

Adjabi, I., Ouahabi, A., Benzaoui, A. and Taleb-Ahmed, A. 2020. Past, present, and future of face recognition: A review. *Electronics,* 9(8).

Ahlfeldt, S., Mehta, S. and Sellnow, T. 2005. Measurement and analysis of student engagement in university classes where varying levels of PBL methods of instruction are in use. *Higher Education Research & Development*, 24(1): 5–20.

André, M., De Vecchi, R. and Lamberts, R. 2020. User-centered environmental control: A review of current findings on personal conditioning systems and personal comfort models. *Energy and Buildings*, 222: 110011.

Anitha, J. 2014. Determinants of employee engagement and their impact on employee performance. *International Journal of Productivity and Performance Management*, 63(3): 308–323.

Appel-Meulenbroek, R., Groenen, P. and Janssen, I. 2011. An end-user's perspective on activity-based office concepts. *Journal of Corporate Real Estate*, 13(2): 122–135.

Arundell, L., Sudholz, B., Teychenne, M., Salmon, J., Hayward, B., Healy, G.N. and Timperio, A. 2018. The impact of Activity Based Working (ABW) on workplace activity, eating behaviours, productivity, and satisfaction. *International Journal of Environmental Research and Public Health*, 15(5).

ASHRAE. 2017. Standard 55-2017, Thermal Environmental Conditions for Human Occupancy, Atlanta USA.

Astolfi, L., Fallani, F.D.V., Cincotti, F., Mattia, D., Bianchi, L., Marciani, M.G., Salinari, S., Colosimo, A., Tocci, A., Soranzo, R. and Babiloni, F. 2008. Neural basis for brain responses to TV commercials: A high-resolution EEG study. *IEEE Transactions on Neural Systems and Rehabilitation Engineering*, 16(6): 522–531.

Chang, A.M., Scheer, F.A.J.L., Czeisler, C.A. and Aeschbach, D. 2013. Direct effects of light on alertness, vigilance, and the waking electroencephalogram in humans depend on prior light history. *Sleep*, 36(8): 1239–1246.

Chang, K.M., Dzeng, R.J. and Wu, Y.J.J.A.s. 2018. An automated IoT visualization BIM platform for decision support in facilities management. *Applied Sciences*, 8(7): 1086.

Chen, T.T., Wang, K.P., Cheng, M.Y., Chang, Y.T., Huang, C.J. and Hung, T.M. 2019. Impact of emotional and motivational regulation on putting performance: A frontal alpha asymmetry study. *PeerJ*, 7: e6777.

Cheung, T., Schiavon, S., Parkinson, T., Li, P. and Brager, G. 2019. Analysis of the accuracy on PMV – PPD model using the ASHRAE Global Thermal Comfort Database II. *Building and Environment*, 153: 205–217.

Coan, J.A. and Allen, J.J.B. 2004. Frontal EEG asymmetry as a moderator and mediator of emotion. *Biological Psychology*, 67(1): 7–50.

Davidson, R.J. 2004. What does the prefrontal cortex "do" in affect: Perspectives on frontal EEG asymmetry research. *Biological Psychology*, 67(1): 219–234.

Deng, M., Fu, B. and Menassa, C. 2021a. Room match: Achieving thermal comfort through smart space allocation and environmental control in buildings. *Proceedings of the 2021 Winter Simulation Conference*, pp. 1–11.

Deng, M., Menassa, C.C. and Kamat, V.R. 2021b. From BIM to digital twins: A systematic review of the evolution of intelligent building representations in the AEC-FM industry. *Journal of Information Technology in Construction (ITcon)*, 26(5): 58–83.

Deng, M., Wang, X. and Menassa, C.C. 2021c. Measurement and prediction of work engagement under different indoor lighting conditions using physiological sensing. *Building and Environment*, 203: 108098.

Deng, M., Wang, X., Li, D. and Menassa, C.C. 2022. Digital ID framework for human-centric monitoring and control of smart buildings. *Building Simulation*.

Djukanovic, R., Wargocki, P. and Fanger, P.O. 2002. Cost-benefit analysis of improved air quality in an office building. *Proceedings of Indoor Air, 2002*.

Dong, B., Prakash, V., Feng, F. and O'Neill, Z. 2019. A review of smart building sensing system for better indoor environment control. *Energy and Buildings*, 199: 29–46.

Echols, M.E. 2005. Engaging employees to impact performance. *Chief Learning Officer*, 4(2): 44–48.

Engelen, L., Chau, J., Young, S., Mackey, M., Jeyapalan, D. and Bauman, A. 2019. Is activity-based working impacting health, work performance and perceptions? A systematic review. *Building Research & Information*, 47(4): 468–479.

Ferreira, J., Resende, R. and Martinho, S. 2018. Beacons and BIM models for indoor guidance and location. *Sensors*, 18(12): 4374.

Fischer, N.L., Peres, R. and Fiorani, M. 2018. Frontal alpha asymmetry and theta oscillations associated with information sharing intention. *Biological Psychology*, 12(166).

Földváry Ličina, V., Cheung, T., Zhang, H., de Dear, R., Parkinson, T., Arens, E., Chun, C., Schiavon, S., Luo, M., Brager, G., Li, P., Kaam, S., Adebamowo, M.A., Andamon, M.M., Babich, F., Bouden, C., Bukovianska, H., Candido, C., Cao, B., Carlucci, S., Cheong, D.K.W., Choi, J.H., Cook, M., Cropper, P., Deuble, M., Heidari, S., Indraganti, M., Jin, Q., Kim, H., Kim, J., Konis, K., Singh, M.K., Kwok, A., Lamberts, R., Loveday, D., Langevin, J., Manu, S., Moosmann, C., Nicol, F., Ooka, R., Oseland, N.A., Pagliano, L., Petráš, D., Rawal, R., Romero, R., Rijal, H.B., Sekhar, C., Schweiker, M., Tartarini, F., Tanabe, S.I., Tham, K.W., Teli, D., Toftum, J., Toledo, L., Tsuzuki, K., De Vecchi, R., Wagner, A., Wang, Z., Wallbaum, H., Webb, L., Yang, L., Zhu, Y., Zhai, Y., Zhang, Y. and Zhou, X. 2018. Development of the ASHRAE Global Thermal Comfort Database II. *Building and Environment*, 142: 502–512.

Frontczak, M., Schiavon, S., Goins, J., Arens, E., Zhang, H. and Wargocki, P. 2012. Quantitative relationships between occupant satisfaction and satisfaction aspects of indoor environmental quality and building design. Indoor Air, 22(2): 119–131.

Gan, V.J.L., Deng, M., Tan, Y., Chen, W. and Cheng, J.C.P. 2019. BIM-based framework to analyze the effect of natural ventilation on thermal comfort and energy performance in buildings. *Energy Procedia*, 158: 3319–3324.

Gan, V.J.L., Luo, H., Tan, Y., Deng, M. and Kwok, H.L. 2021. BIM and data-driven predictive analysis of optimum thermal comfort for indoor environment. *Sensors*, 21(13).

Gupta, S.K., Atkinson, S., O'Boyle, I., Drogo, J., Kar, K., Mishra, S. and Wen, J.T. 2016. BEES: Real-time occupant feedback and environmental learning framework for collaborative thermal management in multi-zone, multi-occupant buildings. *Energy and Buildings*, 125: 142–152.

Hanaysha, J. 2016. Improving employee productivity through work engagement: Evidence from higher education sector. *Management Science Letters*, 6(1): 61–70.

Harmon-Jones, E. and Gable, P.A. 2018. On the role of asymmetric frontal cortical activity in approach and withdrawal motivation: An updated review of the evidence. *Psychophysiology*, 55(1): e12879.

Ho, K., Hirai, K.W., Kuo, Y., Meng, H.M. and Tsoi, K.K.F. 2015. Indoor air monitoring platform and personal health reporting system: Big data analytics for public health research. *2015 IEEE International Congress on Big Data*.

Huizenga, C., Abbaszadeh, S., Zagreus, L. and Arens, E.A. 2006. Air quality and thermal comfort in office buildings: Results of a large indoor environmental quality survey. *Proceeding of Healthy Buildings*, 3: 393–397.

Humanyze. 2018. Data to Design - Bringing the Right Intelligence to Redesigning the Workplace. from https://cdn.worktechacademy.com/uploads/2018/12/WORKTECH-Academy-Humanyze-Data-to-Design-Report.pdf?_ga=2.40387493.628437762.1577049988-1390632762.1577049988.

iMotions. 2019. Electroencephalography-The Complete Pocket Guide. from https://imotions.com/guides/electroencephalography-eeg/.

Ioannou, A., Itard, L. and Agarwal, T. 2018. *In-situ* real time measurements of thermal comfort and comparison with the adaptive comfort theory in Dutch residential dwellings. *Energy and Buildings*, 170: 229–241.

Jaworska, N., Blier, P., Fusee, W. and Knott, V. 2012. Alpha power, alpha asymmetry and anterior cingulate cortex activity in depressed males and females. *Journal of Psychiatric Research*, 46(11): 1483–1491.

Kakitsuba, N. 2020. Comfortable indoor lighting conditions for LED lights evaluated from psychological and physiological responses. *Applied Ergonomics*, 82: 102941.

Kang, K., Lin, J. and Zhang, J. 2018. BIM- and IoT-based monitoring framework for building performance management. *Journal of Structural Integrity and Maintenance*, 3(4): 254–261.

Kim, J., Schiavon, S. and Brager, G. 2018. Personal comfort models – A new paradigm in thermal comfort for occupant-centric environmental control. *Building and Environment*, 132: 114–124.

Kuh, G.D. 2001. Assessing what really matters to student learning inside the national survey of student engagement. *The Magazine of Higher Learning*, 33: 10–17.

Lee, D., Cha, G. and Park, S. 2016. A study on data visualization of embedded sensors for building energy monitoring using BIM. *International Journal of Precision Engineering and Manufacturing*, 17(6): 807–814.

Li, D., Menassa, C.C. and Kamat, V.R. 2017. Personalized human comfort in indoor building environments under diverse conditioning modes. *Building and Environment*, 126: 304–317.

Li, D., Menassa, C.C. and Kamat, V.R. 2018. Non-intrusive interpretation of human thermal comfort through analysis of facial infrared thermography. *Energy and Buildings*, 176: 246–261.

Li, D., Menassa, C.C. and Kamat, V.R. 2019. Robust non-intrusive interpretation of occupant thermal comfort in built environments with low-cost networked thermal cameras. *Applied Energy*, 251: 113336.

Lu, Q., Parlikad, A.K., Woodall, P., Ranasinghe, G.D. and Heaton, J. 2019. Developing a dynamic digital twin at a building level: Using cambridge campus as case study. *International Conference on Smart Infrastructure and Construction 2019 (ICSIC)*, 67–75.

Ma, G., Liu, Y. and Shang, S. 2019. A building information model (BIM) and artificial neural network (ANN) based system for personal thermal comfort evaluation and energy efficient design of interior space. *Sustainability*, 11(18): 4972.

Machado, F.A., Dezotti, C.G. and Ruschel, R.C. 2019. The interface layer of a BIM-IoT prototype for energy consumption monitoring. *Advances in Informatics and Computing in Civil and Construction Engineering, Cham, Springer International Publishing.*

Marzouk, M. and Abdelaty, A. 2014. Monitoring thermal comfort in subways using building information modeling. *Energy and Buildings*, 84: 252–257.

Masoso, O.T. and Grobler, L.J. 2010. The dark side of occupants' behaviour on building energy use. *Energy and Buildings*, 42(2): 173–177.

Medithe, J.W.C. and Nelakuditi, U.R. 2016. Study on the impact of light on human physiology and electroencephalogram. *Journal of Biomimetics, Biomaterials and Biomedical Engineering, Trans Tech Publ.*, 28: 36–43.

Min, B.K., Jung, Y.C., Kim, E. and Park, J.Y. 2013. Bright illumination reduces parietal EEG alpha activity during a sustained attention task. *Brain Research*, 1538: 83–92.

MIRVAC. 2019. The Super Experience - Designing for Talent in the Digital Workplace from https://cdn.worktechacademy.com/uploads/2019/09/WORKTECH-Academy-Mirvac-The-Super-Experience-White-Paper-2019.pdf?_ga=2.79728144.628437762.1577049988-1390632762.1577049988.

Morys, F., Janssen, L.K., Cesnaite, E., Beyer, F., Garcia-Garcia, I., Kube, J., Kumral, D., Liem, F., Mehl, N., Mahjoory, K., Schrimpf, A., Gaebler, M., Margulies, D., Villringer, A., Neumann, J., Nikulin, V.V. and Horstmann, A. 2020. Hemispheric asymmetries in resting-state EEG and fMRI are related to approach and avoidance behaviour, but not to eating behaviour or BMI. *Human Brain Mapping*, 41(5): 1136–1152.

Nakama, Y., Onishi, Y. and Iki, K. 2015. Development of building information management system with data collecting functions based on IoT technology. *33rd eCAADe Conference Proceedings*, Vienna, Austria.

Papousek, I., Weiss, E.M., Schulter, G., Fink, A., Reiser, E.M. and Lackner, H.K. 2014. Prefrontal EEG alpha asymmetry changes while observing disaster happening to other people: Cardiac correlates and prediction of emotional impact. *Biological Psychology*, 103: 184–194.

Pasini, D. 2018. Connecting BIM and IoT for addressing user awareness toward energy savings. *Journal of Structural Integrity and Maintenance*, 3(4): 243–253.

Pasini, D., Ventura, S.M., Rinaldi, S., Bellagente, P., Flammini, A. and Ciribini, A.L.C. 2016. Exploiting Internet of Things and building information modeling framework for management of cognitive buildings. *2016 IEEE International Smart Cities Conference (ISC2)*.

Pisinger, D. and Ropke, S. 2010. Large neighborhood search. pp. 399–419. *In*: Gendreau, M. and Potvin, J.-Y. (eds.). *Handbook of Metaheuristics*. Boston, MA, Springer US.

Rafsanjani, H.N. and Ghahramani, A. 2020. Towards utilizing internet of things (IoT) devices for understanding individual occupants' energy usage of personal and shared appliances in office buildings. *Journal of Building Engineering*, 27: 100948.

Rahaman, M.S., Pare, H., Liono, J., Salim, F.D., Ren, Y., Chan, J., Kudo, S., Rawling, T. and Sinickas, A. 2019. OccuSpace: Towards a robust occupancy prediction system for activity based workplace. *2019 IEEE International Conference on Pervasive Computing and Communications Workshops (PerCom Workshops)*.

Rathore, M.M., Ahmad, A., Paul, A. and Rho, S. 2016. Urban planning and building smart cities based on the Internet of Things using Big Data analytics. *Computer Networks*, 101: 63–80.

Riaz, Z., Arslan, M. and Peña-Mora, F. 2015. Challenges in data management when monitoring confined spaces using BIM and wireless sensor technology. *Computing in Civil Engineering*, 2015: 123–130.

Saxena, V. and Srivastava, R. 2015. Impact of employee engagement on employee performance–Case of manufacturing sectors. *International Journal of Management Research and Business Strategy*, 4(2): 139–174.

Schaffer, C.E., Davidson, R.J. and Saron, C. 1983. Frontal and parietal electroencephalogram asymmetry in depressed and nondepressed subjects. *Biological Psychiatry*, 18(7): 753–762.

Schaufeli, W.B., Bakker, A.B. and Salanova, M. 2006. The measurement of work engagement with a short questionnaire: A cross-national study. *Educational and Psychological Measurement*, 66(4): 701–716.

Schaufeli, W.B., Salanova, M., González-romá, V. and Bakker, A.B. 2002. The measurement of engagement and burnout: A two sample confirmatory factor analytic approach. *Journal of Happiness Studies*, 3(1): 71–92.

Schmid, P.C., Hackel, L.M., Jasperse, L. and Amodio, D.M. 2018. Frontal cortical effects on feedback processing and reinforcement learning: Relation of EEG asymmetry with the feedback-related negativity and behavior. *Psychophysiology*, 55(1): e12911.

Seppanen, O. and Fisk, W.J. 2004. A model to estimate the cost effectiveness of the indoor environment improvements in office work. *Lawrence Berkeley National Laboratory*.

Shuck, M.B., Tonette, S.R. and Carlos, A.A. (2011). Exploring employee engagement from the employee perspective: Implications for HRD. *Journal of European Industrial Training*, 35(4): 300–25.

Smolders, K.C.H.J., De Kort, Y. and Cluitmans, P. 2016. Higher light intensity induces modulations in brain activity even during regular daytime working hours. *Lighting Research & Technology*, 48(4): 433–448.

Smolders, K.C.H.J., de Kort, Y.A.W. and Cluitmans, P.J.M. 2012. A higher illuminance induces alertness even during office hours: Findings on subjective measures, task performance and heart rate measures. *Physiology & Behavior*, 107(1): 7–16.

Sood, T., Janssen, P. and Miller, C. 2020. Spacematch: Using environmental preferences to match occupants to suitable activity-based workspaces. *Frontiers in Built Environment*, 6: 113.

Stone, P.J. and Luchetti, R. 1985. Your office is where you are. *Harvard Business Review*, 63(2): 102–117.

Sun, L., Peräkylä, J. and Hartikainen, K.M. 2017. Frontal Alpha asymmetry, a potential biomarker for the effect of neuromodulation on brain's affective circuitry—preliminary evidence from a deep brain stimulation study. *Frontiers in Human Neuroscience*, 11(584).

Tang, S., Shelden, D.R., Eastman, C.M., Pishdad-Bozorgi, P. and Gao, X. 2019. A review of building information modeling (BIM) and the internet of things (IoT) devices integration: Present status and future trends. *Automation in Construction*, 101: 127–139.

Teizer, J., Wolf, M., Golovina, O., Perschewski, M., Propach, M., Neges, M. and König, M. 2017. Internet of Things (IoT) for integrating environmental and localization data in Building Information Modeling (BIM). *Waterloo, IAARC Publications*, 34: 1–7.

Vecchiato, G., Toppi, J., Astolfi, L., Cincotti, F., Fallani, F.D.V., Maglione, A., Borghini, G., Cherubino, P., Mattia, D. and Babiloni, F. 2012. The added value of the electrical neuroimaging for the evaluation of marketing stimuli. *Bulletin of the Polish Academy of Sciences: Technical Sciences*, 419–426.

Wang, Z., Wang, J., He, Y., Liu, Y., Lin, B. and Hong, T. 2020. Dimension analysis of subjective thermal comfort metrics based on ASHRAE Global Thermal Comfort Database using machine learning. *Journal of Building Engineering*, 29: 101120.

Zhan, S., Chong, A. and Lasternas, B. 2021. Automated recognition and mapping of building management system (BMS) data points for building energy modeling (BEM). *Building Simulation*, 14(1): 43–52.

Chapter 8

Semi-Autonomous Digital Twins to Support Sustainable Outcomes in Construction 4.0

Marzia Bolpagni,[1,]* Angelo Luigi Camillo Ciribini,[2] Davide Simeone,[3] Sara Comai,[2] Silvia Mastrolembo[2] and Maud Santamaria[4]

8.1 Introduction

The construction industry is more and more implementing the key principles of the Industry 4.0 paradigm supporting the so called "Construction 4.0". Historically we can identify four industrial revolutions: the first relates to the invention of the steam engine, the second to electric energy, the third to the use of computers, the internet and renewable energies, and the fourth to the connection between the digital and physical environments and use of robotics and artificial intelligence (AI) (Bolpagni et al. (2022). The successful implementations of those revolutions are not yet equally

[1] Mace, London EC2M 6XB, UK; Department of Mechanical and Construction Engineering, Northumbria University, Newcastle upon Tyne, NE1 8ST, UK.
[2] Department of Civil and Environmental Engineering, Architecture and Mathematics, University of Brescia, Via Branze 43, 25123 Brescia, Italy.
[3] Department of Civil, Construction and Environmental Engineering, Sapienza University of Rome, Rome, Italy.
[4] Mace, London EC2M 6XB, UK.
Emails: angelo.ciribini@unibs.it; davide.simeone@uniromal.it; sara.comai@unibs.it; silvia.mastrolemboventura@unibs.it; maud.santamaria@macegroup.com
* Corresponding author: marzia.bolpagni@macegroup.com

distributed internationally, for example 17% of the world still lacks access to electricity and more than half of the world's population lack Internet access (Schwab 2017). On the other side, it is possible to observe an increasing use of technologies such as AI, sensors, the Internet of Things (IoT), and robots that are radically changing the way we work and interact with each other. Another key driver is the will to deliver sustainable assets to face climate change and the Environmental Social and Governance (ESG) criteria. Thus, following the Paris agreement (2015), countries such as the UK are introducing zero net paths with the ambition to reach zero net targets by 2050. The Construction sector plays a key role in this challenge as it is responsible for 40% of emissions of CO_2. To reduce those emissions and be more sustainable different initiatives are emerging such as the use of innovative materials, tools to calculate carbon (embodied carbon and operational carbon) as well as sensors to monitor the usage of our assets. The concept of "Digital Twin" (DT) rapidly emerged in both academia and industry in recent years. Despite there being no official definition yet, the term was introduced by NASA in 2010 and it represents the digital information structure of the physical system that forms an independent whole (Halmetoja 2022). This structure is a copy of data embedded in and attached to a physical system throughout its life cycle (Halmetoja 2022). Different countries such as Singapore and the UK launched a national initiative to create DT programmes. For example, the UK National Digital Twin Programme was launched in 2018 with the aim to enable an ecosystem of connected digital twins to foster better outcomes from the built environment, ensure secure resilient data sharing and effective information management and provide coordination and alignment with different key players (NDTP 2022). On the other hand, private and public organizations started to develop DT solutions for their assets by linking a virtual replica to a physical one using sensors. DT can be used to evaluate different aspects including built assets performance as well as behaviours of users. One increased application is the occupancy analysis of assets at different stages of the project: from design to evaluate user flow, to construction to study the usage of sites to operation to evaluate effective usage of spaces.

The first occupancy analyses were developed in CAD in a static environment, but with the emergence of Building Information Modelling (BIM), a 3D environment has been preferred as it allows more effective results (Simeone et al. 2013). The agent/user dimension is added to the virtual representation of assets to study the interaction between humans and spaces. In this way, the models started to become dynamic. After setting up the digital representation of the space, it is essential to define constraints/rules to be applied to occupants' simulation behaviours. This approach relates to the simulation of human behaviour in videogames, and it is the reason why game engines such as Unity3D have been incorporated into BIM in the past years (Simeone et al. 2013, Simeone et al. 2017, Simeone et al. 2015, Feng et al. 2022). Occupancy simulations can be used in the early phases of design to plan spaces as well as to train professionals before using an asset (e.g., how to access/navigate a hospital even if not built yet). In addition, thanks to sensors, occupancy analyses are now used more and more to monitor and analyse the actual usage of spaces and to compare the planned scenario with the actual one. This approach allows us to have a better idea of how users interact with the built environment and to detect areas of improvement. For example, if an area is not used, it is possible to investigate why (e.g., poor light, thermal comfort, safety, etc). The building would be able to provide alerts if benchmarks are passed and autonomously adapt its operation according to specific performance levels, which have been defined through the interaction with the environment (both internal and external) and the building occupants (Cadene et al. 2019). The process described a bidirectional flow of information between physical assets and a virtual replica. What is described is the function of "cognitive" buildings. Several terms have been used in literature including "smart", "intelligent", "interactive" and "reactive".

This chapter presents two case studies on occupancy analyses to investigate the current applications, limitations, and opportunities. The first case study is an office building in the UK while the second is a school project in Italy. The chapter concludes with discussions of the results and conclusions.

8.2 Case Study 1: Integration of IoT for Office Buildings in the UK to Improve Customer Service

This case study presents the results of a smart cleaning application in an office building in London. The case study has been conducted by Mace, an international consultancy and construction company operating also in development and facility management. Mace has been piloting the use of IoT to monitor space usage by different users to improve the workplace experience. Mace is aware of the impact that effective workplaces have on business objectives and the role it plays in supporting a healthy and sustainable workforce.

8.2.1 Background

As part of the services provided, cleaning plays a massive part in the Maslow pyramid of needs (under "safety needs") (Maslow 1943), thus cleaning needs to be a solid foundation of any facility management (FM) contracts. FM services are starting to digitalize exponentially as the IoT is developing, costs are more affordable, and skills are entering the sector contributing to activities such as data analytics (e.g., creating data models and insightful real time dashboards). However several sources estimate that cleaning labor accounts for approximately 80–95% of the total cost of cleaning (Klungseth and Blakstad 2016). This shows that the FM service of cleaning has always been slow to fully digitalize.

To overcome this gap, Mace wanted to monitor the usage of toilets in an office building to better understand if it would be possible to move from fixed cleaning (on a routine-based format) to on demand cleaning promoting a "smart cleaning" approach.

The office building was reaching capacity in terms of users (both employees and external guests). And therefore, the growth in headcount placed greater pressure on the amenities. At the same time, the transformation of the workforce gender mixes increased, while the gender mix of the building users is 65% male and 35% female. The bathroom configuration is split equally between men and women with five each on each floor of the five stories building. Within these configurations, there are 14 male cubicles and 20 female cubicles in total. In the first application, disabled facilities were excluded from the study.

Historically the FM service delivery has cleaned/replenished the female toilets up to six times a day and the male toilets three times a day on a routine-based format, same route, same time approach. Later the scope evolved, and it has been tailored over time based on cleaners' experience and understanding of usage, as well as per the fault reporting database. The way the end user could report an issue was to go to the 1st floor Building Services helpdesk and report verbally the issue or use the Building Services email or phone number. However, an external visitor would have limited access to or knowledge of this procedure.

The bathrooms were cleaned evenly throughout the day and remained open whilst being cleaned. Male and female operatives were required in the cleaning team to attend to both gender amenities (as the toilet were staying open whilst the cleaning regime was happening).

The reporting format for the cleaning team was a very traditional paper-based attendance sheet on the toilet door. This was then collected at the end of the day and put on excel manually for weekly reporting to the FM manager. This will form part of the Key Performance Indicators (KPIs) reporting data.

8.2.2 Challenges and Goals

The cleaning process involved an equal effort in cleaning all areas regardless of how much each space was used, generating inefficiencies and waste. In addition, the manual sheets to record staff attendance was not effective as everyone had access to them and cleaners might forget to fill in after completing the cleaning. Moreover, it was not possible to quickly identify and react to occasional anomalies, such as leakages, blockages, or lack of supplies to improve the user's experience.

To overcome those challenges Mace wanted to adopt a smart cleaning strategy with the following main goals:

- To drive operational actions that improve resource allocations and customer experiences
- To establish a cleaner, safer, and 'healthier' buildings
- To predict and react to usage fluctuation on a day-by-day basis

8.2.3 Solutions

The solution focused on three main areas:

a) Use data to calculate the optimum cleaning regimes based on the actual usage of each space.

b) Attendance is recorded electronically (via the feedback station and the cleaner unique key).

c) Feedback stations allow to logging cleaning and maintenance requests as well as recording user satisfaction.

To implement the solution, initially passive infrared sensors (PIR sensors) were attached to the bathroom entrance doors to count the number of people entering (the physical count was halved to count as one user – however tailgating could not be counted). A feedback station - 'smiley face' loop - was incorporated into all 10 bathrooms with option buttons for 'poor', 'indifferent', and 'good' choices. In addition, it was created a feedback console to gather all end users' feedback with the data automatically on the site dashboard and alert for the most negative or pressing issues created as seen in Fig. 8.1. All cleaners were trained on the new procedure, and they carried a keyring and taps the feedback station when attending the facility. This records attendance and feeds the Service Levels Agreements (SLA) compliance sheet electronically (also feeding the dashboard).

Later, a further set of PIR sensors were then placed inside the cubicle doors to measure the actual usage of the cubicles throughout the day. Manual data was collected on how often each cubicle was empty to enable the cleaning whilst the bathrooms remained open.

The value for Smart Cleaning tools and processes to be developed by an FM provider can benefit the following users:

i. End user: while the fundamental requirement for cleaning services is well understood within office space as per the Covid pandemic from

Figure 8.1: Electronic attendance records and feedback stations.

a safety point of view, it is also clear as per a psychological factor that a clean office provides a greater experience. It may affect behavior on its own based on the Broken Window Theory (Kelling and Wilson 1982). The broken windows theory states that visible signs of disorder and misbehavior in an environment encourage further disorder and misbehavior (Kelling and Wilson 1982).

ii. Client: as per a greater and augmented satisfaction of its end users, the client can gain in experience satisfaction level and Net Promoter Score (NPS) score. The cleaning regime may also affect the wellbeing of the user, and stop the spread of germs and viruses that may have left the end user becoming ill and therefore unproductive. As per a more efficient cleaning regime, savings may be targeted as per the reduction of the cleaning team or frequency resulting in true bottom line budget savings.

iii. FM provider (if not in-house provider): by having access to large a amount of data on its amenities, the FM team can start using predictive maintenance to predict issues and services requirement as well as rota planning for its cleaning staff. This can also result in cost savings.

iv. Cleaning team: now the cleaning team has the responsibility to check the data and act upon requirements as opposed to simply following a very basic, unfulfilling routine. This is encouraging the satisfaction of the cleaning team, becoming more productive and loyal to the current organization, and eventually, saves the company money in terms of talent attraction and retention.

8.2.4 Results

The deployment of IoT technology (including Passive Infra Red Sensors and Feedback stations) in the office bathrooms has enlightened the organisation's views, challenged paradigms, shaped thinking, and enabled to make cost reductions whilst simultaneously increasing the standard and consistency of the cleaning.

Data was collected for three months and analysed by a data analyst as seen in Fig. 8.2. The main insights from the data showed:

- Less than 8% (total feedback divided by building users) actually left feedback and this could be less than 4% if the same users left feedback

BATHROOM DOOR ENTRY DATA		FEMALE BATHROOMS						MALE BATHROOMS					
> 50 USERS IN THE HOUR													
> 70 USERS IN THE HOUR		1st	2nd	3rd	4th	5th		1st	2nd	3rd	4th	5th	
Monday 09:00 - 10:00	03/06/2019	23	27	40	55	34		25	74	51	53	37	
Monday 10:00 - 11:00	03/06/2019	34	47	43	78	50		24	76	31	48	45	
Monday 11:00 - 12:00	03/06/2019	33	38	47	58	50		35	83	38	49	55	
Monday 12:00 - 13:00	03/06/2019	34	31	48	66	39		30	82	35	40	21	
Monday 13:00 - 14:00	03/06/2019	29	32	39	79	39		40	51	30	60	30	
Monday 14:00 - 15:00	03/06/2019	38	35	42	50	39		39	74	35	53	27	
Monday 15:00 - 16:00	03/06/2019	30	27	37	65	42		29	72	34	42	32	
Monday 16:00 - 17:00	03/06/2019	37	28	48	44	45		47	76	29	45	24	
Monday 17:00 - 18:00	03/06/2019	14	6	19	18	8		10	16	14	26	11	
Monday 18:00 - 19:00	03/06/2019	0	0	3	41	64		3	5	2	29	11	
Monday 19:00 - 20:00	03/06/2019	0	6	34	0	0		0	14	30	21	6	
		272	277	400	554	410	1913	282	623	329	466	299	1999
Tuesday 09:00 - 10:00	28/05/2019	25	34	56	47	34		44	87	46	47	29	
Tuesday 10:00 - 11:00	28/05/2019	43	46	47	67	34		30	92	52	44	27	
Tuesday 11:00 - 12:00	28/05/2019	11	38	48	37	43		30	61	60	49	37	
Tuesday 12:00 - 13:00	28/05/2019	47	32	42	35	35		27	66	36	40	8	
Tuesday 13:00 - 14:00	28/05/2019	20	27	53	50	31		25	57	31	54	19	
Tuesday 14:00 - 15:00	28/05/2019	30	25	41	52	39		39	79	35	42	26	
Tuesday 15:00 - 16:00	28/05/2019	22	48	39	70	33		20	55	41	36	24	
Tuesday 16:00 - 17:00	28/05/2019	27	27	44	35	22		29	61	33	42	20	
Tuesday 17:00 - 18:00	28/05/2019	11	5	16	25	9		11	19	11	42	2	
Tuesday 18:00 - 19:00	28/05/2019	1	5	6	40	28		1	4	3	42	1	
Tuesday 19:00 - 20:00	28/05/2019	0	0	49	1	0		1	8	17	4	30	
		237	287	441	459	308	1732	257	589	365	442	223	1876
Wednesd 09:00 - 10:00	29/05/2019	27	41	44	52	52		40	64	37	43	30	
Wednesd 10:00 - 11:00	29/05/2019	31	48	49	54	29		25	60	42	32	28	
Wednesd 11:00 - 12:00	29/05/2019	41	27	24	29	33		38	75	55	53	42	
Wednesd 12:00 - 13:00	29/05/2019	23	44	42	47	37		35	66	28	23	15	
Wednesd 13:00 - 14:00	29/05/2019	33	30	45	41	37		18	81	44	39	30	
Wednesd 14:00 - 15:00	29/05/2019	30	43	44	59	24		30	71	38	43	18	

Figure 8.2: Data sample from sensors.

twice a day, therefore at least 92% indifference or assumed level of satisfaction as no feedback left

- actual usage volumes throughout the different hours of the different days of the week
- monitor which floors within the building had the most bathroom usage
- measure the difference in the peak time usage of men's and women's bathrooms
- cubicle usage of female toilets versus door entry into the bathroom shows a significant extent of non-cubicle use (assumed mirror/sink usage only instead)
- number of cubicles get cleaned with an open bathroom cleaning policy.

The main findings showed that in comparison to male bathroom usage, female cubicle usage does not warrant an enhanced cleaning regime. In addition, less cleaning is required in the late pm for female bathrooms as less cubicle usage was measured as seen in Fig. 8.3.

Cubicle cleaning would be significantly more effective if bathrooms are closed for 15 minutes each (small reduction in evening shift deep clean time). The data enabled us to compile a 'closed' cleaning schedule for the 10 bathrooms that causes the least disruption and matches clean times to post peak usage. Feedback data allowed to modify cleaning regimes and frequencies and measure the impact of changes.

Thanks to those findings the management team proposed a reduction from 45 to 30 bathroom cleans a day with male and female bathrooms both being cleaned three times only daily. This has the financial benefit of reducing the cleaning team by ½ a head which corresponded to an average

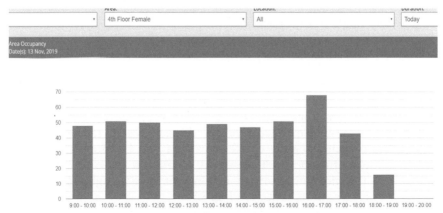

Figure 8.3: Extraction of bathroom usage per floor per gender.

of £ 15k. The ½ head reduction allowed challenging other aspects of the cleaning resource model and when combined with other efficiency gains, it become possible to reduce the cleaning team by a full head (around £ 30k).

Moreover, it was agreed to close all bathrooms for 15 minutes for a full clean instead of keeping them open. This has the potential to increase hygiene and consistency of cleaning standards, better presented bathrooms post peak times, and greater flexibility within the cleaning team as single gender cleaners are required for bathroom cleans.

Figure 8.4 presents a simple data-flow process used in this case study where data was collected using PIR sensors, data was transmitted to a database where an excel file was extracted. The excel file was used for the first analyses and to present the first results. Afterwards, more user-friendly and interactive dashboards in PowerBi have been created.

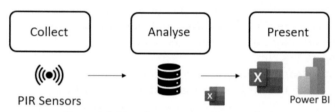

Figure 8.4: Data flow process of case study 1.

8.2.5 *Future Work and Limitations*

The Mace team is planning to scale this approach to other sites and clients to improve the experience by adding a layer of automation of the data into actionable insights. Mace would like to create a standard operation procedure to understand the needs and implement the right smart cleaning regime with the same technology following the following steps:

1. Identify High Traffic Spaces
2. Calibrate resource efforts to space usage
3. Use feedback data to improve service experience
4. Improve service response time

The application showed was limited in monitoring real time bathroom usage, in the future Mace would like to adopt solutions that automatically inform the cleaning team when a threshold is achieved to react to cleaning needs. The cleaning regime of all areas, not just bathrooms, could be monitored using the approach presented. Finally, an app could be created to support the cleaning team to get instant data insights that create cleaning alerts/requests as seen in Fig. 8.5.

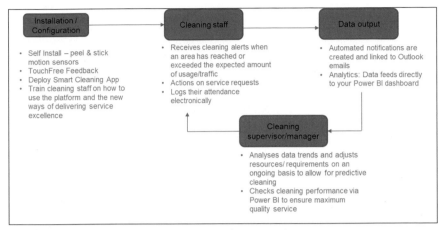

Figure 8.5: Diagram of future application.

8.3 Case Study 2: Agent-based Simulations in Italian Schools to Enable Better User's Experience

8.3.1 Background

In 2020, the pandemic emergency due to the SARS-CoV-2 virus forced many nations to order a total closure of public places and workplaces. In Italy, for example, schools have been closed from mid-February 2020 to September 2020, highlighting the need to use alternative channels of teaching to ensure students' continuity of learning. In those months, the teaching methodology changed from face-to-face to distance learning. Previous studies show that the COVID-19 crisis, as well as the measures taken to contain the pandemic curve, had affected student learning and children's performance with short- and long-term effects, negatively impacting skills acquisition (Di Pietro et al. 2020). For these reasons, during lockdown months, analyses were conducted to reorganize the typical school day and to define behaviors to be maintained outside and inside the building. Such studies had the final goal to reduce the risk of virus transmission among children and allow the return to face-to-face instruction from September 2020. Within this context, the first basic rules defined by the Italian government included:

- social distancing in both circulation paths and learning spaces of educational buildings
- mask wearing in circulation paths
- body temperature checking before school access through thermo-scanner (37.5°C is the maximum temperature allowed)
- frequent hands disinfection with a hydro-alcoholic solution and washing

- micro-community organization and segmentation
- regular and adequate room ventilation.

Subsequently, the Italian government provided several documents containing the guidelines for a safe re-entry to face-to-face teaching, developed thanks to the indications of the Technical Scientific Committee (CTS). Particularly, the protocols defined contain rules regarding interpersonal distances and the maximum number of people allowed in classrooms and in circulation paths. The first guideline was published in May 2020 (CTS 2020a) and states that at least 1 meter of interpersonal distance must be respected between end-users, both sitting at school desks or circulation paths (i.e., dynamic meters). The second protocol was released in July 2020 (CTS 2020b), to facilitate school directors to guarantee in-presence teaching activities and determine the observance of 1 meter of interpersonal distance in classrooms (i.e., static meter).

8.3.2 Case of Study

The research work described in this paragraph has been developed using an existing school building, located in Milan (Italy) as a case study. The selected building consists of three floors above ground and one semi-basement where are located the kitchen and the canteen; the ground floor comprises common spaces such as the atrium and the gymnasium, the nursery classrooms (4–5 years old child), and the kindergarten classroom (2–3 years old child). On the first floor, there is the nursery room (3 years old child) and the administrative offices while the second floor contains the classrooms of the primary school (6–10 years old child). The research described here focuses only on primary school students (6 to 10 years old children).

The aim of the study is the reorganization of the internal spaces and the typical day of the students, ensuring a safe school reopening despite the SARS-CoV-2 pandemic emergency.

The methodology adopted focuses on five fundamental points:

- analysis of the normative texts
- model generation
- occupancy analysis
- simulation-based prediction
- communication of provisions to end-users.

Analysis of the normative texts (Italian protocols): this phase allowed to collect data from the Italian protocols, describing the actions needed to reduce the spread of the covid-19 virus. In addition, in this phase were also collected data regarding the school building was taken as a case study.

Model generation: this phase includes the generation of the building information model of the school (including furniture and devices related to COVID-19 protocols). The 2D drawings in .dwg and .pdf format shared by the school manager were integrated with a digital survey using the Indoor Mobile Mapping Survey (iMMS) technology to acquire three-dimensional geometries and digital photographic documentation of the spaces. The model was generated using Autodesk Revit modelling software. Within the software, the point cloud generated by the digital survey was imported and the information modelling of the building taken as a case study was developed.

Occupancy analysis: this phase allowed the identification of common spaces, teaching spaces, and unused spaces suitable to be converted into new teaching environments. Using Autodesk AutoCad 2D drawing software, the most functional arrangement of furniture inside the classrooms was studied to define how many children the school could accommodate.

Simulation-based prediction: in this phase crowd simulations have been developed to rearrange the organization of the common activities and agent-based simulations have been adopted to assess the behavior of single students.

Communication of provisions to end-users: previously developed simulations were critical to developing this phase of the research. The new rules of behavior to be maintained inside the school building were communicated through new digital technologies. In particular, training videos, interactive mini-games, and a formative survey have been generated.

Figure 8.6 presents a simple data flow of the steps presented above.

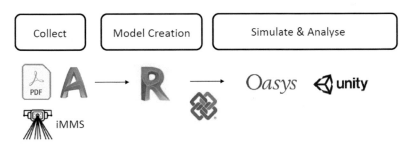

Figure 8.6: Data flow process of case study 2.

8.3.3 Solution Implemented

In this chapter, the focus is on movement simulations. Simulations helps in understanding the behaviour of crowds or individuals within an environment and allow us to predict and prevent dangerous situations due to overcrowding.

In the case study considered, three critical situations were identified: for students of all three levels of education, entrance (1) and exit (2) processes from the building have been studied while for primary school students, that represent the central focus of this work, also the lunch break (3) movements have been considered in the simulations.

To develop the simulations, it was necessary to study the layout of the environment in which the end users would have to wait and circulate. As shown in Fig. 8.7, several areas were identified:

- thermo-scanner checkpoint: placed at the entrance of the school
- hand sanification area: positioned at the entrance of the atrium
- waiting zones: the squares in the central part of the atrium are dedicated to kindergarten and used only for preschool, while the

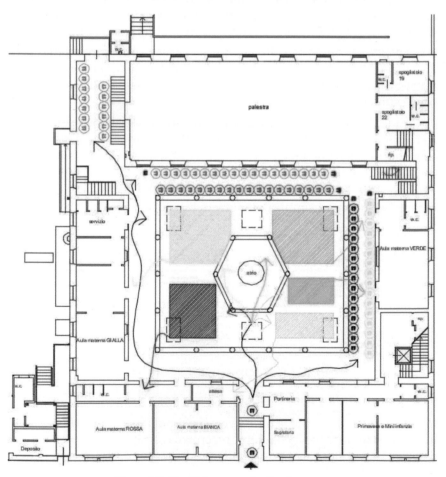

Figure 8.7: The atrium organization in zones.

symbols with little feet are zones where primary students have to queue before going to class accompanied by the teacher

- circulation path: in the Fig. 8.4 identified by the arrows that connect the previous areas.

The study done on the capacity of the learning environments played a key role in the organization of the spaces in the atrium. Since for kindergarten students, no interpersonal distance obligation was imposed, they were allowed to stay within a waiting space, one for each classroom, confined by furniture. On the other side, primary students were supposed to maintain an interpersonal distance of 1 meter, which was necessary to identify areas where to queue and specify the position of each student. Finally, the largest classes were positioned at the top of the atrium (orange and green rows) while the smallest classes were positioned to the right (red and yellow rows).

8.3.3.1 Crowd Simulation

Oasys MassMotion software was used to create the crowd dynamics simulation. Within the software, the ground floor of the building was imported into the open .ifc schema. The building elements were transformed into software elements: slabs became floors and walls became barriers. This step is crucial as it defines where the avatar can or cannot walk. Then, the zones of the atrium were recreated, maintaining the same waiting and circulation zones as previously identified. To obtain a more realistic crowd and individual simulation, the software settings were implemented with realistic values for the speed of children's movements (m/s) and with the rules of interpersonal distancing imposed by the national CTS as seen in Fig. 8.8.

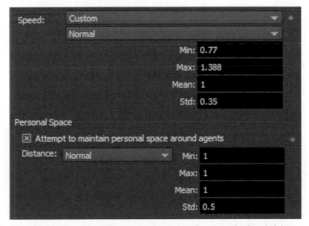

Figure 8.8: Profile settings used in flow simulations. The speed of a child was considered in m/s while the personal space was imposed by the CTS.

The organization of the atrium presented above was useful for both simulated entry and exit of classes as seen in Fig. 8.9. For the exit simulation, it was decided to use the space inside the school yard to allow parents to wait for their children in compliance with the rules of physical spacing. This space was equipped with horizontal signs to highlight the positions where each parent has to wait for their child or children.

The simulation of movement flows prior to the re-opening of the school allowed the identification of critical points in the circulation paths, leading to the generation of behavioral rules for end-users. In this regard, through simulation software, it was possible to create proximity maps. As can be seen from Fig. 8.10, the most critical zone in the atrium is the access

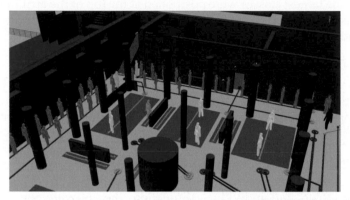

Figure 8.9: Simulation in the collective scenario.

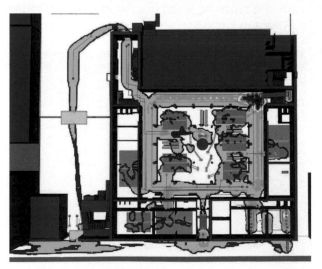

Figure 8.10: Proximity map. Low density identified by the blue colour, high density indicated by the red colour.

point to the second floor, highlighted as a red area, a route that all the classes have to follow to reach the upper floor of the building. Some fairly critical points (marked in yellow in the image) can be identified along the two areas bordering the colonnade, where rows are created. In light of this result, teachers were informed of such issues and asked to avoid the critical situation of overcrowding in the described zone. In addition, each classroom was equipped with a dispenser of sanitizer allowing students to sanitize their hands before entering the class.

8.3.3.2 Agent-based Paradigm and Behavioral Patterns Simulation

To reach reliable simulations of school use processes, the agent-based paradigm has been integrated with behavioral pattern representations, able to simulate the performing of group activities as well as singular actions different from the spatial movement of students. Game engines such as Unity3D provide the perfect environment for this integrated simulation, computationally managing and coordinating individual behaviors and structured activities involving complex, multiple interactions among agents, all performed in the virtual environment derived from the information model of the school as seen in Fig. 8.11. Static and dynamic parameters such as velocity ranges, orientation, and movement capabilities have been introduced in the agents' template to generate a realistic variation in terms of children's behaviors. To control

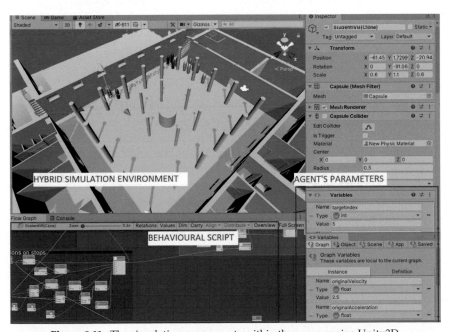

Figure 8.11: The simulation components within the game engine Unity3D.

the simulation of collective activities, specific computational entities have been developed and organized in a simulation plot, coordinating the actions of the involved agents. Each agent has also a set of variables that, updated during the simulation, represent its status concerning COVID-19 risks. Those variables include the distance from other agents, checked/ not checked the temperature, and sanitized hands. In developing the agents' behavioral sets, we relied on the use of bolt scripts to progressively expand the set of behavior libraries and the number of formalized variables. This is particularly important to allow further calibration of the agent-based model as well as its customization as per different schools and protocols.

8.3.4 Results

The collection of geometric data of the school building allowed the creation of a three-dimensional model, which has been used to study the movement flows of the different end users' of the school. Particularly, the crowd simulation has been adopted to study the collective scenarios, leading to the divisions of the different school zones between waiting areas and circulation paths. Although the models and predictions developed have been of great utility to re-organize the school activities, they take into account only the end users' behaviors considered during the models' generation. To solve this issue, it has been developed a second type of simulation that sees the active participation of the student. Each student, being free to move around the school, can independently choose the path to take.

8.3.5 Benefits

The tools applied in this research allowed the description of the different movement patterns occurring in an elementary school. After analyzing the common spaces and hypothesizing their layout, mass simulations allowed to validate or disprove the hypotheses taken. The school principal, always in contact with the research team, was able to visualize the routes that the end users will have to travel and according to them, she could organize the typical school day. Crowd- and agent-based simulations were used to communicate the new rules to be maintained both outside and inside the school. In addition, training videos and an interactive game were developed and shared with end users prior to the opening of the school. These steps played a key role, especially in the first few days of school reopening. In fact, thanks to these tools, most students already knew the route to follow and the waiting areas for the thermo scanner check and hand sanitizing. The methodology of this research, if appropriately tailored to the needs of the end users, can be applied to other schools as well as other types of buildings.

8.3.6 Future Work

This study was the first step in analyzing users' routes in an emergency situation to provide prompt support to Italian schools during COVID-19. For this reason, the effective user's behavior was not considered due to time limitations. This aspect could be evaluated in future works. Moreover, serious games based on the simulations and the games reported in this chapter could be developed with the aim to teach new rules of behavior. These tools could be designed to be used through both immersive and non-immersive virtual reality technologies, with the goal to educate end users. Those tools should have the possibility of anonymized data to protect users' privacy. Other future work could be related to the analysis of data obtained qualitative data by interviewing teaching staff about how the new communication tools affected children's behavior.

8.4 Discussion and Conclusion

This contribution investigates the role of technology to evaluate the user's behaviors in the built environment. Two case studies have been presented from the UK and Italy. Even if the two case studies are quite different in the scope and approaches used; both show the potential of occupancy analyses. The first case study showed how the installation of PIR sensors in office toilets can provide a significant contribution to understanding the actual use of spaces, optimize resources, save money and increase customer satisfaction. The second case study, instead, showed how a virtual environment can be used for a crowd- and agent-based simulations to support final users' training and awareness in critical situations, such as the respect of social distance during a pandemic.

The two applications showed some autonomous functionalities of Digital Twins (DT), however as the processes are not fully autonomous yet, they can be defined as "semi-autonomous". The price of technologies that support DT applications (such as the creation of models, laser scanning, and sensors) are now affordable to most companies and the benefits of their applications have been demonstrated in this chapter as well as in literature presented in the introduction. One of the main gaps in the industry is related to skills needed for those processes and technologies (Bolpagni et al. 2022) that might be considered as a barrier. It is therefore relevant to collaborate with innovation departments within an organizations or partner with consultants or academia to set up those applications.

The use of semi-autonomous digital twin applications also generates potential risks such as violation of privacy, security, and ethical use of data. It is therefore essential to consider those aspects when setting up an initial plan for application. Another area of future work is related to the link of (semi)- autonomous digital twin and ESG Criteria, as more and more it is becoming relevant for Real Estate and Infrastructure Property and Development Management. Finally, in the future, the use of semi-autonomous digital twins can be linked to social networks to explore the interactions with the so called "Metaverse" and further support sustainable outcomes for Construction 4.0.

References

Bolpagni, M., Gavina, R. and Ribeiro, D. (eds.). 2021. *Industry 4.0 for the Built Environment: Methodologies, Technologies and Skills* (Vol. 20). Springer Nature.

Cadena, J.D.B., Moretti, N., Poli, T. and Cecconi, F.R. 2019. Low-cost sensor network in cognitive buildings for maintenance optimisation. *Tema: Technology, Engineering, Materials and Architecture*, 5(1): 93–102.

Comitato Tecnico Scetifico. 2020a. Report Ufficiale n. 82, Modalità di ripresa delle attività didattiche del prossimo anno scolastico.

Comitato Tecnico Scetifico. 2020b. Report Ufficiale n. 94, Quesiti del Ministero dell'Istruzione relativi all'inizio del nuovo anno scolastico.

Di Pietro, G., Biagi, F., Costa, P., Karpiński, Z. and Mazza, J. 2020. The likely impact of COVID-19 on education: Reflections based on the existing literature and recent international datasets (Vol. 30275). Luxembourg: Publications Office of the European Union.

Feng, Z., Gao, Y. and Zhang, T. 2022. Gamification for visualization applications in the construction industry. *In Industry 4.0 for the Built Environment*. Springer, Cham, pp. 495–514.

Halmetoja, E. 2022. The role of digital twins and their application for the built environment. *In Industry 4.0 for the Built Environment*. Springer, Cham, pp. 415–442.

Kelling, G.L. and Wilson, J.Q. 1982. Broken windows: The police and neighborhood safety. *The Atlantic Monthly*. Manhattan Institute.

Klungseth, N.J. and Blakstad, S.H. 2016. Organising in-house cleaning services in public FM. *Facilities*, 34(13-14): 828–854.

Maslow, A. 1946. A theory of human motivation/Maslow A. *Psychological Review*, 50(4): 370–396.

National Digital Twin Programme. 2022. https://www.cdbb.cam.ac.uk/what-we-do/national-digital-twin-programme (accessed May 05, 2022).

Schwab, K. 2017. *The Fourth Industrial Revolution*. Portfolio Penguin.

Simeone, D., Cursi, S. and Coraglia, U.M. 2017. Modelling buildings and their use as systems of agents. *Proc. Int. Conf. Educ. Res. Comput. Aided Archit. Des. Eur.*, 1(September): 85–92.

Simeone, D., Schaumann, D., Kalay, Y.E. and Carrara, G. 2013. Adding users' dimension to BIM. *In 11th Conf. Eur. Archit. Envisioning Assoc.* | *Envisioning Archit. Des. Eval. Commun.* (Track 3) Conceptual Representation: Exploring the Layout of the Built Environment, pp. 483–490.

Simeone, D., Toldo, I., Cursi, S. and Schaumann, D. 2015. A simulation model for building occupancy prediction. *Tema: Technology, Engineering, Materials and Architecture*, 1(2): 166–171.

Chapter 9

Cognitive Digital Twin Framework for Life Cycle Assessment Supporting Building Sustainability

Lavinia Chiara Tagliabue,[1,*] *Tassiane Feijó Brazzalle,*[2]
Stefano Rinaldi[3] and *Giovanni Dotelli*[4]

9.1 Introduction

The building simulation through calculation virtual environments encourages the AEC sector to promote the European collection of strategies in the direction of decarbonization namely the European Green Deal and its package to reach EU Countries' carbon neutrality. These strategies are coherent consequences of the Paris Agreement (2016) key target of blocking global warming to hazardous levels bringing the earth to dramatic effects.

As stated by IEA (International Energy Agency), energy production related to the AEC sector is the most carbon emissive segment responding

[1] Computer Science Department, University of Turin, Italy, Corso Svizzera 185, 10149, Turin, Italy.
[2] Via Don Carlo Gnocchi, 33, Milano, Italy.
[3] Department of Information Engineering, University of Brescia, via Branze 38 - 25123 Brescia (BS), Italy.
[4] Department of Chemistry, Materials and Chemical Engineering "Giulio Natta", Politecnico di Milano, Piazza Leonardo da Vinci, 32, 20133 Milan, Italy.
Emails: tassifb@gmail.com; stefano.rinaldi@unibs.it; giovanni.dotelli@polimi.it
* Corresponding author: laviniachiara.tagliabue@unito.it

to more than 40% in 2018. This percentage comes by 11% from the production of construction materials (embodied carbon) and by 28% from the Operations and Maintenance (O&M) phase (operational carbon) of the built environment. The concept of energy saving is not confined to the O&M phase however now the idea is to consider the life cycle of the buildings and include not only electricity and thermal energy for the daily running although the materials production phase and the dismantling phase. This augmented view of the entire life cycle is increasing the need for knowledge about the energy used in the processes that are part of the building life before and after the running phase. In fact, a relevant amount of energy is likewise associated with the number of resources employed to build up the asset, and it can be calculated by applying the Life Cycle Assessment (LCA) methodology. According to the definitions stated in the scientific literature (De Wolf et al. 2017), embodied energy is the amount of energy used to manufacture a material (from extraction to production processes), whilst embodied CO2e is the number of Greenhouse Gases (GHGs) released to produce the same material. Every material type has a different composition that consumes energy and emits carbon. According to further research (Monticelli et al. 2011), the construction of buildings and their operational phase have extensive direct and indirect effects on the environment during the asset life cycle, which can be reduced by recovering existing buildings dropping the impacts related to the construction waste, repurposing, and extending their useful life, thus supporting the rationale of reuse and recycle not only at material level nevertheless at the whole building level. In the research two approaches that immediately had a leading role in the European effort for action applied to the AEC sector are underlined: the former (a) the Nearly Zero Energy Building (nZEB) concept application as a challenge to trigger existing inefficient buildings into high-energy efficient organisms, powering them up by renewables, considering the possibility to harvest more energy than the required amount such as in the Energy Positive Buildings where energy production is higher than the demand (Sartori et al. 2012, Lu and Huang 2019), and the latter (b) GHG emissions rate decrease during the recovery process evaluated and supported by LCA calculations. In the research, both methods are linked to the building envelope materials such as external walls, floors, roof, and outside openings, as enhancements in the listed elements boost envelope energy efficiency qualifying the building as nZEB when renewable energy systems (RES) are adopted to provide the energy demand (Dall'O et al. 2013). Nevertheless, it is worth noting as the implementation of the building envelope to improve energy efficiency in the running phase can lead to an increase of embodied energy in the construction materials, for example, related to the increased thickness of the insulation layers or in the triple glazing windows that are commonly adopted in nZEB building (Costardi et al. 2021, Wiik et al. 2018). For that reason, parametric studies have been developed (Lobaccaro et al. 2018) to drive the design of nZEB to balance the increase of embodied GHG emissions. The concept of LC-ZEB (life cycle – zero energy building) is not new (Hernandez and Kenny 2008, Hernandez and Kenny 2010) and it has been conceptualized in the last decade however more recent researches on integrating the dimension of economic feasibility and Life Cycle Cost (LLC) are more recent (Sesana and Salvalai 2013, Ritzen Michiel et al. 2016). Nowadays the idea to overcome the nZEB concept hinged on the running phase and extending to the building life cycle phases is supported by some interoperable tools that can boost the process and strongly support the effective approach to LC-ZEB. As required by the energy calculation methodology to evaluate the building energy performance, this approach requires the adoption of tools to implement the LCA calculation and a coherent extraction of the information by the BIM digital model (Potrč Obrecht et al. 2020, Bueno and Fabricio 2018) can enhance and promote the transparency and accuracy of the procedure. However, some interoperable workflows that can be adopted are burdened by inefficiencies and losses of information, and for such a data and meta-data intensive task, the semantic web is the only logical choice of technology. For that reason, updated studies (Sobhkhiz et al. 2021) about the use of the semantic web has been proposed to address the data management issues of BIM-LCA applications. For comparison, the execution is additionally performed by using an LCA tool (Tally), and a method using Relational Database Management Systems (RDBMS). The research results appear to promote the proposed method as superior to RDBMS methods in terms of capturing semantics and can improve LCA tools by providing reliable data in the early design stages.

LCA calculation within the presented research was accomplished by including materials data obtained from a traditional construction materials list for Phase 01 – Baseline; and through the use of EPDs, certified manufacturer documentation containing their LCA data for Phase 02 – Insulation. The LCA calculation was implemented employing a dedicated software, namely One Click LCA, which has a promising interoperable path with BIM tools. The main key approach of the research is to conceive the digital implementation of a BIM-based Digital Twin for LCA (Chen et al. 2021, Ghita et al. 2021). Thus, the process starts from the LCA evaluation supported by BIM for quantity extraction and the definition of which kind of information related to materials and their duration could be automatically checked during the O&M phase to promote replacement procedures that can enhance the energy efficiency of the building and control the embodied energy that increases when refurbishment procedures and new materials are installed.

As the first step this research proposes a methodology to perform Life Cycle Assessment (LCA) using an existing building as a case study adopting data created by virtual modelling using Building Information Modelling (BIM) methodology. The LCA procedure, when employed in the Architecture, Engineering, and Construction (AEC) sector, is used to quantify the environmental impact of the actions during the course of the assembly chain, and its preparation is already applied and extensively demanded in new design projects. When utilized in existing buildings it extends the possibility to decrease the environmental impact of the built structures' renovation, which can be established by the emission of specific Certifications. This research is organized on three main targets: (1) the Nearly Zero Energy Buildings (nZEB) concept development and implementation, considering building performance and energy consumption which have to be reduced during the life cycle according to more restrictive trends in European directive and standards, coupled with the use of renewable energy generated within the calculation boundaries; (2) the environmental impacts decrease during refurbishment planning and works during the life cycle when the useful life of the components ends; (3) envision the technological framework and the digital architecture for the Digital Twin (DT) supporting LCA during the life cycle. The summarized goals stemmed from the sequential use of Calculation Virtual Environments (CVE), starting from a BIM authoring tool as a basis for the LCA calculation and the data organization of the DT for LCA evaluation management. Employing virtual calculation is a way to support predictive performance evaluation to test materials scenarios and retrofitting hypotheses, demonstrated to be a strategy to estimate the efficacy and cost-benefit of revamping processes to reach higher quality goals from a kaizen perspective (Umeda et al. 2020).

9.2 Background

The research method is applied to a case study located in Milan, Lombardy region, Climate zone E Della Repubblica, P. (1993), Italy. At the national level an official nZEB classification is declared in Law 90/2013 (Legge 90 2013) which describes nZEB as a "building characterized by a very high energy performance, where the very low energy demand is significantly covered by renewable sources, produced within the building system boundaries". Italy is a country characterized by undeniable restoration needs, since 37,1% of total energy demand relay on the AEC sector, according to EPBD (Energy Performance in Building Directive) (EPBD 2018). Moreover, the Country relates different constraints corresponding to the intensity of the intervention. The level of intervention identified for the present research development was the Second-level as defined in the

Table 9.1: Thermal transmittance limits for II-level major and minor renovation (EPBD 2018, Climate zone E).

Envelope Components	U-value [W/m²K]
Walls	0,28
Roofs	0,24
Floors	0,29
Doors, windows, shutters	1,4

legislation, i.e., "refurbishment of at least 25% of the external surfaces of the building with or without renovation of the heating and/or cooling plant". According to this level in Table 9.1, the envelope efficiency requirement is summarized.

The requested U-values are achieved for the case study by calculating the thermal properties of the envelope considering the different layers and materials and upgrading the insulation layer with different materials scenarios. A calculation model using the materials data included in the BIM enriched database has been developed to perform the envelope verification and the energy results consequently achieved by changing the insulation materials considering the environmental impacts of these changes and promoting an evaluation towards the LC-ZEB buildings. The further step is to depict the DT structure and organization to implement the procedure as the renovation works occur and propose by AI-based recommendation algorithm, the building renovation installing low embedded carbon materials with additionally positive outcomes on the energy performance during the O&M phase.

9.3 Methodology

A step-by-step procedure is proposed applying as cascade the digital modeling by Autodesk Revit Architecture 2021, the data transfer by Visual Programming Language (VPL) Dynamo add-in to Revit; DiRoots ParaManager and SheetLink add-ins to Revit, to exchange data with the calculation model in Microsoft Excel, then Autodesk Green Building Studio (GBS) for the building energy performance calculation and PVGIS (Photovoltaic Geographical Information System) provided by European Commission for the calculation of the renewable sources; finally, Bionova One Click LCA and Environmental Product Declarations (EPDs) documents for the BIM based LCA evaluation. The procedure utilized data handled and extracted throughout the above-mentioned sequence and empowered a fast data-oriented calculation process to include the LCA procedures as a significant step in refurbishment design for existing buildings.

The calculation has two progressive steps: Phase 01– Baseline and Phase 02– Insulation, where now materials are introduced to refurbish the existing envelope situation.

The Phase 01 cycle delivers data generation, increase, selection, extraction, and iteration focused on the calculation of materials effect in the envelope layers to verify their efficiency in the existing building situation. These data were subsequently incorporated into the LCA calculation to assess the environmental impact of the material choice.

The calculation chain was iterated in Phase 02– Insulation with five materials and compared with the result of the Baseline to evaluate the benefits of the different materials listed below:

01. Rolan Rock Wool

02. Mètisse Recycled Cotton

03. Freudenberg Recyced Plastic

04. Isolconfort EPS

05. Stiferite EPS

The geographic building data was retrieved from the virtual model to be used in the PVGIS to calculate photovoltaic energy production. The LCA evaluation was performed for each insulation material supporting the decision-making process for energy retrofitting of the envelope. The research findings determined the positive results of modelling existing assets enriched with data enabling energy simulation cycles. The process is not fully automated, nevertheless, it allows to save and retrieve data whenever desired.

A single BIM model with clear phase definitions to guarantee the correct data extraction for all the material options was managed. The trustworthiness of the BIM model increased with the data enrichment, and it helped to increase the level of reliability of the outcomes. The more information was added to the model the more trustworthy the results. The connection between data sources and databases in the cloud provided a time saving and regular update.

The parameters were designed with DiRoots ParaManager add-in and added to specific categories according to the digital model structure. A second add-in, DiRoots Sheetlink granted a degree of interoperability between data and Microsoft Excel Spreadsheets in a bi-directional way: a table with category parameters was exported, filled in, and imported back to the model, filling the Parameter values with external data (Fig. 9.1).

Figure 9.1: Workflow for retrieving information from BIM and the calculation model.

Autodesk Revit Architecture 2021 authoring tool was adopted to virtually create the case study of the test existing building to execute the computation of the current energy demand, and then its embodied carbon. BIM database adds data to geometry and fosters bi-directional workflow performing automatic updates when the model is modified, revising linked technical drawings, schedules, and graphical information within a master file, and linked ones. The implementation of the enriched database is obtained by creating parameters that can be grouped, scheduled, exported, complemented, and imported back to fill parameter gaps.

In Fig. 9.2 the new parameters created and managed for the energy definition of the envelope are included in the digital model of the test house and exchanged through SheetLink to the calculation model. The parameters are calculated for the different materials scenarios and the energy performance. The conductivity (λ W/mK), thermal transmittance (U-Value W/m²K), and thermal resistance (R m²K/W) are prepared to include the calculated value in the digital model.

The data are transferred from the calculation model to the BIM database through Sheetlink and the existing situation is compared to a new run with different scenarios and energy performance evaluated in Autodesk Insight and Green Building Studio CVE.

Additionally, scheduling data is used for management purposes and transferred to other platforms. The capability to recover data from the digital model and use them in management platforms allows efficient time saving and control of possible errors and miscommunication, expanding the restrictions of the transmission by sharing these data and creating timely updates.

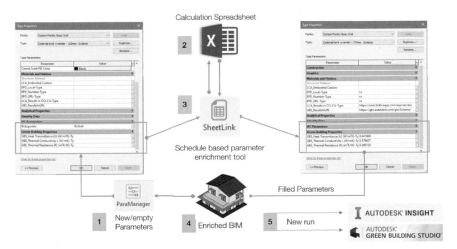

Figure 9.2: New parameters for energy assessment in the enriched digital model.

The thermal properties were calculated with a Microsoft Excel calculation model implementing thermal equations according to ISO 6946/2017 (ISO6946 2017). The thermal properties calculation required the values of each envelope material layer, surface area, and volume; these quantities data were extracted from the digital model and transferred to the calculation model.

In Fig. 9.3 the workflow for the parameters connected to the calculation model is depicted. The value is included in the calculation sheet and the parameters are included in the digital model via a bi-directional link.

The calculated thermal parameters are fundamental to calculating the heat transfer capability and defining the building performance, the main parameters and units are listed as follows:

- thermal conductivity λ [W/mK];
- thermal resistance R-Value [m²K/W];
- multilayered wall's heat transfer coefficient or thermal transmittance U-Value [W/m²K].

The application of Computational Design while creating a BIM model enables to prevent repetitive tasks by using specific scripts provided through Visual Programming Language (VPL). In the present research, the Autodesk Revit add-in Dynamo was utilized to generate Schedules in Revit (Fig. 9.4). The schedules might be transferred for a wide range of uses and to be maintained in the model for checking and data repository.

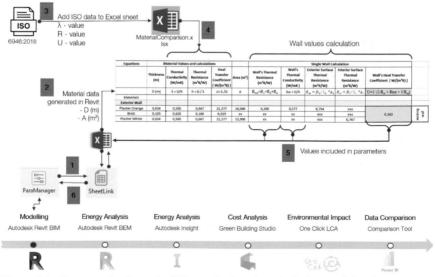

Figure 9.3: Data transfer from the ISO standard to the calculation model and to the BIM model.

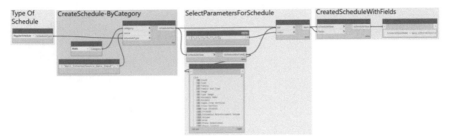

Figure 9.4: Dynamo script for the automatic generation of Schedule in the BIM model.

9.4 Case Study Building and Tested Materials with EPDs

The case study building is a single-family house with constant residential use calculated with an ideal system (i.e., no HVAC heating, ventilation, air conditioning, and cooling setting), located in Milan, Italy, and equipped with solar photovoltaic panels on the south west pitch of the roof. The test house has shading systems to protect the transparent surface from solar radiation and the retrofitting strategy includes the additional insulation of the opaque vertical and horizontal envelope (Fig. 9.5).

The baseline performance (Phase 01) is compared with the scenarios adding insulation materials (Phase 02), which are characterized and defined in their environmental impact by the Environmental Product Declarations (EPDs). According to EPD International, the Environmental Product Declaration (EPD) is shared by manufacturers to demonstrate their commitment to measuring the environmental impact of their products transparently and includes information from phases A1 to A3 (Fig. 9.6), from raw material extraction until selling for installation.

The "Building life cycle information" defines the Cradle to Grave section and the "Supplementary Information" are related to the circularity and the two sections (A+B+C+D) identify the Cradle to Cradle.

The EPDs information provided by manufacturers is verified by third parties and after the EPD can be used. Even though construction materials can come from anywhere, the EPD defines the value of transportation impact according to the availability of the product around the globe. A material with a national line of production tends to show a lower ecological footprint on the transportation phase (A4) of the building life cycle assessment, the worksite is located in the same country. The EPDs are reliable sources of information and can be used for maintenance planning, modelling, communication, approvals, and manual consultation, among others. The EPDs carry, on their written document, the information about emissions released due to its production for evaluation and also properties related to thermal behavior and allow the user to calculate the performance inside a virtual environment for simulation. It is worth noting

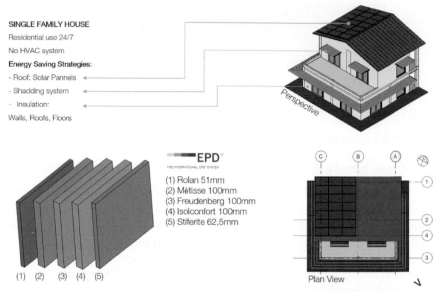

Figure 9.5: BIM model of the test house and tested insulation materials.

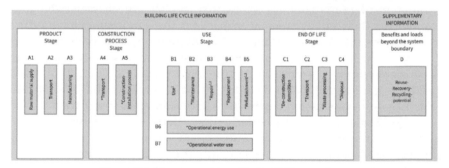

Figure 9.6: Phases considered in the LCA procedure.

as it is possible to access machine Readable EPDs. A machine readable EPD is a document that can be processed by computers and can be used to optimize digital processes due to its structure. EPD International (EPD 2022) has within its database machine-readable EPDs provided by some companies. They can be searched through databases like Environdata, EPDTurkey, Reference_data, and INDATA (INDATA 2022). The results are available online as Process Data Set or downloaded as a .xml structure data file format. An XML file is a structured data format that can be imported into Excel. The imported data can be incorporated into the BIM model using Dynamo scripts for adding value to new or existing parameters (Fig. 9.7).

Figure 9.7: Workflow for machine readable EPD to BIM.

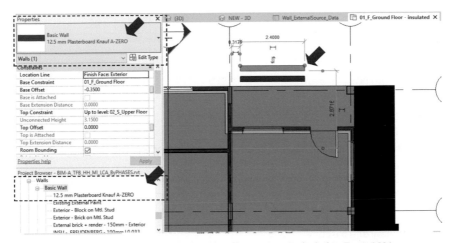

Figure 9.8: The new type created with Dynamo included in Revit 2021.

To access a machine-readable EPD a login and password are needed. Data in EPDs have issuing day and validation day, so any data retrieved by an EPD has to be reviewed from time to time to follow to continuous LCA in case of reapplication of that specific product. The XML importing process to Excel can be added to the digital model by a Dynamo script for creating a new type of wall with data from Machine Readable EPD as shown in Fig. 9.8.

This example relates to an insulation product. The data provided by the EPD can be added to BIM by the means of parameters later added to management systems for reference; it contains the number of the EPD which makes it easier to search for another kind of data, to keep building documentation up to date, etc. The machine readable EPD does not provide data about the thermal properties of the material, however, it provides detailed data about the material's environmental footprint.

9.5 Results

9.5.1 Phase 01 – Baseline Thermal Properties Calculation and Data Transfer to the Model

The estimation was performed initially for Phase 01 – Baseline and subsequently for Phase 02 – Insulation. In Table 9.2 the percentage

Table 9.2: Percentage of recycled material for the insulation materials as reported in the EPD.

Main Component		% Recycled Material
Phase 02 – insulation		
Rolan rock wool	Mineral Wool	70
Mètisse recyc. cotton	Recycled Fabric Fiber	85
Freudenberg recyc. plast.	Recycled Polystyrene PET	100
Isolconfort EPS	EPS	10
Stiferite EPS	EPS	2,7

of recycled material for each main component for a Functional Unit of 1 m² of the insolation panels is resumed.

In Table 9.3 the thermal properties calculation results are exposed.

Table 9.3: Wall thermal properties values for Phase 01 and Phase 02.

	Thickness (mm)	λ (W/mK)	R-value (m²K/W)	U-value (W/m²K)
Phase 01 – baseline				
Existing conditions	150.0	0.577	0.260	0.342
Phase 02 – insulation				
Rolan rock wool	51.0	0.037	1.646	0.331
Mètisse recyc. cotton	100.0	0.039	2.824	0.240
Freudenberg recyc. plast.	100.0	0.033	3.290	0.216
Isolconfort EPS	100.0	0.031	3.486	0.206
Stiferite EPS	62.5	0.022	3.078	0.225

These calculated values were transferred to the digital model as "Green Building Parameters" to be then used by the Building Energy Modelling (BEM) and Calculation Virtual Environments (CVEs), adopted for the energy performance calculation in the present research. The same procedure was repeated for Phase 02 – Insulation.

9.5.2 *Phase 02 – Baseline Thermal Properties Calculation and Data Inclusion into the Model*

The EPDs of the selected and tested materials for energy retrofitting provided the information for the calculation of the five insulation panels. The EPDs included the materials' thermal properties and their life cycle environmental footprint as provided by manufacturers and asserted by a third independent party, which guarantees transparency and reliability.

The selected EPD database proposed, for some specialized materials, Machine Readable EPDs to boost the digital processes as mentioned above. Unfortunately, no machine readable EPD was available for the selected insulation panels, and the data were implemented.

The next step was to retrieve the materials by EPD in the CVE for LCA, namely OneClick LCA (2022); the materials were selected in the database according to their thermal conductivity (Table 9.3) while using the OneClick LCA add-in to Revit, the family types have their materials mapped through the same EPDs. This technique permitted additional automatically implemented use on the LCA CVE.

9.5.3 Energy Demand CVE Applied for both Phase 01 and Phase 02

The BIM to BEM procedure adopted Autodesk Revit 2021 for the BIM modelling and Autodesk Insight and Green Building Studio for the building energy modeling. As the software are belonging to Autodesk software house, the workflow is completely operable, and the CVE can directly transfer the data from the digital model. The in-cloud Software-as-a-Service (SaaS) accepts the analytical model created in Autodesk Revit and it can quickly calculate parametric values of the building's Annual Energy Consumption and Life cycle Energy Consumption (Fig. 9.9).

The Annual Energy Cost was calculated for the Phase 01 – Baseline and Phase 02 – Insulation, for each insulation material, considering the Annual Energy Consumption and the cost of energy (1kW = 0.24 €). The results are summarized in Table 9.4.

Autodesk Insight for the existing building analytical evaluation:

- provides a range of options for energy improvement;
- calculates Energy Use Intensity (EUI) measured by kW/m²/yr;
- Calculates cost of consumption measured by Euros/m²/yr

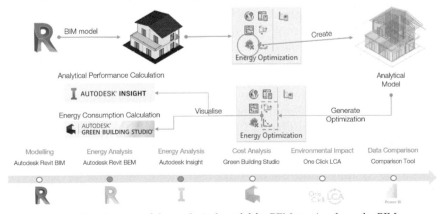

Figure 9.9: Creation of the analytical model for BEM starting from the BIM.

Table 9.4: Consumption and cost – Phase and Materials.

	Annual Energy Consumption (kW)	Annual Energy Cost (€)	Life Cycle Energy Consumption (kW)
Phase 01 – baseline			
Existing conditions	43'605	10'406	1'308'140
Phase 02 – insulation			
Rolan rock wool	21'480	5'155	644'414
Mètisse recyc. Cotton	19'923	4'781	597'698
Freudenberg recyc. Plast.	19'657	4'717	589'718
Isolconfort EPS	19'571	4'697	587'122
Stiferite EPS	19'836	4'760	595'095

9.5.4 *Photovoltaic Energy Generation CVE*

A supplementary value required for LCA alternatives for Phase 02 computation was the potential energy generation by the photovoltaic system (PV) and the portal of the European Commission PVGIS (Photovoltaic Geographical Information System) was utilized as CVE. The software as a service (SaaS) is permitted to manually input the PV system data provided by the manufacturers along with the project's geographic location and climate variables. The CVE provided detailed estimations about PV generation as "Energy Supply" and allowed to export of data files such as .csv and .json files for further elaboration. The value entered in the LCA SaaS resulted in the difference between "Energy Supply" (calculated by the PVGIS CVE) and "Energy Demand" calculated by the BEM CVE.

As introduced above, one of the key objectives of the research was to consider and simulate renewable energy production within the system-boundary by an integrated BiPV (Building Integrated Photovoltaic) system on the pitched roof. The model allowed to arrange the PV area and the solar active surface was included in the PVGIS CVE, as well as technical data supplied by the PV manufacturer. The PVGIS CVE was used to execute the calculation as the building energy demand in the existing situation of the building (Phase 01) was estimated. The results about energy supply, energy demand and exported energy are summarized, and reported in Table 9.5 for Phase 01 and Phase 02 with the insulation panels as retrofitting scenarios.

The digital model is not considering the MEP (Mechanical, Electrical, Plumbing systems) and the consumption due to electrical devices. The additional consideration of that part in the enriched model could increase

Table 9.5: Exported energy calculation results.

	Energy Supply (kWh)	Energy Demand (kWh)	Energy Demand (%)	Exported Energy (kWh)	Exported Energy (%)
Phase 01 – baseline					
Existing conditions	0.00	43'605	--	--	--
Phase 02 – insulation					
Rolan rock wool	451'696	21'480	4.76	430'216	95.5
Mètisse recyc. Cotton	451'696	19'923	4.41	431'773	95.6
Freudenberg recyc. Plast.	451'696	19'657	4.35	432'039	95.6
Isolconfort EPS	451'696	19'571	4.33	432'125	95.6
Stiferite EPS	451'696	19'836	4.39	431'860	95.2

the "energy demand" and correspondingly decrease the "exported energy" rate for each tested material. In any case, the installation of the insulation panel substantially halves the "energy demand" and as the thickness is comparable according to the thermal conductivity of the materials the comparison on this criterion in not strongly suggesting a main preference towards a material however the environmental impacts related can enlighten which could be a most conscious and environmentally aware choice based on the carbon emissions.

9.5.5 Life Cycle Assessment CVE

The tools adopted for the LCA calculation according to ISO series 14040 (BS EN ISO 14040 2006) is cloud-based SaaS, which allows a user to rent/buy/enroll in a service that delivers remote digital and high processing capability, hosting results in the web to be consulted and shared easily. The software is intended for carbon emission computation and as introduced in the methodology section is OneClick LCA. With the support of this specific SaaS, it is possible to calculate the environmental footprint of construction materials by accessing several materials databases of environmental impact reports offered by manufacturers, namely the EPDs based on ISO 14025 (ISO 14025 2006).

A Life Cycle Assessment determines the environmental impact by the means of standardized indicators. The materials manufacture procedure emits gases into the ecosystem and their impacts are evaluated based on the effects listed in Table 9.6.

The total quantity of carbon emissions is assessed through the whole asset life cycle, and it contemplates carbon emissions coming from a range of different crucial factors. The data collection for LCA calculation

Table 9.6: Environmental impacts quantified in the EPDs.

Environmental Effect	Symbol	Unit	Description
Global Warming Potential	GWP_{100}	(gCO_{2eq}/t)	Measures the increase of the concentration of greenhouse gas in the atmosphere
Stratospheric ozone depletion	ODP	$(gCFC_{11eq}/t)$	Depletion of stratospheric ozone layer increasing sun's UV-A and UV-B radiation, impacting fauna and flora
Acidification	AP	$(molH^+_{eq}/t)$	Measures the rate of water acidification, increasing the occurrence of "acid rain"
Formation of Ozone Lower Atmosphere	POCP	(gC_2H_{4eq}/t)	Impact the generation of toxic smog and causing damage to the respiratory system
Eutrophication	EP	(gO_{2eq}/t)	Increase of plants in delicate ecosystems caused by unbalanced amount of nutrients

is supported by the digital model in BIM and by the CVEs, as specified as follows:

- construction material quantification input (BIM connected by add-in) **Mandatory;**
- annual energy consumption (calculated by GBS) **Mandatory;**
- water consumption (calculated by GBS);
- constructions site operations (provided by documentation related to the building, if any);
- building area (retrieved by the BIM model) **Mandatory;**
- calculation period (in years) **Mandatory.**

The LCA computation was completed for the six scenarios, primarily for Phase 01 – Baseline, and later for Phase 02 – Insulation.

The required data input procedure is shown in Table 9.7 where the adopted software, the data retrieved or calculated, the input model, the destination in the LCA SaaS and the obtained results are organized to depict step by step the process and the data.

To calculate the LCA of Phase 01, material data was assigned from the Revit model into the LCA SaaS using an add-in made available by the company and retrieved through Autodesk Revit to map the applied materials with the LCA database options. One of the main challenges was to represent a theoretically damaged existing material employing a database where materials are coupled to their high-performance status. The solution was to map the most basic and traditional ones along the

Table 9.7: Data input for LCA Saas with specification on Input Model and results.

Software/ Documents	Data	Input Mode	Destination LCA SaaS	Result
Revit (By Phase) Digital model BIM	Material quantities (m², m³, pieces)	**Add-in** to the cloud	Building Materials	**Correct input, following mapping and classification system**
Green Building Studio (By Run) CVE/BEM	Annual Electricity Energy	Manual	Energy Consumption	**Correct, updated manually**
Green Building Studio (By Run) CVE	Annual water use (Annual, L/year)	Manual	Water Consumption Annual	**Correct, updated manually**
Non calculated	Construction site operations	Manual	Construction Site Operations	**No input**
Revit/BIM Digital model	Gross building area plan (121 m²)	Manual	Building Area	**Correct, updated manually**
Expected life of the building	Number (60 y)	Manual	Calculation Period	**Correct, updated manually**

database to establish the baseline for the subsequent comparison. The simulation of the revamping process was not considering the demolition phase. With this option, all materials contained in Phase 01 – Baseline were maintained in Phase 02 – Insulation assessment, nevertheless they were reported differently handling a reusable option in the cloud SaaS calculation setup. The LCA results are listed in Table 9.8 where the Total Material Cost (TMC), the environmental impact, the Total Use of Primary Energy (TPE), and the bio-CO_2 Storage (BioS) are the indicators. Moreover, LCA as emissions ($kgCO_2$) and as a percentage is included as required by EN 15978 (BS EN 15978 2011).

The LCA CVE offers data visualization in the shape of comparison graphs where the materials scenarios are compared to the existing situation considering the environmental impact categories listed above. The insulation materials halve the impacts and the total use of primary energy as they reduced the energy needs of the envelope increasing the thermal resistance. The energy performance in the running phase is thus crucially improved and the environmental impacts of the different materials are not dramatically diverging. The rock wool panel and the stiferite EPS have a higher impact compared to the others and the bio-CO_2 storage, which is the process of extracting bioenergy from biomass and capturing and storing the carbon, thereby removing it from the atmosphere, is on the other hand very different. The carbon in the biomass

Table 9.8: Material cost and LCA results by material and LCA calculation.

	GW				OD			Bio	
	TMC (€)	P (%)	AP (%)	EP (%)	P (%)	POCP (%)	TPE (%)	S (%)	LCA (t co$_{2e}$)	LCA (%)
Phase 01 - baseline										
Existing conditions	–	100	100	100	100	100	100	100	1370.03	100
Phase 02 - insulation										
Rolan rock wool	732.66	48.21	48.85	48.84	48.58	47.38	49.03	30.24	660.57	48.22
Mètisse recyc. cotton	435.93	44.53	45.09	45.16	44.95	43.26	45.17	11.88	610.09	44.53
Freudenberg recyc. plast.	818.64	44.21	44.74	44.83	44.79	43.02	45.17	2.19	605.71	44.21
Isolconfort EPS	1.539.87	43.86	44.26	44.24	44.09	42.45	44.47	2.19	601.03	43.87
Stiferite EPS	922.15	46.05	45.45	45.83	48.47	44.74	45.97	36.29	630.97	46.05

comes from the greenhouse gas carbon dioxide (CO_2) which is extracted from the atmosphere by the biomass when it grows. The panels with higher impacts in the other categories have a higher bio-CO_2 storage effect together with the recycled plastic.

The results of the LCA calculation demonstrate the effect of insulation addition in existing buildings and how are distributed the environmental impacts of the compared materials. The workflow adopted needs the management of a number of CVEs and interoperable paths however the possibility to include LCA in the design phase through linked SaaS, which is able to create comparison scenarios based on material choices is fascinating. LCA can be handled using data coming from the BIM database and integrated by BEM analysis and EPDs evaluation through the LCA CVE.

9.5.6 The Cognitive Layer to Enhance the LCA

The workflow described in the previous sections can be further enhanced by the addition of a cognitive layer to optimize the performance of the building over its life cycle and improve the sustainability of the technical solutions (Barni et al. 2018, Miehe et al. 2021) adopted in its renovation strategies as needed in the lifespan period ensuring at the same time an LCA evaluation to promote low carbon buildings (Chen et al. 2021). Studies have been developed about LCA oriented DT both to improve the building assessment and users' wellbeing (Ghita et al. 2021, Boje

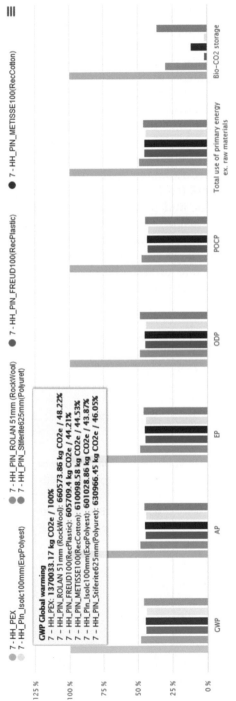

Figure 9.10: LCA, EN-15978 - All impact categories.

et al. 2021) as the inclusion of the embedded carbon and the user centered approach are nowadays core research topics. However, the presented framework is considering the operational life of the building and the embedded energy that is increasing during the building life and that is not only related to the installation during the construction site and the starting activities of the use of the building. Figure 9.11 depicts the proposed system in detail as conceived to enhance the BIM to LCA workflow and extend the suitability of DT (Menassa 2021, Naneva 2022) that can control and define the materials and options to improve energy efficiency and environmental impacts. The approach entails the use of a network of sensors based on Internet of Things (IoT) technology (Riedelsheimer et al. 2021) capable of monitoring various building parameters (such as electricity and energy consumption), the type of use by users, and parameters relating to the state of the environment surrounding the building (such as temperature, relative humidity, irradiation, and weather parameters) that can influence the state of the building or its components in real time (or nearly so) (for example windows, insulation layer, state of the photovoltaic system, state of the roof, condensation in the envelope layers and on the indoor

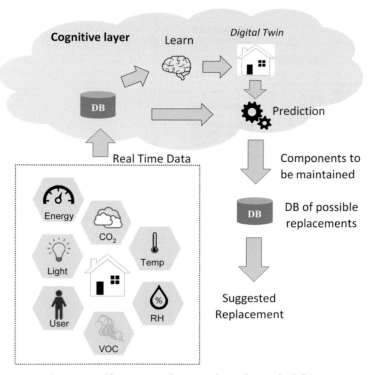

Figure 9.11: The cognitive layer used to enhance the LCA.

surfaces). These sensors do not have a high acquisition frequency because they must monitor the state of deterioration of the building and its components throughout the building's useful life. As a result, these sensors must be optimized to reduce the amount of data transmitted and their transmission frequency, thereby reducing the amount of energy that these devices require and ensuring a useful life of the sensors that is comparable to the life of the building, thus avoiding continuous and time expensive maintenance that would invalidate the benefits brought about by their use.

Furthermore, communication systems should be used, such as those provided by Low Power Wide Area Network (LP-WAN) protocols such as LoRaWAN (Rizzi et al. 2019), which allow for broad connectivity (geographically) by utilizing transmission bands. Industrial Scientific and Medical (ISM) systems and thus not licensed, can significantly reduce the management costs that other transmission technologies, such as 4G or 5G, inevitably have. In fact, these technologies are incompatible, both financially and in terms of energy consumption, with monitoring applications that last tens of years, such as the proposed approach's monitoring campaigns for that reason a review of the applicable and suitable systems and their performance has been performed.

Data generated by sensors installed within the building or on its components (such as windows, insulation system, roof, etc.) can be transmitted to remote data collection systems, as shown in Fig. 9.11. Data is collected in remote databases using appropriate data gathering technologies, such as time series databases (Rinaldi et al. 2019), which are enhanced for data collection from IoT sensors. In order to reduce the problems associated with managing the privacy of user data collected near their homes, sensor data is anonymized and aggregated in Key Performance Indicators (KPIs) in order to eliminate any problem of non-proper data use.

The cognitive level works by utilizing the data collected by the IoT sensors network installed in the building in order to recreate, additionally using information included in the BIM digital model of the building, the so-called Digital Twin of the construction (Pater and Stadnicka 2021, Borjigin et al. 2022), i.e., a digitized model of the building and all of its components, which is used to maintain information regarding the state of the asset instant by instant (Brunone et al. 2021, Li et al. 2020). The DT gives the possibility to verify whether the building behavior, as shown and described by the data provided by the IoT sensors network, presents discrepancies with respect to the behavior of the ideal model designed and represented through the digital model by utilizing the information included in the BIM and providing data exchange between the digitized model of the building and the analytical dashboards for the asset management. The foreseen DT hinged on the green BIM concept (Maltese et al. 2017, Chen et al. 2017) can support sustainable evaluation (Shukra and Zhou 2020, Ansah et al. 2019) and double check when and how the components have a divergent thermal behavior that affects the building. The need for retrofit at the end of life of some components could be seen as not only a step when additional embedded energy is burdening the building energy balance nevertheless the opportunity to install new materials which can reduce the environmental impact improving the whole energy performance, reducing the energy demand, and add a lower quantity of embodied energy. The DT can perform the LCA evaluation of the new components and the possible retrofitting scenarios, as shown in the previous sections, and promote the installation of beneficial technological solutions. Radio-frequency identification (RFID)-technology can be used to organize the DT platform designed for real-time asset tracking in construction and the built environment. Based on the RFID-based digital twin, it is possible to envision an LCA evaluation for the building as the project of the LCA database is consistent with the granularity of the BIM model, enabling a bi-directional automatic data exchange between the two databases.

In the proposed framework, the cognitive system can thus identify deviations in the current behavior of the system compared to the expected performance, and therefore it can identify the components within the building that require potential interventions to restore the building's expected behavior. For example, a progressive increase in the energy required to heat the building from year to year, after normalizing the energy consumption based on the environmental conditions and any variations in the user's usage of the building (parameters that can be monitored or inferred from appropriate IoT sensors), can be attributed to progressive problems in the quality of the building envelope or thermal insulation, requiring technical intervention. Moreover, sensors to provide information about temperature and humidity inside the layer of the wall and the insulation panels can be strongly beneficial in defining the phenomena that are taking place in the hygrothermal conditions of the envelope. If the repairs are ineffective in restoring the building's optimal operating conditions, the damaged components must be thus replaced, or in some cases, the useful life of the product can have a specific date and a planned maintenance program can be linked to the information included in the BIM model and provide alerts when the useful life is coming at its end.

When the replacement is the procedure that can amend the energy deviations, after identifying the components that require to be substituted (as shown in Fig. 9.11), the system will automatically suggest some replacement options for the damaged component.

These alternative components can be chosen based on various cost items, such as minimizing overall consumption, minimizing costs, or minimizing the impact that these new components and the disposal of the replaced one have on the overall LCA calculation (Wang and Wang 2019).

The component is chosen by drawing information from an appropriate LCA database, which must contain up-to-date information on the impact of the various technological solutions available. Furthermore, the various disposal solutions that this component may have must be factored into the overall LCA calculation and they can be supported by the RFID tracking technology (useful in LCA phases A, B, and C Fig. 9.6). Additionally, the blockchain technology can be exploited to validate and notarize the component disposal phase or its new application as a second-hand raw material in a new construction site (LCA phase D Fig. 9.6). It should be noted that this approach allows for the detection of deteriorated building components even before their useful life (a BIM parameter) has expired. In this manner, it is possible to predictably identify building components before they cause a significant loss in building performance, thereby maintaining the building's performance unchanged and promoting predictive maintenance procedures and replacements to maintain an optimized building performance in the running phase. The integration in the DT of the mechanisms of the green building assessment (Ilhan and Yaman 2016) and LCA evaluation could have a key role in boosting and supporting the design and the refurbishment of LC-ZEB buildings and augment the potential of the DT application on the sustainability asset evaluation in the life cycle. The BIM-based workflow for the assessment (Guo et al. 2021, Siddiqui et al. 2009) is crucial in creating an interoperable path and as mentioned to increase the automation of the process as the use of machine readable EPDs will be processed to create the BIM parameters. The cognitive DT can implement the LCA calculation associated with different materials and products selected by artificial intelligence (AI) recommendation algorithms and tested by a simulator to achieve a comparison of LCA for alternative options. In the LCA calculation, first, the embedded carbon of the panels can be compared (LCA Phase A), and subsequently, the energy performance in the running phase can be simulated to be added to the LCA comprehensive value (LCA phase B). When the replacement is actuated the disposal phase is considered and tracked saving the information as immutable data (LCA phase C). The option for the panels' recyclability can finally be simulated and proposed (LCA phase D). Assuming the different stakeholder points of view (Abdelaal and Guo 2022), it is possible to underline as for the owner of the building it could be a key advantage to proceed with an LCA rationale with important outcomes in terms of cost effectiveness, energy saving and, global impact. For the public administration, a similar approach can enhance the public building stock and calculate the environmental impacts that can be avoided by technological choices simulated in the DT.

9.6 Discussion

The process of a virtual model developed with BIM methodology can open many ways to enhance sustainable and green buildings although the interoperability of the workflows needs fine tuning processes and improvements (Huang et al. 2021, Solla et al. 2016). The BIM model in the research is the basic step to organize a wider approach to cognitive digital twin for LCA analysis (Wei and Chen 2020) and upgrading of the building in the life cycle to achieve energy saving and reduced environmental impacts. In the presented research work the digital model allowed the creation of the main database to be exported in the Calculation Virtual Environments to check materials for retrofitting and building performance estimation. In Phase 01 envelope components (i.e., walls, floors, and roofs) both as one multilayered element and with attached independent layers were modeled. The challenge associated with modelling engaged the calculation method of thermal properties with separate layers, when, in an actual survey the complete existing structure would be evaluated, and the fixing methodologies discussed.

The finest approach to obtain thermal results from an existing building would be to consider the multi-layered element, since the thermal value added was a type of parameter in the digital model. In Phase 02, an existing element and the added insulation type have the thermal values summed up, increasing thermal resistance, and promoting a systemic effect.

The generated data by calculation PVGIS was included in the LCA SaaS manually as none of the exported data files (json nor .csv files) were compatible with the upload in the LCA CVE. The solution adopted was to manually implement them in every design option. A further option could be to deploy programming skills to transfer this data. The investigation was completed with the tools provided by public and private suppliers, which implies that they are continuously revised. Possible improvements have the potential to slightly adjust the tested workflow. For example, the LCA SaaS in the version employed during the study calculation phase (v2.2.0) did not allow saving material mapping. The material's EPDs data could be incorporated using the authoring tool Revit Architecture. In the updated version (v.4.0.2) of the add-in, it was then possible to enable the material mapping and save the data improving the interoperability path, allowing time saving in avoiding the rework and pursuing higher reliability of the results. The cognitive DT framework includes the deployment of an IoT sensor network affecting both the indoor environment and outdoor environmental parameters. The monitoring of the users' behavior is functional to infer information about the building behavior which can be possibly enhanced by AI applications. Real time data (e.g., weather related data and users' data) and more static data (e.g., RFID for materials data collection) could be combined to define a platform where the DT can detect anomalies and can promote the replacement of deteriorated materials to preserve energy efficiency and users' comfort. The embedded energy incorporated in the new materials and the disposal of the replaced elements can be mapped and adopted to control the LCA efficiency of the building in the life cycle identifying the optimized solution according to KPIs oriented to lower GWP impacts. In future cities where renovation strategies are mandatory in the life cycle, a supporting cognitive DT for LCA will shift the paradigm from nZEB operational efficiency to a comprehensive LC-ZEB approach to extend efficiency in the life cycle.

9.7 Conclusion

Fostering a BIM-based cognitive digital twin for refurbishment interventions relies crucially on the quality of the existing gathered data, if possible, extracted by site inspections. The collected data turn out to be valuable when it is straightforward to reach and extract them, both tasks are supported by modelling with BIM methodology. Furthermore, the execution of the comparison phases turned data extraction more assertive and effortlessly checked, creating the scenario for a recommendation algorithm that can select materials to be proposed in the retrofitting project.

The calculation of the thermal properties for each material that can be implemented in a DT platform in the cognitive framework, is the main challenge and the research demonstrated the necessity of a multi-skilled team to accurately handle the data (i.e., design expertise, building physic expertise, material expertise, architectural expertise). The treatment of data in Cloud services (namely SaaS) proved to be essential and enabled to quickly check and correct them, when required to shape the materials scenarios and the energy performance changes related.

Additionally, combining paths to check the results locally or online, eased their usability. Nonetheless, they depend on service accessibility and readiness if data are to be saved and retrieved online.

The BIM methodology offers solutions that entail many suppliers, who upgrade their instruments regularly. It is worth to noting as there is the option to involve coding abilities and services to link massive amounts of data generated by computational calculation, even so, it similarly demands specific expertise to provide smooth solutions for complex and regularly revised services.

The use of the LCA CVE to estimate the environmental impacts of the existing situation of the case study has a degree of uncertainty when mapping degraded materials performance are concerned as in the database high performance options are included and retrieved. The comparison of the materials to increase insulation and thus energy performance of the building, can be smoothly performed by the simulator (that can be run by the DT platform) and the results trailed the expectations where the differences between the impacts related to each material were known according to the composition of the elements.

The LCA CVE returned an interactive and cooperative method of explaining the outcomes of the calculations. The tool exposed the correlated results to the quantity of the materials in many interactive charts, offering a clear awareness of the Greenhouse Gases (GHG) Indicator and suggested alternatives to decrease the impact. This mechanism can be reproduced and enhanced by AI systems in the cognitive DT platform for managing LCA.

The combination of CVEs and BIM methodology turned out to be a dynamic and evolving process able to cornerstone the creation of a DT for LCA. It is critical to constantly update the databases to improve results striving for a trustworthy simulation to be part of the cognitive layer of the DT.

Finally, the proposed framework revealed how to structure the simulation layer and the usability of the CVEs to achieve the planned research targets.

The suggested methodology involves a certain level of automation that will be further investigated stemming from the digital modeling tool and ending up in the energy calculation environments. To deal with several data sources an organized and systematic sequence for the allocation of results toward comparative goals is paramount.

The virtual replica of the building required reasonable development to achieve accurate results from LCA CVE and the reliability of the data for the DT for LCA is crucial to increase the life cycle efficiency of the buildings. Additionally, automation of data manipulation processes is essential for data comparison and material recommendation provision.

Existing buildings with damaged structures, when renovated require close monitoring and checking to preserve performance and users' safety and wellbeing. The cognitive DT structure for monitoring and checking to fine tune maintenance planning can likewise be provided by deploying BIM methodology executed for building operations and management tasks for the asset, relying on the gathered accurate data. The Cognitive DT for LCA will be a master topic in the future evaluation of cities' circularity, resilience, and digital transition to support sustainable ways of living.

References

Abdelaal, F. and Guo, B.H. 2022. Stakeholders' perspectives on BIM and LCA for green buildings. *Journal of Building Engineering*, 48: 103931.

Ansah, M.K., Chen, X., Yang, H., Lu, L. and Lam, P.T. 2019. A review and outlook for integrated BIM application in green building assessment. *Sustainable Cities and Society*, 48: 101576.

Barni, A., Fontana, A., Menato, S., Sorlini, M. and Canetta, L. 2018, September. Exploiting the digital twin in the assessment and optimization of sustainability performances. *In 2018 International Conference on Intelligent Systems (IS)*. IEEE, pp. 706–713.

BS EN ISO 14040:2006+A1:2020 Environmental management. Life cycle assessment. Principles and framework ISO 14025:2006 Environmental labels and declarations — Type III environmental declarations — Principles and procedures.

BS EN 15978:2011 Sustainability of construction works. Assessment of environmental performance of buildings. Calculation method.

Boje, C., Marvuglia, A., Menacho, Á.J.H., Kubicki, S., Guerriero, A., Navarrete, T. and Benetto, E. 2021, October. A pilot using a Building Digital Twin for LCA-based human health monitoring. *In Proc. of the Conference CIB W78, 2021*: 11–15.

Borjigin, A.O.B., Sresakoolchai, J., Kaewunruen, S. and Hammond, J. 2022. Digital twin aided sustainability assessment of modern light rail infrastructures. *Frontiers in Built Environment*, 8: 796388.

Brunone, F., Cucuzza, M., Imperadori, M. and Vanossi, A. 2021. From cognitive buildings to digital twin: the frontier of digitalization for the management of the built environment. *In Wood Additive Technologies*. Springer, Cham, pp. 81–95.

Bueno, C. and Fabricio, M.M. 2018. Comparative analysis between a complete LCA study and results from a BIM-LCA plug-in. *Automation in Construction*, 90: 188–200.

Chen, C., Zhao, Z., Xiao, J. and Tiong, R. 2021. A conceptual framework for estimating building embodied carbon based on digital twin technology and life cycle assessment. *Sustainability*, 13(24): 13875.

Chen, C.J., Chen, S.Y., Li, S.H. and Chiu, H.T. 2017. Green BIM-based building energy performance analysis. *Computer-Aided Design and Applications*, 14(5): 650–660.

Costardi, L., Tagliabue, L.C., Hamdy, M. and Dotelli, G. 2021. LCA evaluation and energy performance of a housing building in different technological scenarios. *Journal of Physics: Conference Series, Volume 2042, CISBAT 2021 Carbon-neutral Cities - Energy Efficiency and Renewables in the Digital Era* 8–10 September 2021, EPFL Lausanne, Switzerland.

Dall'O, G., Belli, V., Brolis, M., Mozzi, I. and Fasano, M. 2013. Nearly zero-energy buildings of the lombardy region (Italy), a case study of high-energy performance buildings. *Energies*, 6: 3506–3527. 10.3390/en6073506.

Decreto del Presidente della Repubblica 26 agosto 1993, n. 412 Regolamento recante norme per la progettazione, l'installazione, l'esercizio e la manutenzione degli impianti termici degli edifici ai fini del contenimento dei consumi di energia, in attuazione dell'art. 4, comma 4, della legge 9 gennaio 1991, n. 10.

De Wolf, C., Pomponi, F. and Moncaster, A. 2017. Measuring embodied carbon dioxide equivalent of buildings: A review and critique of current industry practice. *Energy and Buildings*, 140: 68–80, ISSN 0378-7788. https://doi.org/10.1016/j.enbuild.2017.01.075.

EPBD. Implementation of EPBD in Italy. [Online] Available at: https://epbd-ca.eu/ca-outcomes/outcomes-2015-2018/book-2018/countries/italy.

EPD Internationl database. 2022. https://data.environdec.com/processList.xhtml?stock=Environdata.

Ghita, M., Siham, B., Hicham, M. and Griguer, H. 2021. Digital twins based LCA and ISO 20140 for smart and sustainable manufacturing systems. *In Sustainable Intelligent Systems*. Springer, Singapore, pp. 101–145.

Guo, K., Li, Q., Zhang, L. and Wu, X. 2021. BIM-based green building evaluation and optimization: A case study. *Journal of Cleaner Production*, 320: 128824.

Hernandez, P. and Kenny, P. 2008. Defining zero energy buildings—A life cycle perspective. *In PLEA 2008–25th Conference on Passive and Low Energy Architecture, Dublin, 22nd to 24th October 2008*. University College Dublin.

Hernandez, P. and Kenny, P. 2010. From net energy to zero energy buildings: Defining life cycle zero energy buildings (LC-ZEB). *Energy and Buildings*, 42(6): 815–821.

Huang, B., Lei, J., Ren, F., Chen, Y., Zhao, Q., Li, S. and Lin, Y. 2021. Contribution and obstacle analysis of applying BIM in promoting green buildings. *Journal of Cleaner Production*, 278: 123946.

Ilhan, B. and Yaman, H. 2016. Green building assessment tool (GBAT) for integrated BIM-based design decisions. *Automation in Construction*, 70: 26–37.

International Organization for Standardization. 2017. ISO 6946-2017 Building components and building elements - Thermal resistance and thermal transmittance - Calculation methods. ISO

LEGGE 3 agosto 2013, n. 90 Conversione, con modificazioni, del decreto-legge 4 giugno 2013, n. 63 Disposizioni urgenti per il recepimento della Direttiva 2010/31/UE del Parlamento europeo e del Consiglio del 19 maggio 2010, sulla prestazione energetica nell'edilizia per la definizione delle procedure d'infrazione avviate dalla Commissione europea, nonché altre disposizioni in materia di coesione sociale (G.U. n. 181 del 3 agosto 2013).

Li, L., Mao, C., Sun, H., Yuan, Y. and Lei, B. 2020. Digital twin driven green performance evaluation methodology of intelligent manufacturing: Hybrid model based on fuzzy rough-sets AHP, multistage weight synthesis, and PROMETHEE II. *Complexity*, 2020: 3853925 (source: www.scopus.com).

Lobaccaro, G., Wiberg, A.H., Ceci, G., Manni, M., Lolli, N. and Berardi, U. 2018. Parametric design to minimize the embodied GHG emissions in a ZEB. *Energy and Buildings*, 167: 106–123.

Lu, Y. and Huang, Z. 2019. Definition and Design of Zero Energy Buildings. 10.5772/intechopen.80708.

Maltese, S., Tagliabue, L.C., Cecconi, F.R., Pasini, D., Manfren, M. and Ciribini, A.L. 2017. Sustainability assessment through green BIM for environmental, social and economic efficiency. *Procedia Engineering*, 180: 520–530.

Menassa, C.C. 2021. From BIM to digital twins: A systematic review of the evolution of intelligent building representations in the AEC-FM industry. *Journal of Information Technology in Construction (ITcon)*, 26(5): 58–83.

Miehe, R., Waltersmann, L., Sauer, A. and Bauernhansl, T. 2021. Sustainable production and the role of digital twins–Basic reflections and perspectives. *Journal of Advanced Manufacturing and Processing*, 3(2): e10078.

Monticelli, C., Re Cecconi, F., Pansa, G. and Mainini, A. 2011. Influence of degradation and service life of construction materials on the embodied energy and the energy requirements of buildings. *XII DBMC International Conference on Durability of Building Materials and Components*, 4: 1–8.

Naneva, A. 2022. greenBIM, a BIM-based LCA integration using a circular approach based on the example of the Swiss sustainability standard Minergie-ECO. *In E3S Web of Conferences* (Vol. 349, p. 10002). EDP Sciences.

OneClick LCA software, https://www.oneclicklca.com/.

Pater, J. and Stadnicka, D. 2021. Towards digital twins development and implementation to support sustainability—Systematic literature review. *Management and Production Engineering Review*, 13.

Potrč Obrecht, T., Röck, M., Hoxha, E. and Passer, A. 2020. BIM and LCA integration: A systematic literature review. *Sustainability*, 12(14): 5534.

Riedelsheimer, T., Gogineni, S. and Stark, R. 2021. Methodology to develop Digital Twins for energy efficient customizable IoT-Products. *Procedia CIRP*, 98: 258–263.

Rinaldi, S., Bonafini, F., Ferrari, P., Flammini, A., Sisinni, E. and Bianchini, D. 2019. Impact of data model on performance of time series database for internet of things applications. *IEEE International Instrumentation and Measurement Technology Conference (I2MTC)*, *Auckland*, New Zealand, May 20–23, 2019, pp. 1212–1217, ISSN 2642-2077, ISBN 978-1-5386-3460-8, DOI 10.1109/I2MTC.2019.8827164.

Ritzen Michiel, J., Haagen, T., Rovers, R., Vroon, Z.A.E.P. and Geurts, C.P.W. 2016. Environmental impact evaluation of energy saving and energy generation: Case study for two Dutch dwelling types. *Building and Environment*, 108: 73–84.

Rizzi, M., Depari, A., Ferrari, P., Flammini, A., Rinaldi, S. and Sisinni, E. 2019. Synchronization uncertainty versus power efficiency in LoRaWAN networks. *IEEE Trans. Instrumentation and Measurement*, April, 2019, Vol. 68, N. 4, pp. 1101–1111, ISSN 0018-9456, DOI 10.1109/TIM.2018.2859639.

Sartori, I., Napolitano, A. and Voss, K. 2012. Net-zero energy buildingss: A consistent definition framework. *Energy and Buildings*, 48: 220–232. Doi:10.1016/j.enbuild.2012.01.032.

Sesana, M.M. and Salvalai, G. 2013. Overview on life cycle methodologies and economic feasibility for nZEBs. *Building and Environment*, 67: 211–216.

Shukra, Z.A. and Zhou, Y. 2020. Holistic green BIM: A scientometrics and mixed review. *Engineering, Construction and Architectural Management*, 28(9): 2273–2299.

Siddiqui, M.Z., Pearce, A.R., Ku, K., Langar, S., Ahn, Y.H. and Jacocks, K. 2009, May. Green BIM approaches to architectural design for increased sustainability. *In Proceedings of the International Conference on Construction Engineering and Management/Project Management*, pp. 27–30.

Sobhkhiz, S., Taghaddos, H., Rezvani, M. and Ramezanianpour, A.M. 2021. Utilization of semantic web technologies to improve BIM-LCA applications. *Automation in Construction*, 130: 103842.

Solla, M., Ismail, L.H. and Yunus, R. 2016. Investigation on the potential of integrating BIM into green building assessment tools. *ARPN Journal of Engineering and Applied Sciences*, 11(4): 2412–2418.

Umeda, Y., Ota, J., Shirafuji, S., Kojima, F., Saito, M., Matsuzawa, H. and Sukekawa, T. 2020. Exercise of digital kaizen activities based on 'digital triplet' concept. *Procedia Manufacturing*, 45: 325–330.

Wang, X.V. and Wang, L. 2019. Digital twin-based WEEE recycling, recovery and remanufacturing in the background of Industry 4.0. *International Journal of Production Research*, 57(12): 3892–3902.

Wei, T. and Chen, Y. 2020. Green building design based on BIM and value engineering. *Journal of Ambient Intelligence and Humanized Computing*, 11(9): 3699–3706.

Wiik, M.K., Fufa, S.M., Kristjansdottir, T. and Andresen, I. 2018. Lessons learnt from embodied GHG emission calculations in zero emission buildings (ZEBs) from the Norwegian ZEB research centre. *Energy and Buildings*, 165: 25–34.

Index

3D 3, 39, 40, 46, 49, 52, 53, 57, 60, 87, 90, 93, 105, 111, 112, 117, 159
3D printing 3

A

access 24, 27, 40, 51, 56, 57, 94, 102, 128–130, 159–162, 164, 167, 172, 186, 187
accountability 41, 42, 51, 60, 109
actuators 70, 82
adaptability 32
administrators 14, 31
AEC 2, 3, 20, 25, 35, 53, 54, 107, 177, 178, 180
Agent-based simulations 167, 169, 174, 175
air conditioning 2, 133, 147, 185
algorithms 6–10, 15, 29, 30, 43, 44, 57, 66, 67, 70–76, 79, 81, 84, 90, 132, 134–139, 145, 146, 148, 149, 152, 181, 199, 201
Analytics 5, 15, 27, 29, 33, 40, 50, 66, 68, 70, 71, 74, 75, 161
analytics-for-design 33
analyze 5, 7, 15, 69, 125
anomaly detection 5, 74, 75
application layer 33, 58
architecture 1, 2, 12–15, 24, 25, 31–36, 39, 44, 47, 48, 51–53, 67, 72–74, 76, 79, 81, 107, 113, 115, 117, 158, 180, 181, 183, 200
Architecture Engineering Construction and Operation (AECO) 1
artificial bee colony 7, 8
Artificial Intelligence (AI) 3, 6–10, 15, 16, 22, 26, 32, 33, 39–44, 50, 51, 54–57, 61, 65–71, 73–76, 81, 103, 107, 158, 159, 181, 199, 201, 202
asset 5, 6, 16, 21, 31, 33, 45, 47, 59, 60, 65–67, 69, 74–76, 87, 102–105, 114, 117, 140, 159, 160, 178, 182, 191, 197–199, 202
Associative Cognitive Digital Twin 23

augmented 27, 30, 39, 43, 49, 56, 163, 178
Augmented Reality 39, 43, 49
authentication 47, 60
automation 1, 3, 8, 25, 26, 29, 44, 57, 66, 142, 166, 199, 202
autonomous feedback 3
Autonomy capability 26
avatar 41, 42, 44, 46, 47, 49, 52–55, 57, 58, 60, 171

B

Basic Formal Ontology 11
behavioral model 4, 5
benefits 14, 15, 43, 50, 55, 102, 103, 105, 109–112, 114, 116, 117, 162, 165, 174, 175, 180, 182, 197
Big Data 3, 8, 13, 15, 32, 40, 48, 71, 73
Big Data Value Association 32
Blockchain 8, 14, 39–42, 44–48, 50–53, 57, 61, 101, 103, 104, 107–109, 111–117, 199
broadcast network measurements 58
building assets 65, 66, 76
Building Automation Systems (BAS) 66, 142
Building components 2, 112, 199
building facilities 65–67, 70, 76
Building installations 67, 75, 76
Building Lifecycle Management (BLM) 34, 35
building operation 65, 202
built environment 3, 74, 75, 101–109, 116, 117, 130, 159, 160, 175, 178, 198

C

capabilities 2, 14, 21–27, 29, 30, 32, 51, 69, 73, 74, 76, 82, 94, 104, 173
carbon footprint 191

Case Study 36, 86, 117, 127, 132, 137, 152,
        160, 166–170, 175, 180, 181, 183, 185, 202
causes of failures 67, 68
CDTs 5, 14, 23–25, 28–30, 33–35
CDTsBLM 34
challenges 2, 3, 5, 8, 11, 14, 16, 17, 30, 35,
        36, 39, 50, 54, 57, 59, 65–67, 70, 79, 81,
        112, 116, 117, 136, 159, 161, 162, 178, 192,
        200, 201
classification 3, 9, 71, 106, 107, 145, 146,
        180, 193
Classification models 71
Cloud Computing 1, 13, 14, 41, 42, 48
cloud services 42, 201
cloud/fog/edge computing 13, 16
clusters 7–9
cognition capabilities 21, 26
Cognition capability 24
cognition-driven knowledge 82, 94
Cognitive 1, 4–6, 11, 15, 16, 20–33, 35, 73,
        76, 79–86, 94, 142, 143, 160, 177, 194,
        196–202
cognitive capability 11, 28, 29, 35
cognitive computing 1, 15, 16, 22, 82
cognitive intelligence 80–83
cognitive modular production 80–83, 94
cognitive production methods 81
cognitive systems 11, 23, 198
cognitive twins 5, 6, 23–25, 33
COGNITWIN 25, 32, 33
collective space 172
comfortable 3, 138, 139
communication 2, 8, 15, 24, 27, 40, 48, 51,
        54, 55, 70, 83, 91–93, 95, 105, 124, 168,
        169, 175, 185, 197
communication channel 2, 93
communications & control systems 8
complex 4, 5, 8, 9, 11, 13, 20–22, 24, 27, 29,
        30, 33, 35, 36, 56, 57, 66, 71, 72, 80, 82,
        88, 95, 96, 134, 173, 201
complex systems 11, 21, 22, 27, 29, 30, 35,
        36, 88
component 1, 2, 11, 14, 20–24, 28–31, 35,
        48, 49, 52, 54, 61, 65, 67–69, 73, 80, 85,
        87–89, 94, 95, 102, 104–106, 109, 110, 112,
        125, 126, 130, 173, 180, 181, 188, 196–200
computation methodology 82
computational approaches 5
computer readable 6
computer services 3
computer vision 7, 9, 41–43, 51, 55–57, 61,
        129

concepts 4, 7, 13, 14, 16, 20, 22–24, 26–28,
        30, 32, 34, 36, 53, 55, 58, 66, 68, 69, 82,
        102–107, 109, 113, 123, 125, 152, 159,
        178–180, 198
condition assessment 9
condition monitoring 29, 33, 87
condition-based maintenance 68
connected edges 12
Construction 4.0 1–4, 8, 16, 20, 158, 176
construction automation 3
construction industry 3, 4, 10, 15, 101–104,
        107, 108, 116, 117, 158
construction performance 2, 21, 102, 106,
        108
Construction projects 2, 21, 102, 106, 108
construction sites 3, 193, 196, 199
Content Creation 40, 42, 49, 58
content production 41, 59
Continuous Dynamic Transformation 4
Continuous evolving 26
control 2, 3, 5, 8, 25, 32, 42, 56, 69, 80–82, 88,
        94, 112, 123–126, 130, 132, 142, 147, 148,
        152, 173, 179, 183, 196, 201
conventional mobile network performance
        parameters 58
Convolutional neural networks (CNN) 43,
        84
corrective 67, 68
Corrective maintenance 67, 68
correlation 3, 7, 83
customer service 160
CYB 47
cyber components 1, 2
cyber systems 1
cyberinfrastructure 2
Cyber-physical Production System
        (CPPS) 79, 80, 84–86, 94, 95
cyber-physical systems (CPS) 1, 2, 3, 16,
        79, 80
cybersecurity systems 12
Cybex 47

D

data 1–9, 11–16, 20–23, 26, 27, 29–36, 40,
        42–44, 48–53, 56–58, 60, 65–76, 80–96,
        102–115, 117, 123–131, 133, 135, 136,
        141–143, 145–149, 151, 159, 161, 162,
        164–166, 168, 169, 174, 175, 179–184,
        186–194, 197–202
data captured 68, 75
data distribution 70, 107

data exchange 1, 14, 197, 198
data fading 3
data fusion 80–83, 94
data management 2, 22, 56, 65, 179
data mining 8, 34, 82
data science 7, 69
data security 14, 57
data synchronization 89, 90
Data verification 44, 57
data-driven 6, 13, 21, 30, 33, 34, 70
dataset 9, 71, 72, 75, 127, 135, 136, 145, 146, 149
decentralized 14, 40, 44–48, 50–52, 59
Decentralized Exchange 45, 47, 50
Decentralized finance 46
Decentralized infrastructure 52
decision making 3, 5, 6, 8, 10, 15, 23, 25–27, 30, 33, 35, 36, 43, 56, 69, 73–75, 80–82, 102, 105, 106, 110, 111, 114, 117, 124–126, 137, 182
deep learning (DL) 2, 6, 7, 21, 42, 43, 50, 57, 70, 72, 73, 82
deep neural networks 43
defensive systems 31
DeFi 46, 47, 50
Descriptive Ontology for Linguistic and Cognitive Engineering (DOLCE) 11
design, construction, and operation 2, 4
design-for-analytics 33
detection 5, 7–9, 26, 29, 30, 60, 65, 66, 68, 70, 74–76, 199
device 6, 13, 14, 23, 33, 40, 42, 48, 49, 54, 56–58, 60, 66, 69, 70, 74, 81–85, 104, 109, 112, 114, 115, 123, 142, 169, 190, 197
DEX 47, 50
Digital 1–6, 8, 9, 13–17, 20–24, 26–29, 31, 33, 34, 39–42, 46, 47, 49–56, 58–61, 65, 66, 68, 69, 73, 76, 79, 80, 83, 84, 86, 87, 95, 101–106, 109–117, 123, 125, 126, 158, 159, 169, 175–177, 179–184, 186–193, 197, 198, 200–202
digital entities 56
digital replica 5, 73, 125
digital representation 9, 22, 23, 27, 28, 31, 52, 58, 102, 159
digital technologies 169
digital transformation 4, 8, 16
digital twin (DT) 1–6, 8, 13, 15, 16, 20–25, 27–31, 33, 35, 36, 39–41, 49, 51–54, 60, 65, 66–69, 73–76, 79–81, 86, 87, 101, 103–105, 107, 109–117, 158, 159, 175–177, 179–181, 194, 196–202

digital virtual environment 61
digitalization 1, 3, 9, 15
Distributed Ledger Technologies (DLT) 14, 15, 103
distributed ledger technology (DLT) 14, 16, 103
distributed networks 41
diversified 44
domain 3, 5, 7, 11, 12, 15, 21, 22, 24, 31, 69, 89, 93, 102, 107, 108, 116
domain ontologies 11, 12
domain-level reference ontologies 12
drivers 55, 159
dynamic 4, 5, 8, 10, 22, 23, 27, 29–31, 33, 43, 60, 80, 82, 87, 88, 95, 96, 112, 125–128, 148, 159, 168, 171, 173, 202
dynamic design-time 5

E

ecosystem 15, 16, 24, 40–44, 47, 48, 50, 55, 58, 60, 61, 159, 191, 192
Edge 2–4, 12–16, 24, 39, 40, 42, 46, 50, 54, 55, 57, 58, 61, 75
edge devices 14, 40, 42, 54, 57
efficiency 3, 9, 10, 15, 42, 49, 54, 65, 67, 69, 75, 76, 86, 105, 133, 166, 178, 179, 181, 182, 196, 201, 202
elements 4, 20, 20, 23, 24, 27, 28, 32, 59, 69, 93, 95, 106, 171, 178, 200–202
emerging trends 4
end-to-end 3, 9, 46
energy consumption 10, 67, 69, 73, 75, 84, 85, 105, 110, 124, 132, 133, 137–139, 152, 180, 189, 190, 192, 193, 196–198
energy-efficient 3, 110
engineering system modeling 2
Enhanced Cognitive Twin (ECT) 6
entities 11, 12, 20, 21, 23, 27, 28, 31, 45, 51, 54, 56, 59, 69, 73, 84, 94, 174
environment 3, 14, 35, 40, 43–45, 48–50, 53, 54, 56, 57, 59, 61, 69, 74, 75, 80, 81, 83, 88, 89, 101–105, 108, 109, 116, 117, 123–126, 129–134, 139–142, 147–152, 159, 160, 163, 169, 170, 173, 175, 178, 185, 196, 198, 201
environmental data 3, 123, 126, 131, 151
estimation 5, 10, 57, 124, 127–129, 131, 141, 148, 187, 190, 200
event of failures 67
expert systems 6–8
exploratory data analysis 72
extended reality 3, 41, 55

F

FACTLOG 33
forecasts 10, 81, 88
framework 5, 6, 11, 12, 16, 17, 22, 23, 25,
    31, 33, 34, 36, 44, 60, 66–68, 70, 73–76,
    83, 86, 87, 92, 95, 103, 104, 107, 109, 110,
    112–117, 123, 125, 127, 141, 142, 145, 146,
    150, 152, 177, 180, 196, 198, 200–202
functions 1, 3, 5, 8, 14, 15, 23, 24, 30, 31, 33,
    41, 43, 50, 66, 87, 90, 94, 95, 107, 108,
    132, 133, 135–137, 160
Fungible Token (FT) 47, 50
fuzzy logic 6–8
fuzzy rules 6

G

genetic algorithm 8
graphics processing unit 2
guardians 31

H

heterogeneous 11, 21, 22, 60, 81, 82, 84, 96,
    107
heuristic knowledge 9
holistic approach 59
holography 56
human comfort 125
human-centered 6, 44, 61
human-centric 123–125, 130, 152
human-machine 23
humans 5, 6, 8, 11, 15, 23–27, 42–44, 46, 56,
    58, 60, 61, 69, 71, 80, 81, 83, 84, 87, 88,
    90–92, 94, 123–130, 132, 136, 141, 144,
    148, 150–152, 159
hybrid 5, 7, 8, 23, 25, 27, 32
hybrid twins 23

I

identification 8, 10, 41, 60, 70, 73, 82, 115,
    129, 169, 172, 198
immersive 49, 55–57, 175
immutability 51
indoor environment 123–126, 130–132, 134,
    137–139, 147, 148, 152
industrial 4, 5, 12–16, 22, 31, 33, 36, 40, 52,
    53, 79–83, 87, 94, 158, 197
industrial data 13, 80, 83, 94
Industrial Ontologies Foundry (IOF) 12

industrial systems 5, 13, 14, 31
Industry 4.0 1, 3, 13, 15, 20, 158
information flow 125
information fusion 7
information systems 6, 25, 83, 181, 190
infrastructure 9, 10, 14, 42, 47, 48, 51, 52, 61,
    70, 74, 82, 87, 107, 176
inspecting 67
integrating 13, 16, 23, 30, 35, 41, 81, 103,
    108, 109, 113, 179
intellectual property 14, 16
intelligent agents 8
intelligent applications 83
intelligent building systems 2
intelligent systems 1, 21
interaction 5, 6, 8, 15, 20, 23, 26, 28, 30, 31,
    33, 41, 42, 46, 47, 49, 55–57, 60, 69, 80,
    86, 87, 94, 95, 125, 132, 152, 159, 160,
    173, 176
interchangeably 3
interconnect 5
interface 31, 49, 51, 52, 56, 89, 94, 111, 113,
    130, 152
Internet 1, 3, 5, 8, 13, 20, 39, 40, 46, 56, 59,
    60, 68–70, 79, 87, 90, 102, 123, 158, 159,
    196
Internet of Things (Iot) 1, 3, 5, 8, 13, 20,
    22, 23, 26, 27, 31, 33, 34, 39, 42, 49, 55,
    56, 68–70, 73–76, 79, 82, 87, 90, 91, 94,
    102–104, 112, 116, 159, 160, 164, 196–198,
    200
interoperability 11, 12, 16, 21, 31, 32, 35, 36,
    87, 106, 107, 182, 200
interrelationships 5, 10, 21, 23

K

KARMA 36
knowledge 2, 5–9, 11–13, 15, 16, 21–26, 31,
    33–35, 53, 57, 69, 71, 73, 76, 79–85, 90,
    94, 103, 107, 111, 161, 178
knowledge acquisition 16, 35
Knowledge Core 5
knowledge graph 6, 11–13, 15, 16, 21–23, 31,
    33, 73, 76, 79–83, 85, 94
knowledge representation 7–9, 16, 35
knowledge updating 35

L

large displays 56
large-scale 2, 22, 48, 55

learning 5–9, 15, 21, 22, 27, 32, 40, 42–44, 50, 57, 58, 60, 66, 68–73, 75, 76, 82, 86, 104, 127, 129, 132, 142, 145, 167, 171
lifecycle 8, 11, 20, 21, 23, 26–30, 32–36, 51, 67, 70, 87, 103, 104, 108, 114, 117

M

machine learning (ML) 5–9, 15, 40, 43, 44, 60, 66, 68–71, 75, 127, 129, 142, 145
machines 5, 6, 8, 9, 15, 23, 40, 43, 44, 51, 60, 66, 68–72, 75, 81, 82, 85, 88–90, 94, 127, 129, 133, 136, 142, 145, 186, 187, 189, 199
maintenance procedures 68, 69, 199
maintenance requirements 68
maintenance strategy 68
management 1, 2, 4, 7–10, 13, 16, 20, 22, 23, 25, 26, 29–31, 33–36, 39, 46, 50, 51, 53, 56, 58, 65–69, 79, 83, 86–88, 109, 123, 124, 152, 159, 160, 165, 176, 179, 180, 183, 187, 194, 197, 198, 202
management layer 31, 35
Markov Decision Processes 43
memory 24, 27, 72
meta 9, 10, 39, 42, 56, 179
metacyberspace 55
Metaverse 39 61, 176
methodological framework 11
miner extractable value (MEV) 46, 47
mirror 40, 165
mobile headsets 56
model 2, 4, 5, 7–9, 11, 12, 14–16, 20–24, 26, 28–35, 36, 44, 49, 50, 53, 57, 66, 70–72, 75, 76, 80, 82, 84, 87–96, 102–108, 110–117, 124–130, 133, 135, 136, 146, 148–152, 159, 161, 166, 168, 169, 173–175, 179, 181–190, 192, 193, 197, 198, 200
modular construction 101, 103–105, 108, 109, 112, 116, 117
modular production 79–83, 94
modularized 80
monitor 2, 7, 80, 105, 159–161, 165, 197
MR 55, 56
Multi-access edge computing (MEC) 57
multidimensional 60
multivariate regression 8

N

nanotechnology 3
network capacity 3
neural language processing 7

Neural networks 7, 8, 36, 43, 72, 133, 136, 148
nexDT 22
next generation 3, 22, 36, 40, 54, 152
NFT 41, 45–47, 50–53
nodes 12, 46, 47, 53, 82–85
nonlinear distribution 82
nonlinear processing units 72

O

O&M 10, 65–68, 178, 179, 181
office buildings 124, 127, 129, 160, 161
ontology development 12
ontology engineering 11, 16
operation and maintenance 65–67, 70, 73, 75, 82, 105
operational and maintenance 65, 112
operational conditions 5, 96
operations 1, 2, 4, 8, 10, 13, 26, 33, 35, 48, 49, 56, 57, 65–70, 73–76, 80, 82, 86–91, 95, 104, 105, 109, 111, 114, 115, 159, 160, 166, 178, 192, 193, 202
optimal condition 73
optimization 2, 5, 6–8, 10, 24, 26, 27, 31, 33, 43, 68, 69, 73, 76, 81, 86, 132–134, 136–140
optimization algorithm 6, 7, 10, 132
optimizing resource allocation 80

P

peer-to-peer 47
perception 24, 26, 27, 58, 80, 81, 84, 94, 127, 130
Perception cognition systems 81
performance 2, 3, 10, 13, 30, 34, 42, 58, 66, 68–70, 86–88, 102, 107, 113, 116, 125, 137, 141, 145, 146, 159–161, 167, 179–181, 183–185, 188, 192–194, 197–202
physical assets 5, 6, 66, 69, 103, 104, 114, 160
physical components 1, 69
physical construction 3
physical environment 49, 56, 158
physical resources 2
physical system 1, 2, 6, 23, 28, 30, 35, 36, 79, 159
physical twin 5, 22, 27
physical/real-world layer 52
platform 14, 15, 23, 25, 33, 46, 47, 53, 66, 69, 70, 87, 108, 111, 113, 116, 117, 123, 125, 126, 128, 130–132, 150–152, 183, 198, 201, 202

policies 3, 59, 67
prediction 3, 5, 6, 9, 10, 24, 26, 66, 69–73,
    75, 80, 84–88, 96, 125–129, 131, 135, 136,
    140, 142, 145, 146, 148–150, 152, 168,
    169, 174
prediction models 75, 84, 96, 125–129, 135,
    136, 140, 146, 148–150, 152
predictive maintenance 29, 30, 66–68, 70,
    73, 76, 84, 87, 164, 199
prefabricated 101, 103–105, 108, 110, 112,
    116, 117
preventive 67, 68
privacy 14–16, 36, 41, 42, 55, 57, 59, 60, 130,
    175, 197
proactive 10, 32, 67, 81
problem-solving 5, 24, 26, 27, 43
problem-solving abilities 5
procedures 9, 15, 35, 45, 59, 68, 69, 76, 80,
    84, 86, 88, 92, 113, 143, 161, 162, 166,
    179–181, 186, 188, 189, 191, 192, 198, 199
process 3–11, 21, 24, 25, 27, 30–35, 51, 53, 57,
    68–72, 76, 79–86, 89, 91–93, 95, 103, 105,
    106, 108, 110–113, 116, 127, 129, 133, 134,
    137, 146, 160, 161, 166, 169, 178, 179,
    181, 182, 186, 187, 192, 193, 199, 200, 202
process model 9
processes 2–6, 11, 14, 15, 26, 34, 43, 56, 68,
    69, 73, 75, 84, 88, 103, 106–109, 111, 112,
    116, 162, 170, 173, 175, 178, 180, 186,
    189, 200, 202
product 8, 20, 23, 29, 30, 33, 34, 42, 47, 51,
    53, 81–83, 86–88, 90, 92, 94, 102, 181,
    185, 187, 198, 199
Product Lifecycle Management 23, 30, 34,
    51
productivity 1, 3, 10, 69, 86, 123, 140, 141,
    146
prohibitive cost 65
project's progress 10
Proof of Deposit 45
Public Private Partnershi 32

Q

QoE 58
QU4LITY 33

R

reaction 26, 84
real time 3, 6, 13, 14, 22, 27, 28, 33, 40, 49,
    54, 67, 69, 70, 73, 75, 76, 80, 82, 84–86,
    88–90, 92, 94–96, 102–105, 109, 110, 112,
    114, 115, 124–126, 130–132, 141, 147, 148,
    150–152, 161, 166, 196, 198, 201
Reality in Zero Defect Manufacturing 33
real-time monitoring 33, 80, 85, 94, 126, 132
real-time visualization 3, 130, 150, 151
reason 27, 84, 124, 160, 175, 179, 197
reasoning 6–9, 22, 24, 26, 27, 30, 33, 73, 80,
    81–85, 107
recognition 5, 9, 43, 49, 55, 70, 75, 126, 129
reference model 32, 87
reinforcement learning 6, 7, 43, 50, 82, 86
reliability 1, 9, 68, 106, 114, 182, 188, 200,
    202
reliable 2, 5, 10, 13, 14, 57, 86, 173, 179, 185
resilient 2, 159
resource utilization 2
resources 2, 3, 10, 33, 46, 54, 57, 67, 68,
    80–86, 94, 95, 101, 108, 129, 162, 166,
    175, 178
risk reduction 8
RMPFQ 33
robotic systems 56
robotics 3, 56, 105, 158
run-time process 4, 5

S

safe 2, 3, 14, 47, 51, 52, 168
scalability 57, 59, 80, 87, 95
scenarios 3, 5, 14, 22, 24, 30, 33, 45, 58, 75,
    80, 84–87, 91, 93, 102, 107, 129, 142,
    160, 172, 174, 180, 181, 183, 185, 190,
    192–194, 198, 201
schema 21, 87, 106, 107, 171
security 3, 13, 14, 16, 36, 41, 42, 51, 57, 59,
    60, 75, 76, 103, 107, 109, 111, 113, 175
self-correcting 6
self-defense 31
semantic models 2, 21
semantic technologies 11, 16, 21–23, 26, 34
semantically interconnected 23
semantic-driven 5
semantics 2, 5, 11–13, 16, 21–24, 26, 29,
    30, 34, 35, 80, 83, 84, 94, 102, 107, 113,
    115–117, 179
semi-supervision learning methods 72
sensing 13, 26, 27, 29, 30, 49, 54, 70, 79, 80,
    82, 83, 94, 147, 151
sensitivity 72
sensor network data 2

sensors 1–3, 5, 6, 22, 27, 40, 56, 58, 66–70, 73–76, 79, 82, 104, 109, 112, 114, 115, 123, 127, 131, 142, 147, 151, 159, 160, 162, 164, 166, 175, 196–198, 200
service interruptions 67
service management layer 31
service robots 56
shop-floor 79–81, 86–96
simulate 67, 87, 173, 190
simulation 3, 6, 22, 29, 31, 36, 40, 44, 52, 88–95, 102, 103, 105, 111–115, 159, 160, 167–175, 177–182, 185, 193, 202
site-monitoring systems 2
smart 1–4, 6, 8, 13, 20, 24, 25, 33, 45, 47, 48, 50, 53, 54, 58, 66, 67, 69, 70, 80, 86, 105, 107, 108, 111, 113, 123–125, 131, 132, 152, 158, 160–162, 166
Smart contracts 8, 45, 47, 48, 50, 53, 108, 111
social acceptability 41, 42, 59
software incompatibility 3
specifications 12, 21, 24, 30, 32, 40, 79, 106, 107, 112, 193
standardization 16, 31
standards 12, 16, 21, 30–32, 35, 36, 58–60, 88, 107, 114, 116, 124, 132, 164, 166, 180, 184
storage 2, 3, 8, 13, 14, 42, 45, 48, 74, 94, 107, 128, 193, 194
storage systems 2
strategies 4, 14, 26, 27, 30, 43, 68, 132, 177, 194, 201
structure 13, 16, 21, 27, 35, 44, 47, 69, 71, 72, 75, 80, 87, 89, 90, 93, 95, 102, 107, 159, 180–182, 186, 200, 202
subsystems 21–24, 27, 29, 30, 35, 89, 93
supply chain 5, 6, 33
sustainability 8, 10, 34, 53, 81, 95, 101–103, 105, 108–113, 116, 117, 177, 194, 199
sustainable 3, 10, 48, 105, 108–110, 113, 114, 116, 117, 158–160, 176, 198, 200, 202
Symbiotic Autonomous Systems (SAS) 23
synchronization 54, 87, 89–91, 93
syntax 21
system 1–3, 5–8, 10–14, 16, 20–36, 40, 43–46, 48, 50, 55–57, 60, 66, 67, 69, 71, 73, 75, 76, 79–96, 103, 105, 106, 111, 114, 124–133, 142, 144, 145, 147–149, 152, 159, 178–181, 185, 187, 190, 192, 193, 196–198, 202

system applications 67
systems engineering 30, 36, 88

T

technologies 1–6, 8, 11–17, 20–23, 26, 29 30, 34, 35, 39–44, 48, 49, 55, 56, 60, 61, 66, 68–70, 80, 82, 86, 89, 90, 102, 104, 107, 109, 124, 125, 152, 159, 169, 175, 197
three-dimension 20
three-layer framework 5
tiered network 58
tool-chain 23, 36
top-level ontologies 11, 12
topology specifications 24
training set 75
transformations 3, 4, 8, 16, 161
transmission 2, 14, 44, 57, 89, 167, 183, 197
transparency 14, 51, 109, 111–113, 179, 188
transport layer 58
trustworthy 44, 45, 51, 57, 69, 182, 202
twin management layer 31, 35
Twins 1, 2, 4–6, 8, 13, 15, 20–25, 27, 31, 33, 35, 39, 49, 51, 54, 60, 65, 66, 68, 69, 73, 76, 79, 80, 86, 87, 101, 103–105, 109–117, 158, 159, 175–177, 179, 180, 197, 198, 200, 201

U

uncertain scenarios 5
unexpected failures 67, 68
universe 39, 49, 56
unmanned aerial vehicles (UAV) 3, 54
unpredictable 8, 24, 26, 29, 30, 33
unpredicted behavior 27
unsupervised learning 9, 71, 75
use-cases 24, 32, 33, 70, 89
User Interactivity 56
user's experience 162, 167
user-generated content (UAC) 49, 50

V

value-added 2
variable 4, 8, 50, 71, 72, 92, 96, 132, 133, 141, 174, 190
virtual 4, 5, 20, 23, 24, 27, 28, 31, 39, 40, 42, 45, 47–50, 53–61, 66, 80, 86, 87, 90, 103,

104, 112, 151, 159, 160, 173, 175, 177, 180, 182, 185, 188, 200, 202
virtual economy 42, 59
virtual entities 20, 28, 56
virtual model 5, 23, 182, 200
virtual reality 39, 59, 175
virtual space 4, 20, 28, 31, 55, 66
virtualization 3, 4, 126
visibility 29

W

work engagement 125, 127, 140–142, 144–146, 148, 149, 152
workforce 6, 160, 161

X

XR 3, 41, 42, 55, 56, 59, 60

About the Editor

Ibrahim Yitmen received his Ph.D. in Architecture from Istanbul Technical University, Turkey. He is currently an Associate Professor in Management of Construction Production at Jönköping University, Sweden since February 2018. His research focus is mainly on Innovation in Construction involving socio-technical issues regarding digital transformation in AEC industry, and his recent special interest is on Digital Twin-based Smart Built Environment, Augmented Reality/Mixed Reality for Cognitive Buildings, Integration of Digital Twins and Deep Learning for Smart Planning and Construction, Blockchain Technology in Construction Supply Chains, Cyber Physical Systems for Construction 4.0, Integration of Unmanned Aerial Vehicles and BIM for Construction Safety Planning and Monitoring. Dr. Yitmen has published more than 100 research papers in refereed international journals and peer reviewed conference proceedings. He has recently been the editor of the book titled "BIM-enabled Cognitive Computing for Smart Built Environment: Potential, Requirements, and Implementation" published by CRC Press. He was one of the guest editors of the MDPI Journal Applied Sciences for the Special Issue "Cognitive Buildings". Dr. Yitmen is currently leading research projects titled "Integration of Blockchain and Digital Twins for Smart Asset Lifecycle Management" financed by Smart Built Environment (Sweden), titled "Adapting Cognitive Digital Twins for the Production of Sustainable Modular Houses" financed by Vinnova (Sweden), and titled "Collaborative Digital Platform for Dynamic Workflows in Construction Production and Information Exchange Planning financed by Jönköpings Läns Byggmästareförening". Dr. Yitmen serves on the scientific committees of the international conferences held by the International Council for Research and Innovation in Building and Construction (CIB), the American Society of Civil Engineers (ASCE), and the European Council on Computing in Construction (EC3). He is an active Member of the American Society for Engineering Management, USA since 2010.